Just Like Us

Just Like Us

Digital Debates on Feminism and Fame

CAITLIN E. LAWSON

Rutgers University Press

New Brunswick, Camden, and Newark, New Jersey, and London

Library of Congress Cataloging-in-Publication Data
Names: Lawson, Caitlin E., author.
Title: Just like us: digital debates on feminism and fame / Caitlin E. Lawson.
Description: New Brunswick, New Jersey: Rutgers University Press, [2023] |
    Includes bibliographical references and index.
Identifiers: LCCN 2022009358 | ISBN 9781978830912 (paperback; alk. paper) |
    ISBN 9781978830929 (hardback; alk. paper) | ISBN 9781978830936 (epub) |
    ISBN 9781978830943 (pdf)
Subjects: LCSH: Feminism. | Fame. | Celebrities—Political activity.
Classification: LCC HQ1155 .L39 2023 | DDC 305.42—dc23/eng/20220303
LC record available at https://lccn.loc.gov/2022009358

A British Cataloging-in-Publication record for this book is available from the British Library.

Chapter 1 is a revised version of an article previously published in *Feminist Media Studies* 18,
no. 5 (2018): 825–841 as "Innocent Victims, Creepy Boys: Discursive Framings of Sexuality in
Online News Coverage of the Celebrity Nude Photo Hack." Reprinted with permission,
https://www.tandfonline.com/.

Chapter 4 is a revised version of an article previously published in *Communication & Society*
21, no. 6 (2018): 818–833 as "Platform Vulnerabilities: Harassment and Misogynoir in the
Digital Attack on Leslie Jones." Reprinted with permission, https://www.tandfonline.com/.
References to internet websites (URLs) were accurate at the time of writing. Neither the
author nor Rutgers University Press is responsible for URLs that may have expired or changed
since the manuscript was prepared.

Unless specified otherwise, all images are screenshots captured by the author.

♾ The paper used in this publication meets the requirements of the American National
Standard for Information Sciences—Permanence of Paper for Printed Library Materials,
ANSI Z39.48-1992.

www.rutgersuniversitypress.org

Manufactured in the United States of America

For Ben, Jack, and Lorelei

Contents

Introduction: The Rise of Celebrity Feminism   1

1   Hacking Celebrity: Sexuality, Privacy, and Networked
Misogyny in the Celebrity Nude Photo Hack   23

2   Staging Feminism: Negotiating Labor and Calling
Out Racism at the 2015 Academy Awards   43

3   Nasty Women, Silly Girls: Feminist Generation Gaps
and Hillary Clinton's 2016 Presidential Campaign   70

4   Platform Vulnerabilities: Fighting Harassment and
Misogynoir in the Digital Attack on Leslie Jones   94

5   TIME'S UP: Celebrity Feminism after #MeToo   117

Conclusion: Celebrity Feminist Futures   145

Acknowledgments   155
Notes   157
References   161
Index   183

Just Like Us

Introduction

The Rise of Celebrity Feminism

On October 5, 2017, *New York Times* reporters Jodi Kantor and Megan Twohey published an exposé that formalized what had long been an open secret in Hollywood: for decades, the famed film producer Harvey Weinstein had been a serial sexual harasser and assailant who preyed on young actresses and used his clout to threaten their careers if they dared refuse his advances or speak out. While his predatory behavior was well known in Hollywood and among industry gossip hounds, the article painted a picture of systematic abuse and its cover-up on a horrifying scale. This bombshell report was corroborated and expanded five days later when Ronan Farrow (2017) published yet another report in the *New Yorker* that detailed Weinstein's pattern of harassment and assault. In both articles, women bravely recounted the intimidation, their isolation, and their feelings of powerlessness in gut-wrenching detail. These revelations about Weinstein piled atop a growing mountain of accounts about other serial sexual harassers in the media industries such as Bill Cosby, Roger Ailes, and Bill O'Reilly. While none of these men had yet faced legal retribution by that October, many lost work and were publicly shamed. Still others had received no such consequences; one former reality television star, who has been accused of sexual harassment by over a dozen women and was caught admitting to a proclivity for such behavior on tape, had even ascended to the White House.

Compounded by mounting frustration at the Trump administration and bolstered by an overall uptick in social activism, the Weinstein allegations

1

opened the floodgates, and a rush of sexual harassment and assault survivors came forth. On October 15, 2017, actress Alyssa Milano took to Twitter and posted an image that read, "Suggested by a friend: 'If all the women who have been sexually harassed or assaulted wrote "Me too." as a status, we might give people a sense of the magnitude of the problem.'" With this tweet, Milano unknowingly co-opted a movement that had begun with activist Tarana Burke, who started the campaign in 2006 on MySpace to promote empowerment and solidarity among girls and women of color who had experienced sexual abuse. However, amplified by the media attention afforded to celebrity culture (in particular, to white celebrities) and the spreadability of social media discourse, #MeToo exploded across digital platforms and spawned a wave of calls for powerful abusers in Hollywood and beyond to be held accountable. In just twenty-four hours, Facebook reported that there had been 12 million posts, comments, and reactions to #MeToo; after a week, the hashtag had been used more than 1.7 million times on Twitter by users in eighty-five countries (Park 2017). Survivors shared their stories of harassment and abuse, and the final months of 2017 turned into an almost daily series of allegations and firings of men across media and other industries. So powerful was the movement that *Time* magazine's Person of the Year was "The Silence Breakers" (Zacharek, Dockterman, and Edwards 2017).

This explosion of frustration, righteous anger, and digital feminism may have seemed sudden and even surprising, especially given its deep connections to celebrity culture. However, the interrelated phenomena of the Weinstein scandal and #MeToo demonstrate the increasing prominence and global impact of three intersecting platforms: the sociopolitical platform of feminism, the platform given to celebrities by virtue of their fame, and the various digital platforms on which networked publics cohere and communicate. While the "#MeToo moment" of 2017 was spectacular in its discursive omnipresence and longevity, the ways in which it blended popular, activist, and academic feminisms with celebrity culture and social media are not unique but developed over the prior decade. *Just Like Us: Digital Debates on Feminism and Fame* tells the story of celebrity culture's role in the new visibilities of feminism during the early twenty-first century by examining its intersections with digital platforms. Through in-depth analyses of recent celebrity-centered controversies related to gender and the feminist movement, as well as tensions between digital feminisms and networked misogyny, this book shows that digital platforms are a key force in transforming popular feminisms today because they open up more public, collective modes of holding individuals and groups accountable for their actions. Together, celebrity culture and digital platforms form a crucial discursive arena where postfeminist logics can be unsettled, opening up the possibility of more progressive, activist, and intersectional popular feminisms.

Whether we like it or not, celebrities, popular culture, and social media have significantly transformed the feminist movement during the 2010s, and their centrality shows no signs of waning. My goal in this book is to map the processes by which celebrity culture, digital platforms, and feminism transform one another, providing theoretical tools for making sense of their intersections going forward as we work toward a more just and equitable world.

Under Pressure: Intersectional Contestations of White Feminist Perspectives

Throughout this book, my arguments center on the role that celebrity culture can play in making newsworthy and thus hypervisible existing issues surrounding feminist and anti-feminist movements. The cliché that celebrities are "just like us"—us, the boring, nonfamous folk—often appears alongside images of A-list movie stars shopping for groceries or pop megastars filling their cars with gas. The phrase is meant to emphasize their relatability by showing them engaging in everyday activities. But the phrase is a contradiction. While, yes, the unfamous also pick their kids up from school or walk their dogs, our photos do not appear on blogs and in magazines when we do so. The actions may be the same, but the hypervisibility and newsworthiness afforded to celebrities render them very unlike "us." This contradiction structures many of the tensions I explore in this book. Throughout the following chapters, commentators often draw parallels between the experiences of celebrities and those of everyday people, particularly women, to draw attention to systemic sexism and racism. Moreover, the myopia of white privilege that many celebrity feminists convey is also indicative of broader issues within the feminist movement that shape nonfamous white feminist behavior. However, celebrities' hypervisibility, their privilege, and the praise afforded to them set them apart and, as we will see, further problematize celebrity feminist enactments.

As celebrities enter into feminist conversations and as celebrity events or scandals become the subjects of discussions related to feminism, publics often gather online to negotiate interpretations of and responses to these celebrity stories. Through my analysis of those negotiations, I demonstrate that online discussions of celebrity culture can be important sites where networked publics debate the merits of various feminist positions and actions—debates that, in prior decades, were often siloed within activist and academic circles. The publicness of these debates, afforded by the publicness of both celebrity and social media discourse, is a key force in transforming popular feminism.

These debates about feminism around celebrity culture via digital platforms are complex and multifaceted. Just as feminism is a diverse movement (more accurately described as the plural "feminisms"), so too are digital feminist negotiations of celebrity culture. However, my analyses show that two perspectives, frequently in tension with one another, structure many popular feminist conversations online in ways that resonate with long-standing tensions in the feminist movement. These perspectives often translate into what I call *imperatives*. This term indicates that networked publics coalesce around particular feminist orientations and principles, exerting pressure on individuals and institutions to perform that orientation toward feminism properly. In many cases, these pressures stem from the mainstreaming and whitewashing of digital accountability practices pioneered by Black Twitter users (see M. D. Clark 2020), but they extend beyond "calling out" bad actors to describe a broader technosocial environment in which expectations exert pressure even when a direct callout does not take place. These expectations center on holding actors accountable to dynamic, ever-evolving, and often contentious sets of actions, and social media function as highly public forums where feminist issue publics utilize the affordances of various platforms to watch and hold them responsible. Indeed, the hypervisibility of celebrity amplifies this practice of accountability. These pressures are often discursive, taking the form of hashtag campaigns or callouts, or they may incorporate actions such as voting, boycotting, or donating. In this book, I focus on two "imperatives"—the white feminist imperative and the intersectional imperative—as key structuring pressures in the negotiation of digital popular feminisms.

Rafia Zakaria (2021) defines a white feminist as "someone who refuses to consider the role that whiteness and the racial privilege attached to it have played and continue to play in universalizing white feminist concerns, agendas, and beliefs as being those of all of feminism and all of feminists" (ix). Pulling on the threads in this definition, the white feminist imperative centers on inclusion, equality, and reformation. Most closely aligned with liberal feminisms, those who exert the pressures of the white feminist imperative agitate for the equal treatment of men and women and greater opportunities for women to "have a seat at the table." Their goals are focused on reforming existing systems of power to be more hospitable to women. Because these goals do not fundamentally challenge the structures of patriarchy, they are often more easily integrated into mainstream discourses. But, crucially, the white feminist imperative treats "women" as a universal category and ignores the different experiences of women, particularly women of color. Absent from the white feminist imperative is an analysis of the ways that race, in particular, shapes women's experiences; or, if those exerting white feminist pressures do acknowledge the role of race for women's experiences of sexism, they refuse to cede space to women of color. For these reasons, the goals of the white feminist imperative center on the needs, desires, and achievements of white women, often to the explicit exclusion of women of color. As I will discuss in much more depth later in this introduction and throughout the book, when women of color challenge white feminism, white feminists often respond with anger and resistance.

While the white feminist imperative remains, in many ways, the dominant set of popular feminist pressures, it is increasingly challenged by the intersectional imperative. Coined by Kimberlé Crenshaw (1991), the term *intersectionality* refers to "the various ways in which race and gender intersect in shaping structural and political aspects of violence against women of color" (1242). In contrast to the white feminist imperative, the intersectional imperative begins from the premise that women experience sexism differently based on their race, ethnicity, sexuality, ability, socioeconomic status, religion, citizenship status, and so forth and agitates for the centering of women of color's experiences in setting feminist goals. The pressures of the intersectional imperative tend to be more radical and disruptive, calling for a restructuring of sociopolitical power dynamics. Often this places those who exert the intersectional imperative in conflict not only with racist, anti-feminist publics but also with white feminists, provoking intense backlash. I trace these conflicts and tensions throughout the book, demonstrating how those who exert the intersectional imperative work toward a more equitable society and feminist movement.

However, the increasing popularity and buzzwordiness of *intersectionality* does not always (or often) translate into a popular feminism that radically incorporates the experiences, expertise, and priorities of women of color. White women are still overwhelmingly at the center of popular feminism, as are white feminist perspectives. Indeed, the growing popularity of the concept of intersectionality brings with it similar concerns to those that activists and academics have been voicing about the popularity of certain feminist ideals for years: that intersectionality may be sapped of its political potency and rendered inert. "Intersectionality" risks becoming simply another feather in the cap of white celebrity feminists, signaling their "wokeness" while allowing them to remain the power brokers of popular feminism, performing as white saviors who empathize with the plight of women of color but ultimately retain the privilege afforded them by their whiteness. This tension and the roles of legacy and social media in shaping who has the power to speak and stand in for popular feminism are at the heart of my arguments.

Transforming Celebrity Feminism

The often-conflicting pressures of the white feminist imperative and the intersectional imperative, enacted via social media and often coalescing around celebrity stories, are transforming popular feminism. In my analysis of these transformational processes, I contest the notion that there is a "real" feminism separable from and thus outside of popular culture. Instead of evaluating how well celebrity feminism reflects "real" feminism, I conceptualize feminism and celebrity culture as ideological and discursive spaces with semipermeable, intersecting boundaries and focus on the ways those boundaries are negotiated on digital platforms. As networked publics discuss various incidents in celebrity culture that relate to issues of gender, sexuality, race, and class, they engage in boundary work around feminism. This negotiation relies on three interlinked processes: filtration, accumulation, and amplification.

Because the boundaries around feminism and celebrity culture are semipermeable and intersecting, they are not immutable but change and develop over time. They overlap as celebrities engage with feminist ideas, celebrity culture provides fodder for negotiations of feminism among networked publics, and feminist organizing incorporates some aspects of celebrity branding. Such change—both to the makeup of what constitutes feminism and celebrity culture and to the overlap between them—happens as certain ideas, positions, and actions from the broader social, political, economic, and technological environments *filter* through the boundaries surrounding feminism and celebrity and become incorporated into them. At the same time, changes in these environments also mean that certain ideas, positions, and actions filter out of dominant conceptions of feminism and of celebrity culture, and in the overlap between them. In the chapters to come, I explore this process on a granular level, mapping the aspects of feminism that filter across platforms and become amplified within and through celebrity culture. This filtration increasingly occurs on digital platforms, which also have their own processes of filtration. Filtration at the platform level functions in two key ways: a failure to filter out toxic content, which leaves it present to infiltrate spaces like celebrity culture; and algorithmic curation, which sorts and filters what content merits attention. I will explore the complexities of these multilayered filtration systems in much more detail in the case studies.

As ideas, positions, and actions discursively filter into and out of negotiations of feminism when networked publics discuss and debate celebrity events, certain ideas, positions, and actions that stay *accumulate*. Accumulation helps to explain how "dominant conceptions" become dominant, and why a case study approach can be a useful way to analyze these relationships. Some critiques of social media activism are that it is reactive and fleeting and ultimately results in little action. Some incident will occur, networked publics will mobilize in response, and then the controversy soon dies down. However, as Bonilla and Rosa (2015) argue, the persistence of multiple online activist movements can provide users with a broader understanding of the social contexts and conversations in which each individual movement is located. This means that each occurrence does not happen in a vacuum but rather within the context of other responses and campaigns that have accumulated within the public imaginary. For this reason, this book takes a case study approach to map this process of accumulation. Each chapter provides a deep dive into a particular celebrity incident to explore the interconnected dynamics that shape and evolve intersectional feminist negotiations; rather than merely providing a catalog of key moments in celebrity culture, these case studies analyze the ebb and flow of ideas, discourses, and actions as popular feminism evolves, and my arguments focus not on the specifics of individual incidents but rather on the dynamics that shape these incidents as indicative of broader, systemic shifts.

Another key dynamic at work in this negotiation process is amplification. These case studies demonstrate that celebrity culture does not reveal phenomena or dynamics that exist solely within the world of celebrity. Rather, the attention and newsworthiness afforded to celebrities by virtue of their fame *amplify* phenomena and dynamics that are embedded within broader structures of power that noncelebrity women also experience. Sexual harassment, objectification, wage inequality, and/or online harassment impact or have impacted most women. While the privilege and newsworthiness afforded to celebrities transform their experiences and the remediation of those experiences, their hypervisibility also amplifies these issues, propelling them into the spotlight while various media platforms, particularly social media platforms, provide spaces for publics to discuss them. However, celebrity discourses amplify people, ideas, and events unevenly. As the chapters that follow demonstrate, white celebrities and white feminist positions are often amplified over and above celebrities of color, feminist activists, and women of color feminisms. Increasingly, however, these white feminists and white feminist perspectives are challenged by intersectional feminist activists and ideas. The tensions around who and what get amplified across social and legacy media are central to the arguments of this book.

Further, the circulation and recirculation of certain texts, framings, and reactions to these celebrity incidents through legacy and digital platforms also serve to amplify and make dominant particular understandings of each event. The various affordances of digital platforms, such as retweeting, hyperlinking, and trending, amplify certain voices, texts, and perspectives on the incidents I discuss. Beyond social media platforms, legacy media outlets like television news, newspapers and magazines and their online counterparts amplify stories and discourses beyond the confines of social media platforms. Thus the logics of newsworthiness (which stories make the news?) and framing (how do writers and commentators tell those stories?) further amplify certain people, ideas, and ways of thinking about feminism, race, and celebrities' places in conversations around social justice. The individuals, groups, ideas, and evaluations that social media users and digital and legacy media outlets amplify the most will be a central focus of this book as I explore how popular conceptualizations of feminism shift and who comes to personify them.

Uneasy Bedfellows: Understanding Celebrities and the Feminist Movement

Before I jump into the case studies and tease out this argument, I will lay some groundwork. First, how should we think about the role celebrities play in American culture? While scholars have approached the study of celebrity culture in myriad ways, I define celebrities as discursively constructed, commodified representations of spectacular individuality.[1] First, for most audiences, celebrities are more or less a collection of texts such as interviews, social media posts, gossip magazine stories, paparazzi photos, movies, or concerts. Most of us only know celebrities through media texts that represent and talk about them, and through these texts and our discussions, we construct understandings and images of them. Celebrities are thus hypermediated, existing *as stars* almost exclusively through discourses and representations. Second, celebrities are commodities (Marshall 1997). If Hollywood is an industry, one of its products is undoubtedly stars. Stars are produced by the complex machinery of publicists, managers, stylists, voice and acting coaches, and other professionals to be sold to audiences and other folks in the industry. Celebrity personas are carefully constructed as brands, and those brands are marketed to directors, producers, and advertisers. Valuable celebrity brands generate revenue for film studios, record companies, companies whose products they endorse, and more. For this reason, celebrities are deeply embedded in capitalist logics. Finally, celebrities represent an "ideological shoring up of triumphant individuality" (Dyer 1986, 18). In many ways, they embody cultural ideals of beauty, wealth, success, consumption, charisma, and the American dream (Sternheimer 2011). As Turner (2010) explains, celebrities thus participate "in the field of expectations that many, particularly the young, have of everyday life" (14). That participation is not always positive; celebrities frequently make mistakes and fall from grace, functioning as cautionary tales. The point is that celebrities, the texts that inform our understanding of them, the ways in which those texts commodify ways of being, and the discussions we have about celebrities and celebrity stories can help publics negotiate shared cultural values around success and worth. The next chapter will delve more deeply into the cultural power of celebrity gossip.

Most integral to my discussion of celebrities in this book is the increasing integration of feminist language, themes, and action into celebrity brands during the 2010s, and the ways in which that integration shapes public understandings of feminism. Some background on American feminist movements and theories is useful here. The second wave of feminism lasted roughly from the early 1960s through the early 1980s. Whereas the first wave, which took place in the late nineteenth and early twentieth centuries, focused primarily on women's suffrage, feminists of the second wave worked toward a broader range of legal and social reforms. Reinvigorated by the publication of Betty Friedan's book, *The Feminist Mystique* (2010, originally published in 1963), second wave feminist activists and academics sought to reform or totally dismantle patriarchal structures by, among many initiatives, expanding women's reproductive rights, agitating for workplace and wage equality, mobilizing against domestic violence, and fighting against sexist media representations. But, even as the mass media provided fodder for feminists to critique, many women first came into contact with feminist thought through its representations in the news, on television, and in film. More radical feminists were often portrayed as deviant, man-hating bra burners. However, reformist feminist goals that could be incorporated into a liberal individualist framework and did not radically challenge patriarchal power structures gained some traction throughout the 1960s and 1970s (Beck 1998; Douglas 1995; Lilburn, Magarey, and Sheridan 2000; Mendes 2011).

The liberal feminism that achieved limited mainstream acceptance also demonstrated a lack of diversity. As many women of color and LGBTQIA women pointed out, the reformist feminist work that grew out of Friedan's lily-white depiction of heterosexual women's ennui often marginalized or totally ignored the experiences of women of color and queer women (e.g., Combahee River Collective 1982; Rich 1980). Such critiques of the lack of diversity within the feminist movement translated into an interest among many feminists in what Crenshaw (1991) called "intersectionality," which describes how race and other aspects of identity shape women's experiences of sexism. Intersectionality does not mean that racism and sexism have simple additive effects for women of color; rather, it focuses on the ways that racism fundamentally transforms women of color's experiences of sexism and vice versa. Moya Bailey (2021) calls this racialized sexism "misogynoir," defining it as "the unique co-constitutive racialized and sexist violence that befalls Black women as a result of their simultaneous and interlocking oppression at the intersection of racial and gender marginalization" (1). This focus on multiple axes of oppression built on the foundations of Black feminist critique from theorists like bell hooks and Audre Lorde and became a key focus of the third wave of feminism that began in the 1990s. In some ways a reaction to stereotypes of second wave feminists as uptight and judgmental of individual decisions deemed unfeminist, particularly around sex, the third wave sought to redefine what it meant to be a feminist by opening up the definition to allow for greater diversity and individual expression (see Baumgardner and Richards 2000). However, this openness moved many feminists to critique third wave feminism as politically inert. In particular, some second wave feminists critiqued the third wave's focus on apolitical individual choice over collective action without examining the (white supremacist patriarchal) cultural context that shapes those individual choices.

Alongside the third wave, the 1990s, particularly that decade's pop culture, was marked by what feminist scholars called "postfeminism." Postfeminism is the notion that gender equality has been achieved so the collective action of the feminist movement is no longer necessary, meaning that women can focus on individual achievement and get back to enjoying the trappings of traditional femininity (see McRobbie 2009; Gill 2007). Postfeminist analyses point out that mainstream media texts like *Bridget Jones's Diary* or *Buffy the Vampire Slayer* (two oft-cited targets of postfeminist critique) take for granted certain feminist ideas, like access to birth control and women's ability to enter the workplace, while repudiating feminism itself as the antiquated, unattractive "f-word." Rosalind Gill (2009) argues that the entanglement of prefeminist, feminist, and anti-feminist ideas that make up postfeminist popular cultural texts render gender ideologies more difficult to contest.

However, many feminist scholars have noted a "new visibility" of feminism in the popular culture of the 2010s (Gill 2016). In contrast to the "lifestyle" feminism so derided during the third wave, and unlike the postfeminist repudiation of the label and movement, the 2010s saw the emergence of a more vocal, positive orientation toward feminism. In response, journalist Kira Cochrane (2013) announced the arrival of the "fourth wave" and its "rebel women," pointing to the uptick in interest in feminism, particularly among young women. Ealasaid Munro (2013) linked the rise of the fourth wave to the increasing role of digital platforms. She argued that the fourth wave is marked by a focus on intersectionality and the increasing prominence of the practice of "privilege-checking," and one of its central features is how feminists use digital technologies to call out misogyny, sexism, and the continuing "exclusionary nature of mainstream feminism" (Munro 2013, 25).

However, these cultural shifts around popular feminism have by no means been smooth or uncontested. Alongside the rise in discourses and representations of feminism in popular culture, the United States in particular has seen a concurrent rise in popular misogyny, racism, and far right politics (Banet-Weiser 2018). From targeted harassment campaigns such as Gamergate to anger and protest over perceived increases in diversity across the media landscape, instances of popular misogyny and misogynoir are increasingly digital, frequent, and prominent within current media cultures (Massanari 2017). Moreover, activists such as Mikki Kendall (2020) and Rafia Zakaria (2021) point out that women of color continue to be sidelined and harmed by white feminist perspectives, questioning "what it means to stand in solidarity as a movement meant to encompass all women when there is the distinct likelihood that some women are oppressing others" (Kendall 2020, 7). These tensions both within the feminist movement and against misogyny more broadly form the central struggles that are explored in this book. Before we examine these shifting orientations toward feminism in more detail, and the ways it is articulated through both digital platforms and celebrity culture, we first need a theoretical basis for understanding social media.

Hate and Resistance on Digital Platforms

In the early days of the internet, some hoped that digital spaces would provide a utopia free of inequalities, where subjectivities inflected by race, gender, sexuality, ability, and class could be fluid or altogether erased. However, these subjectivities and the inequalities that structure their relationships followed us online, manifesting in ways that are shaped by the affordances of digital technologies yet tied to off-line forms of oppression (Nakamura 2013; Daniels 2013). Soon it became clear that, far from being neutral spaces, platforms are deeply political. Gillespie (2010) defines platforms as programmable "infrastructures that support the design and use of particular applications, be they computer hardware, operating systems, gaming devices, mobile devices or digital disc formats" (349). Eventually this definition extended to include online environments like Facebook that allow users to design and use third-party applications. Crucial to platform studies is the notion of platforms' programmability, which allows users to go beyond the original programmers' vision. This notion of programmability—possibility and agency within the constraints delimited by the platforms' designers and channeled into profit by their creators—spawned great critical interest in the implications of the participatory media practices that occur on commercial platforms.

This project is most indebted to scholarship that explores how platforms shape sociality through their affordances, including the ways that racial and gender differences shape that sociality. Affordances are "functional and relational aspects which frame, while not determining, the possibilities for agentic action in relation to an object" (Hutchby 2001, 444). In other words, affordances refer to the features and design of a platform that shape how users interact with that platform, limiting the possibilities of use and encouraging, but not determining, certain modes of interaction. As a result of the ways in which platforms and sociality are increasingly intertwined, as José van Dijck, Thomas Poell, and Martijn de Waal (2018) argue, we are living in a "platform society." Digital platforms and their computational logics now infiltrate nearly every facet of our social, economic, and interpersonal lives. Despite these platforms' integral, infrastructural roles in many people's lives, they are not held to the same standards and regulations as other institutions and often do not take responsibility for anchoring public values. To deny such responsibility, spokespeople for platforms like Google and Twitter often rely on the rhetoric of neutrality, discursively constructing these sites as blank slates on which users disseminate information and ignoring how features of the platform afford certain behaviors while discouraging others (Gillespie 2018). However, the algorithms and features that make up the platform are not neutral but rather have deep sociopolitical implications. Two broad categories of online sociality that are particularly relevant to this project are online harassment and digital activism.

Many scholars have explored dynamics of online identity-based harassment, paying special attention to how interface design, affordances such as anonymity or pseudonymity, and content moderation policies enable toxicity. While it is important to understand how technologies shape and facilitate racist, misogynistic harassment, it is crucial to remember that such technologies are embedded within social relations that are toxic both online and off-line (Massanari 2017; Matamoros-Fernandez 2016; Daniels 2009; Banet-Weiser and Miltner 2016). Bigoted harassment did not begin with the internet; rather, digital platforms afford new avenues for such harassment and shape that harassment in particular ways. Safiya Noble (2018), in her analysis of racism embedded in search engines, demonstrates that the algorithmic infrastructures that shape our experiences of online spaces are encoded with racist, sexist assumptions. Her work encourages readers to contend with the reality that technologies are made by humans, and just as humans are enculturated by oppressive ideologies, so too are the technologies they create. Ruha Benjamin (2019) calls these phenomena the "New Jim Code," describing "new technologies that reflect and reproduce existing inequities but that are promoted and perceived as more objective or progressive than the discriminatory systems of a previous era" (3). Overall, the logics used to program and to govern digital platforms often leave open spaces for online harassment and violence, particularly against women of color.

However, feminists, anti-racist activists, and queer activists have also mobilized the affordances of digital platforms to resist structural inequalities. Activists use social media to engage in a range of activities, including calling out oppression and offering ways to fight back; dialoguing to share their experiences and form support networks; and organizing boycotts, demonstrations, and more. Crucially, individuals often gather to circulate counternarratives, pushing back on the sexist, racist, and/or homophobic discourses that dominate mainstream media in the form of creative output like web series, hashtag campaigns, and digital community formation (e.g., Baer 2016; Jackson, Bailey, and Foucault Welles 2020; Bailey 2021). In doing so, these networked activists find transformative connections, even as barriers to access and the intense, often emotionally taxing labor of their work shape their experiences (Mendes, Ringrose, and Keller 2019). For women of color engaging in digital feminist work, that emotional labor can be even more intense as they often have to battle against feminists who take umbrage at their critiques of white feminism's myopia. Indeed, digital feminism can reproduce the ongoing failings of previous waves of feminism by excluding women of color and even labeling them "toxic" when they call out their marginalization (Daniels 2015; Loza 2014; Risam 2015).

Even as digital platforms open new spaces for feminist activism and afford new modes of mobilization, feminism remains a contested movement in which activists continue to agitate for the importance of decentering whiteness.

Some of the most common strategies for raising awareness and organizing stem from a range of digital accountability practices pioneered by communities of color, particularly women and/or queer people of color, who use social media platforms to point out and resist bigotry and call for the accountability of offending parties (M. D. Clark 2020). Often referred to (increasingly dismissively) as "calling out," "dragging," or "canceling," these practices center on marginalized groups gathering in digital spaces to discuss, evaluate, and sometimes prescribe a remedy for the offensive behavior of those with more power (see Nakamura 2015). These strategies can be seen as a "last-ditch appeal for justice" from communities of color that are often disenfranchised from more traditional forms of justice (M. D. Clark 2020, 2). As social media have given people who would not previously have had the ability to speak to a wide audience and share their critiques of individuals and institutions a platform to do so, powerful individuals and institutions have blanched at this restructuring of discursive power dynamics. Most recently, these anxieties have surfaced over "callouts" and "cancel culture," an updated version of panics around "political correctness" from prior decades, and have spilled over from conservative discourses to become mainstream. Typified by texts like the infamous "A Letter on Justice and Open Debate" published in July 2020 in *Harper's Magazine* and signed by a litany of powerful public figures, including progressives, critiques of "cancel culture" center on the notion that oversensitive networked publics have the power to destroy individuals for perceived wrongdoing, no matter how minimal, with a mere tweet, which has a chilling effect on public discourse and unfairly victimizes targets. However, this argument ignores the reality that nearly all "canceled" privileged individuals retain their wealth and power, with many returning to their public lives and careers with minimal interruption. This panic over the demise of free speech wrought by "cancel culture" threatens to obscure and reify systemic power differentials by dismissing calls for accountability as toxic. Interrogating these dynamics is critical to examining the complex relationships between celebrity, feminisms, and digital cultures.

Celebrity Feminism in the Digital Age

So how are we to draw these areas of inquiry—celebrity culture, feminist media studies, and digital media theory—together to understand how popular culture and social media are transforming feminism in the twenty-first century? Many feminist scholars and activists have approached this issue with a healthy skepticism, leery of popular feminism's embeddedness within capitalist logics. Indeed, much of this skepticism can be summed up by Roxane Gay's (2014b) oft-cited piece from *The Guardian* titled, "Emma Watson? Jennifer Lawrence? These Aren't the Feminists You're Looking For." In this piece, Gay asserts that celebrity feminism is "a gateway to feminism, not the movement itself," and raises concerns about celebrities' use of feminism as a marketing ploy. Her critiques reflect larger suspicions of popular feminism and celebrity feminism in particular as overly individualized, capitalistic, and politically inert, and other scholars echo these worries. Andi Zeisler (2016) calls the current form of popular feminism "marketplace feminism," emphasizing its media-friendly marketability that she argues renders much of what comes to stand in for mainstream feminism depoliticized, decontextualized, simplified, and deradicalized—ultimately, many of the critiques leveled at postfeminist media cultures. Similarly, Gill (2016) cautions us not to be too enchanted with the new visibilities of feminism, arguing that feminist media scholars still need the insights of postfeminism. Banet-Weiser and Portwood-Stacer (2017) argue that today's popular feminism is "decidedly not post-feminist" because it recognizes the need for some version of feminism but fails to reckon with or work to disrupt the "political economic conditions that allow that inequality to be profitable," so it "has a similar effect to postfeminism" (886). In other words, while we might take a different route to get there in today's analyses of popular feminism, all roads through the popular lead back to postfeminist conclusions—a reformist version of white liberal feminism that is marketable but ultimately serves to contain radical critique of the systemic roots of white supremacist patriarchal capitalism.

As the following chapters will show, these scholars and activists are often correct in their assessment of popular feminism as articulated through celebrity culture. However, this book focuses on how those articulations are debated and contested. As Anita Brady (2016) points out, part of what is at stake in the discourse around celebrity feminists is the determination of "what counts as feminist action, and who gets to adjudicate on its political veracity" (4). Further, she emphasizes that social media is a crucial site at which this jockeying and debate over feminist authenticity take place. Due to the affordances of digital media, to encounter news of and commentary on feminist celebrities "is to always encounter a debate over . . . feminism" (10). Brady concludes that the goal should not to be to pin down or define feminism by saying who is and who is not authentic in their politics; rather, the diversity of celebrity definitions of feminism and the resultant debates highlight that "the production of a field of feminist politics . . . cannot be definitively resolved" (11). And, as Janell Hobson (2017) argues in response to Gay's (2014b) article, "Celebrity feminist discourses occur in sustained dialogue with other feminist discourses, which further complicates the meanings of and possibilities for a celebrity feminism that might coexist alongside grassroots feminism, academic feminism, and other spheres of influence." While Hobson acknowledges that celebrity feminism "continues to assert privilege and prestige" over other forms of feminism because of the platform afforded to celebrities, she emphasizes that it exists in dialogue with multiple feminisms, particularly in online spaces where audiences (who are often feminists) interact with and speak back to celebrity feminism. For this reason, she argues that it is "more than the gateway to the movement" that Gay suggests, but rather is a part of the movement. Those digital conversations around celebrity feminism and the ways that celebrity feminism fits into the broader feminist movement are the focus of this book.

When Feminism Became Cool

Just Like Us covers a selection of celebrity events that incited discussion around gender, sexuality, race, and feminism between 2014 and 2018. While its growing presence within pop culture began anew around the start of the 2010s, popular feminism, particularly celebrity feminism, skyrocketed into public consciousness in a profound way in 2014. Rather than the stereotypes of bra-burning, man-hating lesbians, "new visibilities" of feminism began to emerge across the media landscape (Gill 2016) as more and more celebrities began openly identifying as feminists, incorporating feminist themes into their work, and even working alongside various campaigns for gender equality. One of the most noteworthy examples was former Harry Potter star Emma Watson, who began to work as a United Nations women goodwill ambassador on behalf of the new #HeForShe movement, a campaign intended to encourage both women and men to fight for gender equality. In September, she gave a much-discussed speech promoting the campaign's formation, arguing for the continued need for feminist activism and attempting to correct misconceptions about the movement (United Nations 2014). She said, in part, "The more I have spoken about feminism, the more I have realized that fighting for women's rights has too often become synonymous with man-hating. If there is one thing I know for certain, it is that this has to stop."

Watson was not the only female celebrity who sparked a flurry of press for her emerging identity as a feminist. A few years earlier, writer, actress, and director Lena Dunham created the explicitly feminist (and very, very white) HBO series *Girls*. In 2014, Dunham even managed to convince her friend mega–pop star Taylor Swift that feminism was not so bad, and Swift spent the majority of her summer promotional tour for her album *1989* heralding her feminist awakening courtesy of the *Girls* showrunner. Her comments echoed Watson's; speaking with *The Guardian*, she stated, "What [feminism] seemed to me, the way it was phrased in culture, society, was that you hate men. And now, I think a lot of girls have had a feminist awakening because they understand what the word means. For so long it's been made to seem like something where you'd picket against the opposite sex, whereas it's not about that at all" (Hoby 2014). At the MTV Video Music Awards just two days after Swift made these comments, Beyoncé performed "***Flawless" standing in front of a screen with the word *FEMINIST* emblazoned in huge, bold lettering as writer and activist Chimamanda Ngozi Adichie's definition of feminism blared through the speakers (J. Valenti 2014). The change of heart these women expressed (for Beyoncé, too, previously had shunned the moniker of "feminist") functioned as both evidence and catalyst for a broader cultural reimagining of feminism. According to these women, feminists were no longer misrepresented as militant man-haters; instead, they were sophisticated young actresses and powerful, highly successful recording artists who simply wanted gender equality.

Within the span of a year, the question "Are you a feminist?," which had become de rigueur in interviews with celebrity women throughout 2014, transformed from a genuine query into a formality; feminism was cool now, the hip new celebrity identity, and the tables had radically turned. Just a few years before, identifying as a feminist might have threatened a female celebrity's brand. But now, those who said they were not feminist were subjected to a chorus of online outrage and asked again and again until they acquiesced—just ask actresses Kaley Cuoco or Shailene Woodley, whose shaky denials of the term garnered headlines for months until they eventually recanted and accepted the moniker (Puente 2015a; Donahue 2017). Over the course of 2014 and into 2015, it became clear that there was a correct answer, and that answer was "yes," regardless of how minimal a celebrity's understanding of the word, let alone the movement, might be. So pervasive was celebrity feminism that two unlikely bedfellows—*Cosmopolitan* magazine and Gloria Steinem's Ms. Foundation— teamed up to survey readers and subsequently published a list of the Top Ten Feminist Celebrities of the Year (Filipovic 2014). This astonishing tidal wave of celebrity feminism spawned myriad commentaries and critiques across legacy and social media outlets as well as in academic circles. Why would Watson's campaign seek to water down feminism to appeal to men (Bajwa 2015)? Why is Dunham garnering such accolades for a "feminist" show set in a New York City full of privileged white characters (Berman 2013)? Oh, of course, now that feminism is popular, Swift decides to jump on the bandwagon, careful to ensure people know she is still comfortably enamored with men despite her political awakening. How is a feminist to square Beyoncé's hyper-self-sexualization with her messaging about gender equality (Gay 2014a)? Even as a feminist media studies scholar obsessed with celebrity culture, I found the flood of think pieces and Twitter threads overwhelming and at times exhausting. This exhaustion at the term's ubiquity landed *feminism* on *Time*'s survey of "Words to Ban in 2015." Unsurprisingly, anti-feminist trolls bombarded the poll, and the term won handily, leading to a chagrined apology from the outlet (Steinmetz 2014).

This book traces mediated conversations around celebrity and feminism from this pivotal year of 2014, when they began to pervade mainstream media, through 2018 and beyond as stars grappled with the fallout from the Weinstein scandal and #MeToo. Across this period, I chose moments that typified tensions that continually emerged in social and legacy media discussions of celebrity and feminism. My analyses of the 2014 celebrity nude photo hack in chapter 1 and the 2016 harassment of *Ghostbusters* star Leslie Jones in chapter 4 highlight emerging understandings of celebrities as vulnerable, linking conversations around the irresponsibility of digital platforms and their lax security to conversations around sexist, racist harassment and national political shifts. The discussion in chapter 2 of feminist interventions around the 2015 Academy Awards and my examination of the Time's Up initiative launched at the 2018 Golden Globes in chapter 5 trace the possibilities and limitations of celebrity culture as a site of feminist activism. And my analysis of feminist icons Gloria Steinem, Madeleine Albright, and Hillary Clinton in chapter 3 explicitly links fame, feminism, and politics within the broader context of generation gaps and feminist rage.

While each chapter focuses on particular case studies, the insights they provide extend beyond each individual scenario to map the meandering evolution of popular feminist discussions around celebrity culture as shaped by digital platforms. Moreover, this book aims neither to outline the ways celebrity feminisms or feminist celebrities fail to achieve the nuances of academic feminism nor to praise new visibilities of popular feminism as ideal iterations of the movement. Rather, my goal is to unpack how negotiations of feminism constantly circulate around celebrity culture, facilitated and shaped by the affordances of digital platforms. For that reason, although chapters may focus on individual celebrities, I do not analyze or evaluate their expressions of feminism in isolation; such analyses are not only limited in their transferability to other contexts but, more important, risk oversimplifying popular feminism by focusing on the words and actions of individual stars rather than on the larger set of popular discourses about what feminism is and should be that often emerge around stars.

The case studies in this book and the celebrities I discuss are located almost exclusively in the United States. While celebrities across the world have long been and continue to be deeply involved in social justice and political activism, the particulars of celebrity culture, feminism, and anti-Black racism in the United States are unique and undergird the analyses to follow. Hollywood as a symbolic center of wealth, fame, and beauty holds a particular mystique, and the United States' emphasis on upward mobility means that celebrities come to function as stand-ins for the American dream and its supposedly attainable wild success (Sternheimer 2011). American celebrities simultaneously embody accessibility (stars, they are just like us!) and otherworldly glitz and glamour.

That inherent tension and its entanglements with capitalist ideologies and neo-liberalism provide a central context for the arguments that follow. Moreover, my analyses focus on racism, particularly antiblackness, which is informed by the legacy of chattel slavery in the United States. Thus I draw on U.S.-based Black feminist thought to make sense of racism in the States more generally and within the American feminist movement specifically. While this focus on the United States means that my arguments will not directly transfer to other national contexts, I believe the underlying mechanisms and theoretical frameworks may be useful, and the limitation allows me to attend to the specific historical and cultural contexts of the United States.

Additionally, the celebrity events described in this book focus primarily on how networked publics contest white feminist perspectives in and around celebrity culture that ignore and/or rebuke as toxic the critiques of women of color, specifically Black, feminists who assert the centrality of an intersectional feminist politics. Surprisingly absent from the conversations around the incidents analyzed here is an acknowledgment not only of celebrity feminism's whiteness but also of the overwhelmingly cisgender and heterosexual identities of its key emissaries. Just as the 2010s saw a massive uptick in the popularity of feminism in celebrity circles, the decade was also marked by an increase in LGBTQIA visibility, particularly trans visibility and activism. However, despite the increase in complex media representations of trans experiences and celebrities, there are two important things to note: first, the Trump administration enacted and supported draconian anti-trans legislation from day one, and Republican-controlled state legislatures across the country continue to target trans people, particularly trans youth. As is so often the case, media representations do not translate into expanded rights but often engender deep-seated backlash. Second, despite the concurrent rise in popular discourses on LGBTQIA rights, those conversations did not often intersect with popular feminism. The case studies analyzed here—some of the most widely discussed and prominent moments of cultural rupture around feminism and celebrity—leave unsaid what is readily apparent: that celebrity feminism in particular is focused on the needs and desires not only of white women but of cisgender, heterosexual white women. While the following chapters chart a reckoning with the overwhelming whiteness of feminism, discussions of its deeply cis focus have been mostly absent. So much of the role celebrities have played in elevating feminism as a brand over the last decade centers on the cishet attractiveness they lend it. As dominant cultural images of feminism shift away from the angry, braless, man-hating lesbian toward the straight, cis, sophisticated, hip starlet, feminism's cultural cachet has blossomed. Going forward, the intersectional imperative around celebrity feminism will need to reckon with its elision of LGBTQIA and, in particular, trans politics.

Analyzing the Transformation of Digital and Popular Feminisms

My research design for this book centers on what I call "multiplatform discourse analysis." This method combines a qualitative interpretation of Burgess and Matamoros-Fernández's (2016) approach to multiplatform issue mapping with techniques derived from Brock's (2020) critical technocultural discourse analysis. In bringing together these two sets of methods and techniques, I track each celebrity incident across platforms, including social media, online news and commentary, and legacy media news and commentary, mapping and analyzing media objects—from tweets to newspaper articles, from YouTube videos to red carpet photos—associated with it. Drawing from Burgess and Matamoros-Fernandez's multiplatform mapping techniques, I orient my analysis around the notion of networked "issue publics." Issue publics are groups of individuals, from journalists and commentators to everyday social media users, who pay attention to and converse about the events I analyze, and these conversations form the basis of my analysis. In sampling and mapping each event, I follow the discourse analytic method used by Braithwaite (2016) in her analysis of Gamergate. Like Braithwaite, my mapping "resembles the 'snowball' approach" (3), following the links between social media, online news, YouTube, newspapers, magazines, and so forth to demonstrate the most salient features of each controversy rather than provide an exhaustive account of all media objects related to them.

While this process of data collection operated differently across case studies as each celebrity incident involved different dynamics, I followed the same general protocol. I began by collecting data from Twitter using relevant search terms and hashtags over a period of several days around each incident. Then, using digital snowball sampling, I added any links to webpages, videos, and similar sources included in these tweets to my dataset. Next, I searched the top newspapers, news and commentary websites (including websites for network and cable news channels, which post much of their television content online), and magazines for articles about each incident and added any other articles, videos, social media posts, and so forth that were hyperlinked or embedded in those articles to my dataset. To augment these methods of snowball sampling, I set my Google Chrome web browser to "incognito" to deindividuate my search results and conducted Google and YouTube searches of relevant terms over relevant time periods for each incident. For each case study I went to at least the tenth page of search results for each term and added the relevant media objects to my dataset. The resulting dataset is drawn from Twitter, YouTube, television, online news and commentary sites, newspapers, and magazines.[2] In choosing which data to highlight in each chapter, I selected the most highly circulated texts as well as those that most clearly illustrate themes that resonated across platforms.

To analyze the data, I engaged in critical discourse analysis. Drawing from the work of Michel Foucault, Gillian Rose (2007) defines *discourse* as "groups of statements which structure the way a thing is thought, and the way we act on the basis of that thinking. In other words, discourse is a particular knowledge about the world which shapes how the world is understood and how things are done in it" (136). For this reason, discourse is deeply ideological, reinforcing and producing what constitutes "truth" in a given time and place. Critical discourse analysis aims to map the linguistic, contextual, and intertextual meanings within and between texts to understand how they produce "truth" about a particular topic. Because these discourses span digital platforms, I not only focus on the content of each media object but also, in the vein of Brock's (2020) critical technocultural discourse analysis, examine how that content is shaped by digital platforms. I considered the ways in which the specificities of each platform's design, norms of use, and affordances shape the discourse in each space. These insights of critical technocultural discourse analysis allow for a richer and more nuanced analysis. In addition, by utilizing this method comparatively across platforms, I am able to explore the interrelatedness of platforms across the media ecosystem while remaining attentive to the specificities of each platform. Further, I conducted this analysis through an intersectional feminist theoretical lens. While intersectionality has been a somewhat contested term since Crenshaw's seminal argument (e.g., Lutz, Vivar, and Supik 2011), I adopt what Nirmala Erevelles and Andrea Minear (2010) refer to as the "intercategorical framework of intersectionality." Instead of piling on identity categories in their analysis of race, gender, sex, sexuality, disability, and so forth, they call for an examination of the structural conditions that mutually constitute these categories and their relationships to identity construction.

Chapter Breakdown

Chapter 1 explores the summer of 2014 as a key moment when popular feminism emerged with renewed visibility within celebrity culture, only to be met with virulent networked misogyny. In particular, I focus on the celebrity nude photo hack, which leaked only a few short weeks after the Gamergate controversy began. Through an analysis of online news coverage, I argue that the online news discourse around the hack demonstrates the burgeoning prominence of popular feminist ideas within the mainstream media as the celebrity victims' sexuality and right to digital privacy were sympathetically affirmed rather than shamed, and the hackers and disseminators of the photos were derided as disgusting, misogynistic criminals. Overall, this chapter establishes the role of *celebrity gossip* as a discursive space for negotiating social norms and moral consensus, laying the groundwork for more in-depth discussions of digital accountability practices, moral outrage, and digital vulnerabilities in subsequent chapters.

The second chapter shifts from a focus on popular feminist discourses around sexuality in celebrity culture to examine discussions around women's labor and value. Following yet another 2014 hack that rocked Hollywood—the Sony hack—discussions about female objectification and wage inequality reemerged into public discourse. Here, I focus on the 2015 Academy Awards as a site at which these tensions were explored and negotiated. I demonstrate that the superficiality and lack of intersectionality in discussions of Hollywood women's labor and value around the awards show motivated networked publics to employ *hashtag activism* and engage in digital accountability practices like *calling out* to agitate for more inclusive, more politically motivated feminisms from both celebrities and media outlets that cover celebrities. Building on the previous chapter's contention that certain popular feminist ideas are gaining dominance in some mainstream media spaces, this chapter explores in more detail two strategies networked publics use—hashtags and callouts—to negotiate and pressure celebrities and media companies to engage in representations and performances of self that incorporate feminist ideas.

These feminist negotiations, however, are not confined to entertainment celebrity culture; they also suffuse political and activist celebrity spaces. Chapter 3 transitions out of Hollywood to explore how feminist negotiations and *anger* map onto *political choice* through an analysis of discourse around Madeleine Albright and Gloria Steinem's participation in Hillary Clinton's 2016 presidential campaign. Following my discussion of Steinem's and Albright's controversial comments about young female voters, I argue that mainstream news discourses drew from and amplified contention among networked publics to emphasize feminist generation gaps as progressive feminists pushed for a more intersectional feminist politics of choice. Foregrounding and interrogating the role of outrage in intrafeminist conflict, this chapter explores how this politics of choice stems from a sense of responsibility that feminist voters should educate themselves and make political decisions that decenter white, Western, middle-class women's issues and reject imperialism.

As tensions around the 2016 presidential race intensified, lines between entertainment and politics grew blurrier. This fuzziness was made abundantly clear through yet another instance of online abuse and hacking. Focusing on the far right–led harassment of actress Leslie Jones, chapter 4 examines how *backlash* to popular feminism was mobilized to exploit technological and racial vulnerabilities and teases apart the illogical bases of that backlash, providing a detailed corrective that highlights the continuing need for cross-platform accountability practices. Alongside this analysis, I demonstrate that *supportive counterpublics* rallied around Jones to frame this incident as indicative of systemic issues with platform security, misogynoir, and the rise of far-right politics. Far from sensationalizing this incident as an isolated attack, dominant discourses called for platforms to take responsibility for the safety of users and for voters to draw connections between this harassment and the sociopolitical dynamics supporting the rise of Donald Trump.

The intersections between social justice, celebrity culture, and social media came to a head in October 2017 when renewed accusations of sexual misconduct against Harvey Weinstein sparked millions of women across the world, celebrity and noncelebrity alike, to take to social media to share their stories of harassment and assault using the hashtag #MeToo. Chapter 5 focuses on the *celebrity feminist activism* proposed in the wake of #MeToo, the Time's Up legal defense fund, and its publicization via celebrities' social media accounts and their appearances at the 2018 Golden Globe Awards ceremony. Ultimately, despite the admirably intersectional and systemically focused goals of the legal defense fund, its promotion and public rollout were subverted by the self-promotional logics of both social media and celebrity culture, and the organization ultimately collapsed in 2021, mired in scandal. By analyzing one of the few recent examples of sustained feminist mobilization within celebrity circles, this chapter adds nuance to our understandings of the complex entanglements of neoliberal individualism and feminist collectivity that characterize modern celebrity feminism, demonstrating clearly how celebrity feminism extends, amplifies, and makes hypervisible the promises and pitfalls of the feminist movement more broadly.

The book's conclusion considers how the normalization of celebrity involvement in the feminist movement may impact progressive activism for years to come. Alongside and intersecting with this analysis, I critique the rising backlash against feminism and, in particular, digital accountability practices as spawning a supposed "cancel culture." Overall, I interrogate the possibilities and limitations of sociotechnical discursive pressures to agitate for a more equitable society within and beyond celebrity cultures.

1

Hacking Celebrity

Sexuality, Privacy, and
Networked Misogyny in the
Celebrity Nude Photo Hack

As discussed in the introduction, a key dynamic came to define 2014: as feminism gained popularity, so too did misogyny (Banet-Weiser 2018). Few incidents typify the mainstreaming of sexist harassment, and particularly digitally mediated "networked misogyny" (Banet-Weiser and Miltner 2016), better than the targeted campaigns against women in and around the video game industry that came to be known as "Gamergate." Gamergate began in the summer of 2014 when a man named Eron Gjoni alleged that his former girlfriend, indie game developer Zoe Quinn, had slept with a video game reviewer, Nathan Grayson, in exchange for positive coverage of her game, *Depression Quest* (Malone 2017). Although the allegations were later proved false, gaming communities across platforms like Twitter, 4chan, and Reddit, who were already frustrated with the growing inclusion of women and people of color within the video game world, seized onto the narrative. They doxed Quinn, hacked her personal accounts, and threatened violence, so much so that she fled her home. However, Quinn was not the only victim of misogynistic "Gamergaters." They similarly targeted Anita Sarkeesian, a feminist video game critic popular for her *Tropes vs. Women in Video Games* YouTube series, and Brianna Wu, another female indie game developer who mocked Gamergate. While Gamergaters insisted their campaign centered on "ethics in video game journalism," it was clear that the Quinn incident was merely a spark that ignited mainstream knowledge of the already simmering fire of misogyny within the gaming community and gave it a target (see Cote 2020). This was a watershed moment that made mainstream audiences more aware of the realities for women who exist in male-dominated digital spaces and the ways in which technological platforms and tools can be mobilized to harass, harm, and silence.

But Gamergate was not the only incident that exposed mainstream audiences to these realities that summer. On August 31, 2014, the internet was abuzz after hundreds of private nude photos of female celebrities, including actresses Jennifer Lawrence and Kaley Cuoco and model Kate Upton, began appearing on image and message boards. This event was colloquially referred to as "The Fappening," a portmanteau of the words *happening* and *fap*, a slang term for masturbation. For months, hackers worked to penetrate celebrities' Apple iCloud storage, which automatically backs up photos from devices such as iPhones. Hackers engaged in a "spear phishing" scam, sending emails to famous women purporting to be from Apple's security team to gain information about their log in details. Then the hackers began to post the stolen images on AnonIB, an anonymous imageboard where users primarily post pornographic photos. From there, they quickly spread via Imgur, 4chan, and Reddit to various digital networks across the world, and media outlets spent weeks covering the scandal.

To begin theorizing how popular feminist ideas are filtering into and accumulating within celebrity culture, this chapter takes as its focus online news and commentary about the celebrity nude photo hack. The analysis that follows explores how online discourses framed the conflict between popular feminism and anti-feminist online communities in ways that elided discussions of race and focused almost solely on vulnerability, sex positivity, and retribution against male perpetrators. These findings lay the groundwork for deeper examinations of digital feminist negotiations around celebrity culture via the contested pressures of the white feminist imperative in subsequent chapters. This chapter emphasizes the role of celebrity gossip as a meaningful mode of cultural learning, negotiation, and establishing social norms, teasing out the logics of celebrity culture and gossip that inform and, in some cases, hamper the potential of celebrity culture as a site of feminist negotiation and intervention. The hack and subsequent circulation of these photographs, and the publics that coalesced around the incident, constituted a flash point at which mainstream audiences recognized the vulnerability of digital platforms and, in particular, of women who engage with those platforms. This vulnerability was made manifest through an attack on celebrities, but discussions made clear that the incident was embedded within broader patriarchal power structures that impact famous and nonfamous women alike.

This chapter, focusing on the discursive construction of both the female celebrities and the hackers and posters of the photos, provides a case study that explores not only the impact of celebrity culture and gossip on sociocultural discussions of gender and sexuality but also the ways in which their entanglements with digital harassment provide insight into mainstream attitudes toward and contestation around feminist ideas. Overall, I argue that although coverage of the nude photo hack problematizes celebrities' sexuality through their relationships to publicity and occasionally acknowledges the complexity of communities like Reddit, the popular feminist tone of the dominant discourse defends and supports the white celebrities as innocent victims of patriarchal power structures that affect not only celebrities but all women, while constructing the hackers and online communities who shared the photos as disgusting perpetrators of misogyny.

Analyzing Online Discourse about the Nude Photo Hack

In order to explore the roles of celebrity gossip and online conversations in negotiating popular feminist ideals while attending to the specificities of this particular event, I used a different research design for this chapter than for the others. First, cross-platform data collection was problematized by the ephemerality of content on sites like AnonIB and 4chan. By the time most audiences, including me, became aware of the event, the posts had already been deleted. However, these realities emphasize the importance of news and commentary about the hack. The coverage did more than just fix the meaning of the event; for many audiences, it became the event itself. Second, this event lasted longer than most other case studies in the book, with multiple waves of attacks and leaks for months after the initial release. This means there was an overwhelmingly larger potential dataset across online and legacy outlets and social media platforms.

For these reasons, I theoretically sampled two years of coverage of the hack (August 31, 2014–August 31, 2016) from six online news and commentary outlets selected for their prominence and variance, which resulted in a dataset of 118 articles. Three outlets publish more general news and commentary and were the sites of much early breaking news and investigation of the hack: *Gawker*, BuzzFeed, and *Slate*. Next, I selected two celebrity gossip sites to tap into how the hack was understood as a celebrity scandal: Perez Hilton, a much-maligned mainstay of the early celebrity gossip blogosphere who found himself at the center of a scandal around his publication of the photos, and *Celebitchy*, a more feminist-leaning outlet. Finally, I also analyzed coverage in *Variety* to examine how the hack was addressed from an entertainment industry perspective.

I begin by exploring the role of gossip, both interpersonal and celebrity, in community formation and the negotiation of social and moral norms. This background lays a foundation for the importance of gossip and commentary about the nude photo hack as I analyze the discursive constructions of the celebrity victims of the hack. These online news and commentary outlets were overwhelmingly sympathetic to the celebrities, framing them as the victims of misogynistic power structures that affect famous and nonfamous women. Then my focus shifts to the anonymous and pseudonymous online communities where the hack and leaks began—AnonIB, 4chan, and Reddit—through an examination of how various affordances shape the types of online sociality that occur there. Finally, I analyze the discourse around the hackers and sharers of the photographs, demonstrating that, while some articles acknowledged the complexity of platforms like Reddit, the majority discursively constructed the publics that stole and circulated these images as untalented, disgusting, misogynistic criminals.

Gossip Networks: Considering Gossip as an Epistemological Tool

Gossip, defined as "informal, private communication between an individual and a small, selected audience concerning the conduct of absent persons or events," has long been studied within social anthropology (Merry 1984, 275). While popular understandings of gossip tend toward the pejorative and sexist, conjuring notions of women engaged in more or less malicious idle talk behind others' backs, gossip can fulfill important social roles within communities. It can help to build a sense of community among individuals, allowing people to bond and establish social cohesion (Gluckman 1963). As individuals share information and bond, gossip also provides a space for cultural learning as people learn from the experiences of others (Burdick 1990; Baumeister, Zhang, and Vohs 2004). Moreover, the evaluative nature of gossip allows for and encourages the negotiation of moral and cultural norms as community members discuss and adjudicate the actions of others (Jerslev 2014).

By focusing on the important social roles that gossip fulfills, scholars have pushed back on the popular notion that it is merely idle women's talk (McKeown 2015). While researchers emphasize that both male and female members of communities engage in gossip, feminist scholars have explored the particular functions gossip can serve among groups of women. A central thinker on the importance of women's gossip as knowledge building, Patricia Spacks (2012) points to the role of "serious gossip," which is focused on information sharing, as opposed to malicious or belittling talk, among women to build and strengthen their relationships and allow them to explore uncertainties and obtain information about their social worlds. Moreover, gossip can provide a discursive space for women to speak out against oppressive gender norms. Gossip networks can function as subaltern publics where women and other marginalized communities can share knowledge and negotiate a moral consensus that subverts dominant norms. Far from idle talk, in some cases women's gossip can be powerfully important to community formation and even to resistance.

While the work described in the preceding paragraphs concerns gossip about members of and happenings in one's immediate community, mass and social media have greatly expanded our catalog of known others. For decades, media researchers have noted that audiences can develop parasocial relationships with fictional characters and famous figures, feeling a one-sided sense of closeness and forming emotional attachments to people they do not know personally (Horton and Wohl 1956). And while news and gossip about celebrities is as old as fame itself, the past three decades have seen a rapid increase in the number of media outlets, both legacy and digital, devoted to cataloging and evaluating celebrities' behavior, and growing numbers of audiences, particularly women, who consume this content (Sternheimer 2011; McDonnell 2014). In her study of female celebrity magazine readers, Joke Hermes (1995) noted that many spoke about celebrities as though they were part of their "extended family" (126–127), expressing a sense of solidarity and connectedness with them. Perhaps unsurprisingly, then, research on the role of celebrity gossip presents similar findings to research on community gossip: celebrity gossip provides a way for people, particularly women, to build and strengthen bonds (Gamson 1994); its evaluative nature can help women negotiate and establish moral consensus (Bird 1992); and it can open a discursive space in which to explore and even contest dominant gender norms (Wilson 2010; McDonnell 2014).

The rise of celebrity blogs has transformed and expanded the intimacy, immediacy, accessibility, frequency, and participatory potential of celebrity gossip publics (Graefer 2014). The temporal transformations brought on by digital platforms are key to current shifts in celebrity culture. As Anne Helen Petersen (2010) points out, blogs can post dozens of times a day, providing up-to-the-minute updates on celebrity happenings. She demonstrates that this constancy can have a much stronger impact on audiences' understanding and impression of celebrities' personas. Moreover, this digitally enabled increased access to celebrity stories and images (McNamara 2011) can heighten audiences' sense of intimacy with celebrities, and the participatory nature of these sites allows networked publics of celebrity watchers to form community in comments sections (Jerslev 2014) and across other social media sites. However, the greater sense of accessibility to celebrities and networking capabilities afforded by digital technologies can have a dark side, as the celebrity nude photo hack clearly demonstrates. Overall, celebrity gossip can provide a way for publics to negotiate norms and moral consensus around a range of issues, including sexuality and vulnerability, and digital platforms provide broader access both to information about celebrities and to communities that discuss them. The next sections of this chapter explore how news, commentary, and gossip outlets framed the violating nude photo hack and negotiated consensus around victimhood and blame.

Constructing and Problematizing Celebrities as Victims

They're Just Like Us: Encouraging Empathy, Calling Out Victim Blaming, and Connecting the Hack to Systemic Misogyny

The most prominent way these news outlets discussed the celebrities was as victims, orienting their place within the scandal as sympathetic and disempowered. Such a characterization inverts the typical norms of celebrity gossip, which often frames stars simultaneously as objects of critique and admiration. Their status as the focus of public ridicule or praise stems from their privilege and social capital, but most stories in this sample emphasized their vulnerability. Indeed, this controversy marked a moment in which celebrities were presented as "just like us": women who, like their nonfamous counterparts, are vulnerable to misogyny and violation. For example, in Perez Hilton's first post about the story, he informs readers that "Jennifer Lawrence, Victoria Justice, Kate Upton, and A LOT more celebrity women were victims of a HUGE hacking" (Hilton 2014a). His use of all capitals highlights the magnitude of the number of victims and the hack itself, emphasizing the degree of their victimization. Further, writers often deployed the descriptor "victim" to express outrage and empathy. In several early reports on the hack from *Celebitchy*, writer Bedhead (2014) describes how "poor JLaw" and other female celebrities have been "targeted" and "violated" by the hack, which has rendered them "victim[s]" and "vulnerable." The prominence of such descriptors points to an emerging moral consensus within these news and gossip outlets that the women were, above all, wronged and violated in a significant way, encouraging the reading public to sympathize with their experiences.

Further, the majority of the articles made it clear that the women were innocent victims. Except for *Variety*, each source featured one or more articles assessing reactions to the scandal that blamed the celebrities for taking and storing nude photographs. However, the focus of these articles was on the outrage such responses received. For example, BuzzFeed posted an article about British comedian Ricky Gervais's tweet, which read, "Celebrities, make it harder for hackers to get nude pics from your computer by not putting nude pics of yourself on your computer" (Barrow 2014). Although Gervais soon deleted the tweet, fellow members of this issue public took screenshots of his message and were able to disseminate it as an image within and beyond Twitter, such as in the BuzzFeed article. While Twitter allows users to remove a tweet, it cannot prevent others from using functionalities like the screenshot, which renders that tweet permanent. Ironically, Gervais, like the celebrities he shamed, was unable to remove from circulation a text he wished to keep private because others utilized various technical affordances to disseminate information he had attempted to contain. Therefore, networked publics were able to call him out and hold him accountable even after he deleted the tweet. Indeed, BuzzFeed writer Jo Barrow explains that "Twitter was unimpressed" and posts nine users' tweets in response to Gervais, denouncing his joke as victim blaming. By totalizing the diverse, varied, and complex networked publics on Twitter as uniformly disapproving of Gervais's comment, Barrow portrays such a reaction as dominant and common sense; to agree with Gervais is to incur the public's wrath, to be excluded from the dominant moral consensus, wherein the appropriate response is to understand the (overwhelmingly white) celebrities as blameless victims. Years before panics around supposed "cancel culture" began, this small example demonstrates how networked publics were already working to call out behaviors that violated shifting social norms around gender and sexuality; these themes will be explored in much more detail in later chapters.

In addition, much of the coverage focused on the gendered nature of the celebrities' victimhood, not only by pointing out the dearth of male victims but also by connecting the women's victimization to broader structural issues of sexism and misogyny. Much of the coverage foregrounded gender subtly but insistently, referring to the celebrities as "women" or using the descriptor of "female" before "celebrities" or "stars." While such coverage did not always comment directly on the social inequalities and persistent objectification around women's bodies and sexualities, the presence of this gendered language kept the women's sex at the fore. Other writers explicitly critiqued such inequalities by pointing out that almost no male celebrities were included in the hack. In a particularly blunt example, *Celebitchy*'s first article on the subject notes, "Only females were targeted in this hacking scheme. Of course" (Bedhead, 2014). The connection of their victimization to their gender was seen as a given; "of course" the targets of such sexual attacks were only women. For *Celebitchy*'s self-identified feminist gossip writers, such inequalities are expected. Overall, the writers' foregrounding of the celebrities' femaleness begins to connect the scandal to structural sexual inequalities.

Several of the articles, particularly those from *Gawker*, BuzzFeed, and *Slate*, went beyond such subtle connections to explicitly critique the incident as embedded within patriarchal structures of misogyny. These think pieces were framed not episodically but thematically, linking the hack to other celebrity scandals or, often, to broader issues of sexism and sexual assault online. For example, in her *Gawker* article "That Type of Girl Deserves It," lawyer and feminist Reut Amit (2014) frames the celebrities not as famous but as "successful women," claiming the scandal has "nothing to do with celebrity" but rather is one instance of society punishing women for immodesty. Anne Helen Petersen (2014) of BuzzFeed and Amanda Hess (2014a) of *Slate* further debate the connections between the hack, celebrity, and misogyny. Petersen likens the leak of Jennifer Lawrence's photos to nude photos of Marilyn Monroe that surfaced without her consent early in her career, explaining that Monroe refused to be scandalized and rather incorporated the scandal into her star image. Petersen suggests that, as viewers, we do the same and "perform the difficult but necessary labor of not being scandalized at all" by Lawrence's photos. Here, the burden lies with viewers to accept Lawrence's images as normal and unsurprising. While Petersen highlights issues of privacy and consent, ultimately the task is ours to interpret the photos "as feminists, fans of Lawrence, or just culturally progressive people" and not care about them.

Hess takes Petersen to task for such a directive, claiming that "we should all be scandalized" by the hack. To take the nude photo hack in stride is not to rob the hackers of their power but rather to bow to it by failing to decry the various infrastructures that allowed for such violation. These debates around the hack attempt to understand and ultimately fix its meanings within broader systems of inequality. Moreover, what is particularly notable about these articles is that they assume their readership is made up of feminists. Their goal is not to convince readers to approach the incident from a feminist perspective; rather, they debate and negotiate the appropriate way to respond to the hack *as feminists*. This negotiation is made easier through the affordances of digital platforms. For example, Hess links to Petersen's article, so readers can consume both and choose which one they agree with. By subtly or not so subtly pointing out the unfair norms of patriarchal societies in which women's bodies are sexualized and commodified in a way that men's bodies are not, these discursive choices provide a space for writers and readers to negotiate and contest an established gender hierarchy, not only pushing back on misogynistic viewpoints but also debating among fellow feminists. This multivocality and tension within the feminist movement, and the ways those debates take shape across social media platforms, are central themes that will be developed in more detail in chapters 2 and 3.

In further connecting the celebrities' plight to that of women writ large, much of the coverage focused on how celebrities were "just like us," inviting readers to understand celebrities as a part of their community. Many articles used the nude photo hack as a springboard for discussions about account security, revenge porn, and online harassment that also affect "ordinary" women. To that end, every outlet discussed broader issues of iCloud security and/or steps "we" as the viewing public should take to ensure that we are not victims of similar hacks (e.g., Hilton 2014f; Oremus 2014). Further, *Gawker*, BuzzFeed, and *Slate* all featured articles that de-emphasized the uniqueness of this incident by explaining that "ordinary" women are also frequently hacked, and their photos are circulated on AnonIB and 4chan just like those of celebrities. This argument is typified in an in-depth look at AnonIB from Hess (2014b)

FIGURE 1.1 Header image depicting Jennifer Lawrence (left) and Kate Upton (right) from one of many articles on the nude photo hack from Perez Hilton, 2014. (Credit: Perez Hilton, WENN.)

entitled "Inside AnonIB, Where Hacking Is a Sport and Women's Bodies Are the Prize." Here, Hess explains that the hack's famous victims are joined by thousands of ordinary women and treated as "property" and "objects" by members of AnonIB, who buy, sell, and trade their nude images. These articles point to the role of gossip in supporting knowledge sharing and cultural learning: by reading gossip about and analyses of the experiences of these celebrity women, audiences can learn about their own digital vulnerabilities and view them within the context of structural misogyny. Overall, the main thrust of the coverage makes connections between "us" and "them," emphasizing and decrying women's shared experiences at the hands of a digitally enabled system of patriarchal exploitation that commodifies and violates women's bodies.

The Public/Private Divide: Negotiating, Minimizing, and Exploiting Celebrity Victimization

While in many ways the gossip and news discourses positioned celebrities as just like us, celebrities' fame and the magnitude of the publicity around this scandal set them apart by amplifying their victimization and rendering it spectacular and worthy of reportage and commentary. At times, writers deployed the nature of that fame, and various celebrities' relationships to publicity, to articulate differences between those who are innocent victims and those who are less worthy of our sympathy or attention. One key example is an article in *Celebitchy* that details the release of Kim Kardashian's nude photos in a second wave of leaks. Kaiser (2014), the author of the piece asserts, "It's an invasion of privacy, feminism, men do not own our bodies, etc., let's not be gross, you get the picture. But in all honesty . . . no one is going to get worked up about this, are they? Kim Kardashian is famous because of a sex tape." While Kaiser knows that the "appropriate" response is feminist outrage, her article makes it clear Kardashian's exposure is nothing "to get worked up about" by virtue of her history of public sexual display. Just as Gamson (2001) argued in his work on celebrity sex scandals, discourses of publicity map onto discourses of celebrity so that Kardashian, who is already a "publicity whore," is not a victim in the same way as "innocent" victims who have not previously exposed their bodies, such as Lawrence.

These tensions around publicity and privacy, and the role of celebrity news within that dynamic, also surface in Perez Hilton's coverage of the scandal. Unlike many other mainstream bloggers who refused to post or link to the leaked images in order to protect the women's privacy, Hilton posted the photos on his site the day they leaked. He removed them after readers expressed outrage and posted a video apology on YouTube (Hilton 2014d). In the video, Hilton says that he was "guilty" of posting the photos "without really thinking about the repercussions of [his] actions," explaining that he was on vacation with his family, saw the news, and felt it was his responsibility as a celebrity gossip blogger to disseminate the information quickly on his site. His excuse mirrors the dynamics Petersen (2010) and Graefer (2014) discuss in their analysis of changes brought on by the migration of celebrity gossip from print to digital: the ability for immediate and constantly updated access to celebrity news. While Hilton couches this quick decision under the guise of his "responsibility" to his readers, it was almost certainly informed by a desire to capitalize on this spectacular, juicy scandal and drive traffic to his site, particularly because so many others were refusing to post the photos out of courtesy. After readers called him out, he took the photos down, whether because he genuinely felt remorse or was worried that his actions would foster a sufficient backlash as to ostracize him and threaten the financial viability of his site. Visibly distraught (or at least performatively so), Hilton demonstrates the tensions of reporting on celebrity scandals and negotiating the public/private boundary. And while we might read Hilton's response cynically—he has an abhorrent history of bullying celebrities and his livelihood depends on his audience continuing to visit the site—like the dominant discourse around the celebrity victims, his video ultimately agrees with the emergent moral consensus: the appropriate response was outrage at their victimization, not complicity.

Although Hilton apologized, Lawrence remained angry and mentioned him personally in her tell-all interview with *Vanity Fair* published later that year. She explained, "He took it down because people got pissed, and that's the only reason why. . . . 'I just didn't think about it' is not an excuse. That is the exact issue itself" (Kashner 2014). Here, Lawrence takes umbrage with Hilton for thoughtlessly profiting from her victimization, asserting that her privacy should trump his publication of her intimate photos, that he should consider her a "human" rather than simply a celebrity. She makes the same semantic moves as the dominant discourse did, de-emphasizing her fame and instead focusing on what she has in common with "us." Hilton, however, did not appreciate Lawrence's response and posted another, this time furious, video in which he explains that he was "tempted to apologize to her again but, ya know what? No, f-ck that." He tells Lawrence that she "[doesn't] always get what she wants," emphasizing his genuineness in the previous video and expressing his anger at her for describing him as a bad person (Hilton 2014b). Now, when the publicity turns back onto Hilton, when he experiences firsthand a modicum of the embarrassment Lawrence suffered, he flips from contrite to vitriolic. Hilton's angry, dramatic response stands out within this sample as an example of the "smut" that particularly characterized online celebrity gossip outlets around 2006–2010, Hilton's heyday (Petersen 2009). While this antagonistic, gotcha-style celebrity gossip continues, this case study shows that it is increasingly joined, and sometimes even overshadowed, by discourses that are more heavily influenced by the accumulation and amplification of certain sex-positive feminist ideals. This subscandal demonstrates that the commonsense response to the photos' release is anger and empathy, both for news outlets and, by extension, for the viewing public; those who diverge, such as Hilton or Ricky Gervais, are excluded and face public ridicule.

Overall, the dominant discourses within this dataset demonstrate how celebrity gossip reporters and commentators negotiated and established a contested moral consensus around sexual norms. Although problematized by celebrities' relationship to publicity and their fame, which separates them from those of "us" who are not famous, most of the articles centered on the need to support these innocent women who have a right to privacy and to affirm the unfairness of digitally enabled systems of misogyny that victimize celebrity and noncelebrity women alike. Through calls to support these women, we see much of this online discourse begin to establish celebrity as a site of feminist intervention and frame celebrities as vulnerable to digital victimization in ways that are ideologically meaningful and indicative of broader social inequalities. Overall, these articles point to the role of celebrity gossip as a meaningful mode of knowledge making and cultural learning: readers can learn from the experiences of these women and understand those experiences as embedded within patriarchal systems.

"The Web's Sleazier Corners": Understanding AnonIB, 4chan, and Reddit

To understand the celebrity nude photo hack and the online news constructions of the digital communities that solicited and circulated the photos, it is crucial to understand the platforms on which those communities originated. The first of these are the online imageboards 4chan and AnonIB. The two sites appear and function similarly: a bare-bones interface linking to a variety of differently themed imageboards where users post images, comments, and threaded replies. Within these communities, posters remain anonymous, and content is not permanently stored; for example, studies have shown that content remains on the most active board on 4chan for an average of just under four minutes before being "pruned" and disappearing from the servers (Bernstein et al. 2011, 53). These features highlight two key affordances of both sites: anonymity and ephemerality. Users' identities on 4chan and AnonIB are not tied to any other online or off-line identifiers, and the content they post disappears relatively quickly from the site rather than remaining permanent. Michael Bernstein and colleagues (2011) find that these two factors can foster disinhibition and a mob mentality.

This disinhibition is amplified by these sites having few behavioral guidelines and lax to nonexistent content moderation. Thus the design and emergent social norms of 4chan have afforded "subcultural innovation" that has been key to developing web vernacular and meme culture (Tuters and Hagen 2020, 7) as well as communities with a penchant for "trolling"—or engaging in provocative online behavior in order to elicit an emotional response—"normies" who are outsiders to 4chan humor and logics as well as mainstream media (Coleman 2014; W. Phillips 2015, 2019). AnonIB, while it shares the same general platform design and affordances, focuses on pornographic content. Boards are organized by type of pornography or location, with separate boards for each state in the United States as well as different countries. Much of the site features nonconsensual pornography stolen from women's accounts in the same manner as the nude photo hack. The first images stolen from celebrity women appeared on AnonIB before migrating to 4chan via overlapping users. From there, they spread to the more mainstream Reddit, where they eventually received widespread attention.

Similar to 4chan, Reddit is an online message board, but it is more focused on news aggregation and discussion. Reddit is a "community of communities," composed of so-called subreddits organized around a wide range of topics from sports to hobbies to entertainment and beyond. Unlike AnonIB and 4chan, Reddit is pseudonymous, which means users' accounts show their posting history and their accrual of "karma," or the platform's point system. Users upvote or downvote posts and comments, which not only contribute to the poster's karma score but also amplify or bury content on the site. Highly engaging content can make it all the way to the "front page" of Reddit, or the default landing page for users who visit the site. Even though Reddit lacks the anonymity and ephemerality of 4chan and AnonIB and affords stricter moderation practices, other features of the platform can render it similarly toxic. Users may rebel against moderation policies with outrage and subversion (Squirrell 2019). And, as Adrienne Massanari (2017) points out, it is simple to create a new user account and a new subreddit. These features help to explain why the celebrity nude photo hack, or as it was widely known on Reddit, The Fappening, flourished on the site, which enabled it to receive mainstream attention. Users created a dedicated subreddit for photo sharing, r/thefappening, which received so much engagement and so many upvotes that many posts made it to Reddit's front page. In this way, Reddit, like sites such as 4chan and AnonIB, afford what Massanari (2017) calls "toxic technocultures" (333), seemingly leaderless and amorphous online cultures that leverage sociotechnical platforms for coordination and harassment, often against members of marginalized identity groups.

Extending and intersecting with these toxic technocultures, more recent work on 4chan and various bigoted subreddits in the years since The Fappening identify such communities as part of the digital "Manosphere," "an aggregate of diverse communities brought together by a common language that orients them in opposition to the discourse and rhetoric of feminism" (Marwick and Caplan 2018, 553). These explicitly anti-feminist communities, the likes of which participated in both Gamergate and The Fappening, have grown more hostile and violent in the last decade and have been linked to the far right and to white nationalist movements (Hine et al. 2017; Marwick and Caplan 2018). Far from innocuous trolling, these toxic technocultures have become part of a significant and dangerous mainstreaming of white supremacist, misogynistic, xenophobic politics (W. Phillips 2019). The analysis that follows provides insight into shifting norms around popular feminism in mainstream discourses and establishes a basis for understanding a sense of marginalization and backlash among these communities, which will deepen and resurface in subsequent chapters.

"The Unwashed Boys of the Internet": Hackers, AnonIB, 4chan, and Reddit as Networked Publics

Just as the celebrities' victimization was foregrounded in online news discourse, the most consistent description of both the hackers and members of AnonIB, 4chan, and Reddit was "creepy." *Gawker* referred to these groups as "horny creeps," "scum," and "skeevy" (Conaboy 2014; Juzwiak 2014; Cush 2014). *Slate* referred to the hackers as both "creeps" and "wretched little shits" (Honan 2015). Even celebrity and entertainment sites were derisive, with *Celebitchy* calling the thief "some hacker creep" and a "douche," and *Variety* describing these groups

General Boards

Amateur	College Bitches	Feet	Military	Scene v4
Accidental Nude	Celeb Fakes	Girlfriend	Milf	MySpace/Social
Ass/Anal	Creepshots/Candid	GIFs/WEBMs	Models	Teen 18+
Azn Chikz	Cum on Everything	Redheads/Gingers	Muscle	Tattooed
Random	Cosplay	Porn Stars	Panty	Tumbl.R
BDSM	Amputee	Hentai	Camwhoring (paid)	Traps
Oral Sex	Chanwhores	Hairy	Petite	Peeping Toms
BIG TITS	Ebony	Lesbians	Plump	Wincest
Celebs	Ethnic/Indian	Latina	Pregnant	YGWBT
Camwhoring	Fakes/Xray	Midget	Reddit	You Tube
				Rate my Wife

USA

Alaska	Hawaii	Michigan	Nevada	Utah
Alabama	Iowa	Minnesota	New York	Virginia
Arkansas	Idaho	Missouri	Ohio	Vermont
Arizona	Illinois	Mississippi	Oklahoma	Washington
California	Indiana	Montana	Oregon	Wisconsin
Colorado	Kansas	North Carolina	Pennsylvania	West Virginia
Connecticut	Kentucky	North Dakota	Rhode Island	Wyoming
Washington, D.C.	Louisiana	Nebraska	South Carolina	
Delaware	Massachusetts	New Hampshire	South Dakota	
Florida	Maryland	New Jersey	Tennessee	
Georgia	Maine	New Mexico	Texas	

International

Australia	Canada	Germany	United Kingdom

FIGURES 1.2 AND 1.3 AnonIB landing page; images censored to preserve privacy.

as a totality that resides in the "Web's sleazier corners" (Bedhead 2014; *Celebitchy* 2014; Spangler 2014). The abundance of such terms amplifies the contemptibility and repugnance of these groups, not only for their abhorrent actions but also for their general sleaziness; they are, as *Gawker* describes them, "the unwashed boys of the Internet," and we as readers should be repulsed by them (Spangler 2014).

As *Gawker*'s description of 4channers and Redditors as "boys" implies, these gross, sleazy characters are not to be respected. This lack of respect stems from the fact that they are not only "creeps" but also juvenile, immature criminals, and technologically unskilled criminals at that. Coverage across all outlets refers to the hackers as "criminals" and "culprits" and describes the scandal as a "theft." While the focus of the articles, particularly on *Gawker*, centers on the skeeviness of the "creeps" responsible, these news outlets make it clear that the hackers were not just guilty of gross behavior. Their behavior was a crime that can, will, and should be prosecuted. As is particularly evident in Perez Hilton's coverage of the nude photo hack, writers often openly hoped for the arrests of the hackers. He called for the FBI to provide "justice" for the stars, emphasizing that the hackers must be stopped and expressing confusion and

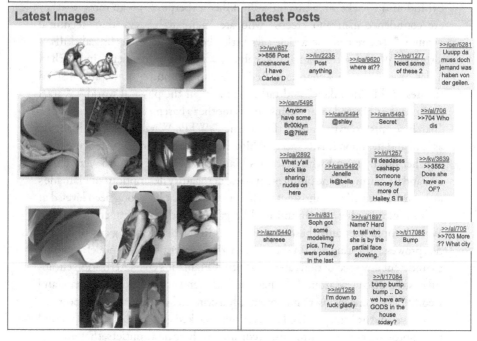

FIGURES 1.2 AND 1.3 (continued)

frustration that the "nefarious" culprits had not yet been caught (2014a, 2015). Overall, this emphasis on the criminality of the hackers furthers a sense of disgust at both their "creepy" personal characteristics and their illegal actions.

However, these outlets—and BuzzFeed in particular—made clear that the hackers are not to be respected for the hacking capabilities that enabled their criminality. While in mainstream conceptions hackers may be thought of as skillful coding wizards able to break into complex systems, the discourse around these hackers works to disabuse readers of those notions. *Gawker* called them "rookie[s]," *Slate* derided them as "not terribly talented criminal[s]," and Perez Hilton pointed out that they "aren't geniuses" (Biddle 2015; Wolff 2015; Hilton 2014f). They explain that the "hackers" did not actually hack but rather scammed celebrities through phishing schemes, which require little technical skill. If any readers were tempted to admire the hackers for their abilities to steal and disseminate the celebrities' photos, such descriptions discourage respect and instead foster derision.

BuzzFeed's coverage of this subject is particularly interesting and featured an investigative piece from Charlie Warzel (2014), who traveled to Georgia to talk with Bryan Hamade, an early suspect in the hack and leak, and his family and acquaintances.[1] While Hamade's neighbor says she understands he is "very, very intelligent" and good with computers, Warzel explains that "the individuals behind most 'hacks' aren't technically skilled cyberpunk programmers—they are confidence men and creeps" who are "more web savvy than technical geniuses." The rest of the article says little about Hamade's technical skills—although Warzel notes Hamade was able to scrub his web presence in less than a day after folks on 4chan and Reddit began hounding him—and instead focuses on his "mundane" and rather sad life "in the physical world." Warzel explains that Hamade was "living in his mother's basement" and notes that he "barely seem[s] to exist outside the internet." While Warzel describes Hamade as "tall and fit" upon finally meeting him, he closes the article with a quote from another family friend who describes Hamade as "'a creep, weird, very childish, and immature.'" The piling on of these derogatory descriptions of Hamade's awkward, lonely life is consistent with stereotypes that have long been leveled at technologically savvy communities like gamers and programmers. However, Warzel emphasizes only these negative traits instead of detailing any of Hamade's prowess, inserting within the article derisive descriptions of modern hackers to undercut any speculations about his skills. Hamade's characterization encapsulates the discourse around the hackers and members of AnonIB, 4chan, and Reddit: he is a creepy loser and potentially a criminal who merits no respect.

However, the "creeps" like Hamade who hacked and/or shared and viewed the photos are not just criminals; according to these news outlets, they are also horny masturbators. *Gawker* engages in such descriptions most frequently, deriding the "horny creeps" on Reddit and 4chan "who like masturbating to non-consenting strangers" (Conaboy 2014; Biddle 2014b). These individuals are described as "horndog[s]" and "enterprising masturbation enthusiast[s]" throughout the majority of *Gawker*'s coverage; indeed, one post detailing an FBI raid of a suspect's home describes him as one of "the brave men of Reddit and 4chan who masturbated" to the stolen nude photos (Cush 2014; Biddle 2014a, 2016). Such a consistent focus on the sexual desire and supposedly autoerotic proclivities of the hackers, sharers, and viewers on these online communities accomplishes several tasks. First, it locates the motive for the crime and violation in the desire for sexual release. While other motives are mentioned—namely, that users on AnonIB attempted to sell the photos in exchange for Bitcoin—*Gawker*'s reliance on sexual descriptors discursively fixes members of these communities as prompted by sexual desire. Second, by continually referring to masturbation, *Gawker* emphasizes the solitariness of both the sexual act and, by extension, the user himself. Drawing again on the same stereotypes of weird, creepy loners that BuzzFeed used to describe Hamade, such descriptions further degrade these users.

Overall, most of the coverage of the hackers and sharers of celebrities' nude photos traded on long-standing stereotypes of geeks and tech nerds to shame them for their illegal and misogynistic actions. These tropes center on emasculation and social ostracization. These men are not skilled, desirable, or respectable but rather creepy losers who masturbate in their mothers' basements. Such disdain was heightened by the contrast between these stereotypes and the glamorous, charismatic celebrities they targeted. If the hackers were a nameless, faceless horde of internet bottom dwellers, their victims were the opposite: women like Jennifer Lawrence, who was and remains one of the most admired, charming, well-known actresses in Hollywood, and whose whiteness almost certainly bolstered outrage at her victimization. This stark difference further enabled media outlets to rally around the celebrities and, coupled with the emerging popularity of some feminist ideas around sexuality such as the rejection of slut shaming, afforded a media narrative that vehemently detested the hackers and often, by extension, the platforms on which they cohered.

While the impacts of such discourses were not clear at the time, this moment would prove to be one instance that men who identified as a part of particularly toxic communities on platforms such as 4chan and Reddit could point to in order to evince feelings of disempowerment and marginalization at the hands of feminism and the "liberal media." Coupled with the negative attention similar communities received earlier in the year because of Gamergate, 2014 marked a turning point when a few corners of the emergent "Manosphere" were exposed to widespread attention, and mainstream outlets overwhelmingly recoiled in disgust. This is not to say the outlets were incorrect in their unequivocal damning of these men; however, this was a moment when toxic geek masculinities came under fire in such a way that the men's feelings of resentment and oppression began to further metastasize, a dynamic that will also shape events discussed in the coming chapters.

The Limits of Empathy: Conclusions on Innocence, Victimization, and Backlash

While they were on opposing ends of the scandal, both the celebrities and the hackers and online communities who shared their nude photos became known and gossiped about by a much larger and broader public than they intended. The celebrities meant for their photos to remain private, shared only with viewers of their choosing. The hackers and traders of the photos circulated the photos under the radar for months, sharing and discussing them among themselves and constituting a relatively unknown public. However, all groups fell victim to the permeability of the digital platforms in which they had placed their trust; the iCloud was fallible, and AnonIB, 4chan, and Reddit are widely accessible, even for users who do not typically frequent those sites. The massive data dump on August 31, 2014, attracted widespread mainstream attention, amplifying backstage practices and making them visible for public consumption, and allowing news and gossip outlets to negotiate and establish a dominant understanding of this event and those involved.

Toward both groups, the commonsense response was inflected with supposedly feminist ideals and a rejection of perspectives that objectify women and blame them for their own victimization. Coverage of the celebrities downplayed the "risky" behavior of taking and storing nude selfies by de-emphasizing the spectacular nature of the scandal and instead emphasizing the interconnectedness of their actions and this scandal with the rest of "us." The celebrities were framed as victims not only of the hack but also of broader structural issues around women's bodies; because this scandal was just one instantiation of bigger issues that can and do affect all of us, the celebrities were, with some notable exceptions, innocent. The popular feminist bent of the gossip and media coverage emphasized their victimization, railing against patriarchal structures of power. However, the celebrities' relationships to publicity sometimes problematized their victimization, and those who were constructed as narcissistic and/or who used their sexuality to gain publicity were considered deserving of such victimization; the tensions around Hilton's coverage of the photos demonstrate how tricky the line between the public and the private can be for the celebrities involved.

In contrast, the hackers and sharers of these photographs were derided because they were considered both sexually and socially deviant. While some of the coverage touched on the potential and promise of sites like AnonIB, 4chan, and Reddit, the dominant discourse focused on "toxic technocultures" that emerged due to the affordances of anonymity and ephemerality on AnonIB and 4chan, and the organizational and moderating features of Reddit (Knuttila 2011; Massanari 2017). The distinctions between these platforms and the varied communities and publics they host were, for the most part, elided, and their members were collapsed into a homogeneous, loathsome totality. The sexual desires of the men within these communities were derided as misogynistic, immoral, and illegal. Further, the focus on their masturbation—encapsulated in the very name of the scandal, The Fappening—again emphasized their isolation from society. The expressions of sexuality the scandal enabled for them are not social but rather solitary.

Overall, the feminist leanings of the discourse around the nude photo hack structured the event as an almost perfect binary that left unexamined the grounds on which these norms and assumptions rest. The actions of the celebrities could be integrated into dominant understandings of sexuality provided the women were understood as "innocent," that is, if they do not seek publicity and self-promote *too much* or, in particular, too sexually. Taking nude selfies meant to be private or shared with a small, intimate public was socially acceptable within this view; utilizing one's nude form as a key factor of fame, as Kim Kardashian does, mitigated a woman's victimization. This disruption of the perfect binary the discourse lays out belies a problematic assumption of popular feminist politics evident in this coverage; in a throwback to regressive dichotomies of the virgin and the whore, innocence is a precondition for privacy. It is also important to note that most of the women whose photos were stolen were white, and race goes completely unmentioned in reporting on the hack. The popular feminist thrust of the discourse, then, lacks a sense of intersectionality. Certainly, the whiteness of most of the victims aided their construction as "innocent." These supposedly virtuous celebrity women are allowed access to innocent victimhood at the hands of the gross, undesirable, misogynistic hackers and sharers of their private photos. These one-dimensionally constructed men are isolated from and bring disorder to the rest of society, and the coverage derides their creepy, sleazy sexuality and criminality as reprehensible; they are thus rejected by and excluded from dominant sexual norms.

The news and commentary around this incident provide foundational insights onto which subsequent chapters will build in order to come to terms with the intersections of celebrity, digital platforms, and feminism at this historical juncture. First, reactions to the nude photo hack demonstrate that celebrity culture functions as a platform on which broader issues around gender, sexuality, and digital platforms can be worked out. Celebrities experience gendered digital vulnerabilities similar to those that often impact all women who engage on these platforms, but the additional platform of celebrities' fame amplifies their victimization, rendering it more visible and gossip-worthy. However, the discourse around this incident explicitly drew connections beyond celebrity culture to patriarchal structures more broadly and how they affect all women vis-à-vis sexual agency and harassment.

This tendency to expose and negotiate broader sexual inequalities through discussing celebrity events repeats in each of the following chapters. Discourse around wage equality and Patricia Arquette's acceptance speech at the 2015 Academy Awards ceremony emphasized that the wage gap exists not just in Hollywood but affects women everywhere, and her lack of intersectionality is not localized to her statement or to Hollywood but points to problems with white-centric feminism more broadly. Similar dynamics emerge around Gloria Steinem and Madeleine Albright's comments while they were campaigning for Hillary Clinton, when the dominant discourse emphasized the conflict as indicative of broader generational disconnects within the feminist movement. Further, discourse around the Leslie Jones attack emphasized that Black women are the objects of vitriolic harassment in digital spaces and beyond all the time. This connection between Hollywood women and "the rest of us" is perhaps the clearest in the post-Weinstein reckoning and the Time's Up initiative: sexual harassment, as well as women's lack of recourse to stop it, spans every industry. Lifted up on the platform of their fame, these "intimate strangers" make visible broader issues and open a space for public debate, providing audiences an opportunity to learn from their experiences and from public reaction to those experiences (Schickel 2000). Further, how social and legacy media discourses treat these issues provides an excellent set of case studies where we can see on a large scale how dominant understandings around popular feminism are developing.

Further, this incident establishes celebrity culture as a space where women are the victims of larger patriarchal structures of power. This opens celebrity culture up as a potential site of feminist intervention and support, consistent with dynamics at work in the #AskHerMore campaign, responses to the attack on Leslie Jones, and the #MeToo movement. Further, the entanglements of celebrity and digital technologies emphasize the role of online platforms as spaces of both possibility and peril where celebrities can be victimized but also defended. Thus, this case study begins to map a time when feminist issues were coming closer to the fore of discussions of celebrity culture, demonstrating how the dynamic pressures of the white feminist imperative are developing. At the same time, the unequivocal (and unnuanced) damning of communities like 4chan and Reddit connects to similar dynamics around the unequivocal damning of far right harassers during the Jones attack and men accused of sexual misconduct during the #MeToo phenomenon, which served to bolster these men's performance of victimhood. While this incident itself is not overtly political in that the discourse does not explicitly connect it to the work of a specific political party, talk around this incident functions as a place where we can see these binary discourses begin to fester.

2

Staging Feminism

Negotiating Labor and Calling
Out Racism at the 2015
Academy Awards

During the celebrity nude photo hack, the hackers and circulators of the images rendered the women they depicted as objects, digital artifacts to be shared and traded. Their actions transformed women into sexual commodities, valuable within the increasingly mainstream digital economy of nonconsensual pornography. The photo hack stimulated discussion about celebrity women—their digital vulnerability, representation, objectification, and value. And as 2014 came to a close, yet another hack—this time of Sony Pictures' servers—amplified and added new layers to the conversation about celebrity women's value. This chapter analyzes the networked negotiations regarding intersectionality, activism, and value that coalesced around the 2015 Academy Awards by studying interactions of cross-platform feminist issue publics and examining how those interactions were amplified and discursively constructed across legacy media. Through these analyses I identify and explore two key strategies that shape digital feminist intersections with celebrity culture: media-focused hashtag activism and calling out.

Even before the winners were announced on February 22, the 2015 Oscars were a site of controversy around issues of identity, particularly race and gender. The failure of the Academy of Motion Picture Arts and Sciences to nominate Black female director Ava Duvernay for Best Director for her work on

Selma, as well as any people of color for the four key acting awards, had sparked the #OscarsSoWhite campaign on social media and moved Hollywood's lack of racial diversity to the forefront of Oscar conversations. Alongside this concern about the whiteness of the impending awards ceremony were questions about how women were represented and compensated. The previous year had planted the seeds for these frustrations. Female celebrities grew increasingly frustrated with their objectification on the red carpet, amplified by various technologies implemented by outlets such as E! Entertainment Television that increased audiences' ability to survey and evaluate celebrities' appearances. For example, E! began using a "Mani Cam," in which actresses walked their fingers down a miniature red carpet to show off their manicure and jewelry, and the "Glam Cam 360," which provided a 360-degree, slow-motion look at celebrities' bodies. While the red carpet had long been an arena of female objectification and evaluation, these technologies amplified the red carpet as a space where celebrity women function as objects of the gaze.

However, conversations about Hollywood's inequities preceded the announcement of the mostly white Oscar nominees and actresses' frustration on the red carpet. On November 24, 2014, a group of hackers who called themselves the Guardians of Peace leaked confidential data stolen from Sony Pictures, including personal information such as salary data and emails. Some of the most widely discussed information to come from this leak had to do with wage disparities between women and men at every level of the company, including A-list actresses such as Jennifer Lawrence. As reported by *The Daily Beast*, emails among Sony executives Andrew Gumpert, Amy Pascal, and Doug Belgrad revealed that actresses Amy Adams and Jennifer Lawrence were paid considerably less than their male counterparts for their roles in the David O. Russell film *American Hustle* (Boot 2014). The Sony hack, similar to the celebrity nude photo hack, revealed not only the vulnerabilities of the platforms we often trust to store our personal information but also the vulnerabilities of the people and institutions that use those platforms. In response, for both industry professionals and audiences, the 2015 Academy Awards became a site of feminist intervention and a space where such inequities could be addressed in a highly public way.

This chapter examines two incidents that framed the 2015 Oscars as a site of feminist negotiation—the #AskHerMore red carpet campaign and Patricia Arquette's acceptance speech for the Best Supporting Actress award. In particular, I focus on the roles of hashtag activism and callouts in these processes of negotiation, further examining the limitations of the white feminist imperative and introducing the intersectional imperative as a challenge to myopic white feminist perspectives. The #AskHerMore campaign serves as a quintessential example of the white feminist imperative: a media-friendly campaign for greater inclusion and equality in a way that is fundamentally not disruptive to established power structures, centers on women who already have a great deal of privilege, and excludes any discussion of inequalities between women. Much of its power lies in its ability to leave its focus on white women tacit. However, Arquette's acceptance speech "said the quiet part out loud," making explicit, if only by mistake, that in popular feminist discussions "women" most often means "white women." In response, networked publics mobilized to contest this white feminist perspective and enact the pressures of the intersectional imperative. Far from constituting a coherent sociopolitical platform, these case studies allow us to explore digital feminist contestations regarding the future of the feminist movement as refracted through popular and celebrity cultures. What should the feminist movement's goals be, and how should we evaluate those goals and engage with allies who fail to live up to them? Whose job should it be to do the labor of exerting pressure towards a more equitable media landscape?

To answer these questions, I begin by providing a historical overview of the Academy Awards, focusing on the evolving roles that fashion and politics have played during this media ritual over the past eight decades. Then I turn to a consideration of #AskHerMore, analyzing the two key readings of the campaign that dominated social and news media discourse: those that framed the campaign as a feminist triumph and those that argued it was too superficial and misguided to enact any substantive change. Alongside an analysis of the questions posed on Twitter, I demonstrate that the struggle over the values of the red carpet in media coverage and in conversations among networked publics revealed a liberal feminist struggle over women's labor and objectification. Then I move from labor on the red carpet to the Oscar stage and social media, examining debates around Arquette's acceptance speech in which she argued for wage equality. After this, I explore the networked publics that mobilized the intersectional imperative to spark a broader conversation about white feminism by examining the critics who called out Arquette and her defenders, highlighting how the labor of calling out often falls to women of color whose actions are maligned as "toxic." I end this section by questioning the role and efficacy of "imperfect" white celebrity feminists in enacting structural change.

Overall, this chapter builds on the foundations of chapter 1, exploring how celebrities and networked publics can use the newsworthiness afforded to stars to amplify feminist issues like labor and wage equality while using the affordances of social media platforms—namely, hashtags and callout campaigns—to exert the discursive pressures of the white feminist and intersectional imperatives. I argue that each of these case studies demonstrates the limits of the incorporation of liberal feminism into popular feminist discourses, amplified by celebrity's deep embeddedness within capitalism. While each of these campaigns achieved varying types and degrees of "success," both ultimately left intact and unquestioned capitalist structures, opting instead to treat symptoms of patriarchal capitalism's impact on women. However, while each strategy demonstrates the complex entanglements of white feminist and postfeminist discourses within popular feminism (Gill 2016), the intersectional imperative as debated and articulated by those who called out these flawed feminist campaigns and emissaries shifted the discourse in a more nuanced direction. Through this analysis, I begin to demonstrate how popular feminist discourses coalesce around celebrity events like the 2015 Academy Awards, rendering these events as spaces of contestation where the broader values of feminist politics and action are negotiated.[1]

Politics and Fashion at the Oscars: A Brief Historical Overview

While the Oscars ceremony and its red carpet have become prominent media rituals since the ceremony was first broadcast via radio in 1932, they have been the subject of relatively little academic research. This section provides historical background on the Academy Awards, reviews some notable politically charged statements made throughout the ceremony's history, and discusses its relationship to celebrity and fashion. This background provides the base for the chapter's theoretical intervention as I analyze the implications of the 2015 Oscars with regard to the intersections of celebrity, feminism, and fashion in an age of real-time social media commentary.

The Academy of Motion Picture Arts and Sciences was the brainchild of film producer and cofounder of MGM, Louis B. Mayer, in 1927. His goals in creating the organization and the awards ceremony were twofold: to tamp down the growing power of below-the-line workers as they unionized, and to assuage public concerns about the immorality of Hollywood. Mayer believed that the formation of the Academy could be a "public relations coup" that would help "establish the industry in the public mind as a respectable and legitimate institution, and its people as reputable individuals" (Levy 2002, 11, 26). An awards ceremony would function as the public face of this respectability. However, despite such lofty, union-busting goals, controversy and politics inflected the awards ceremony from early on. For example, members of the Directors Guild, the Screen Actors Guild, and the Writers Guild boycotted the ceremony in 1936 to protest the Academy's failure to support them in their contract negotiations, as did Bette Davis when the Academy refused her 1941 request to transform the ceremony into a fundraiser for the Red Cross in response to the start of World War II (Sandler 2015; "The 14th Academy Awards" 2014). While the ceremony had been conceived as a platform from which the film industry could present itself as a distinguished, morally reputable group of professionals, some industry insiders recognized that it could also function as a highly public platform of social agitation and political statement. Long before Arquette's acceptance speech in favor of wage equality, other stars made waves for using their time onstage to convey social and political messages. Most famously, in 1973, Marlon Brando refused to attend the ceremony, sending an Apache woman named Sacheen Littlefeather in his stead to protest Hollywood's treatment of Native Americans and in protest of an incident at Wounded Knee earlier in the year. Littlefeather's appearance sparked a great deal of controversy, from the loud jeers from the crowd as she exited the stage to critiques of Brando for using her to manipulate the press. Other Oscar presenters and recipients have similarly used the spotlight to highlight causes they find important, such as Richard Gere's 1993 Oscars statement in favor of freeing Tibet, or director Michael Moore's chastisement of George W. Bush in 2002 (Lewis 2017). As Hollywood and sociopolitical issues have become increasingly intertwined in the last several decades, and especially during the 2010s, such statements have become commonplace as the stage has emerged not only as a place of performative respectability and Hollywood self-congratulation but also as a space where speakers engage with social issues.

However, more than political statements, and often even more than the awards themselves, the Academy Awards have become synonymous with fashion. While today media outlets report breathlessly about the designer gowns, shoes, and jewelry on the Oscars red carpet, this focus on fashion was not always so central. For the first few decades, actresses had dresses made by costume designers they worked closely with, purchased gowns from department stores, or even made their dresses themselves. Then, in 1951, Marlene Dietrich showed up at the ceremony in a stunning black dress by the designer Christian Dior, and for the first time, a star's fashion choice made as many headlines as the winners themselves (Cosgrave 2006). This moment marked a sea change; after this, in addition to costume designers, French couturiers and fashion designers began dressing actresses, often to much fanfare.

While Oscar fashions shifted with the times, fashion continued to grow in importance and garnered publicity for stars who stood out. Designers began to understand that this publicity could work to their advantage, and in 1990 Giorgio Armani asked actresses to wear his gowns to the show, cost-free, launching a whole new approach to Oscar fashion. As the 1990s progressed, designers increasingly began to see dressing stars for the Oscars and beyond as equivalent to launching multimillion-dollar ad campaigns, such was the press they would get from the event (Cosgrave 2006). They wooed stars with extravagant gifts, vying for the chance to clothe them, and the fashion industry as a whole became more intertwined with Hollywood as celebrities often took over from models as the faces of fashion labels. As of the early twenty-first century, designers continue to court stars during the two-month-long award season that culminates with the Oscars. Stylists field requests from major design houses, and stars often try on dozens or more gowns to find the perfect dress. That is not even to mention the jewelers, shoe designers, and hair and makeup artists whose work goes into crafting a perfect look for Oscar night. This focus on the image, framed as a devaluation of the actresses who walk the red carpet, became the target of the #AskHerMore campaign in 2014.

More Than Their Dresses: #AskHerMore, Hashtag Activism, and the Problem of Celebrity Red Carpet Representation

#AskHerMore as Media-Focused Hashtag Activism

#AskHerMore is an example of hashtag activism, or "discursive protest on social media united through a hashtagged word, phrase or sentence" (Yang 2016, 13). Through the affordance of the hashtag, networked publics are able to establish discursive and platform-level connections between posts on social media, particularly Twitter. Users can choose to follow or simply click on a hashtag to view public posts that feature it, allowing individuals to unite around a particular subject, conversation, or cause. Activists often use hashtags to draw attention to issues and exert pressure on individuals and institutions to take action. Media institutions—such as the Academy of Motion Picture Arts and Sciences—can become the focus of such pressure, and when those pressures gain the attention of celebrity advocates, their newsworthiness can amplify them. This strategy is not unique to feminist activism. As mentioned previously, #OscarsSoWhite also emerged as a prominent hashtag campaign around the 2015 awards show, deployed by anti-racist activists, including celebrities, to protest the lack of racial diversity among the Academy's nominees. Social media opens up a space for everyday users and activists to speak back to and intervene in established media rituals like a red carpet broadcast or an awards ceremony, putting change theoretically within reach. This analysis of #AskHerMore explores the particular entanglements of postfeminist and feminist ideals that often emerge at the intersection of feminism and celebrity culture and demonstrates how, far from establishing a unified front, networked publics and media outlets that engaged with this hashtag negotiated which pressures feminists can and should exert and how to assess their efficacy.

Although the #AskHerMore campaign was recognized across mainstream media and addressed by red carpet reporters in 2015, The Representation Project (TRP) actually began the conversation in 2014. The project was founded by filmmaker Jennifer Siebel Newsom as an organization dedicated to critiquing sexist and misogynistic media representations of women and fostering change. It launched the #AskHerMore campaign on February 28, 2014, ahead of the Academy Awards ceremony, as a way to push back on red carpet reporters' focus on women's appearances rather than their accomplishments. With the hashtag #AskHerMore, TRP encouraged users to "send suggested questions to reporters, in real-time, whenever they risk devaluing the accomplishments of women in Hollywood, and to spark deeper conversations in front of a national television audience" (The Representation Project 2014). From the beginning of the campaign, its organizers used the hashtag to contest the meaning and values of the red carpet. They framed a focus on fashion as "devaluing" the actresses as artists, setting achievement and aesthetics in contrast to one another, while emphasizing the importance of the red carpet as a platform of feminist intervention by mentioning its "national television audience."

This short article was expanded in a fifty-minute video conference call via Google Hangouts between TRP allies Soraya Chemaly, Jaclyn Friedman, and Arturo Garcia, which was then posted on YouTube and linked in the post (The Representation Project 2014). This video demonstrates the deeply cross-platform, convergent nature of this particular digital feminist campaign and, indeed, much of the platform ecosystem (Jenkins 2008; van Dijck 2013). Just within this one text, TRP capitalized on the different affordances of at least three platforms—its website, Google Hangouts, and YouTube—to engage in discussion and debate as well as publicize and amplify that discussion. Google Hangouts afforded Chemaly, Friedman, and Garcia the ability to video chat with one another, which they were then able to record and upload to YouTube. YouTube afforded this otherwise ephemeral conversation persistence, which meant it could then be shared via other social media platforms as well as TRP's website. This cross-platform flow expands and deepens the possibility of contention and negotiation, exemplified in this case study as not all members of this issue public cosigned on #AskHerMore's articulation of feminism and were able to express those differing evaluations across a variety of digital and legacy media spaces, utilizing each platform's specific affordances. Through the liveness of the red carpet broadcast, the malleability of the interviewers' questions, and the ability of Twitter users to communicate with media personalities, the 2015 red carpet became a place where intervention seemed possible.

#AskHerMore came and went during the 2014 Oscars with little fanfare. However, it gained traction the following year when it was publicized online by two A-list actresses: Amy Poehler and Reese Witherspoon. Poehler's organization targeted at encouraging young women's education and creativity, Smart Girls, posted both on its own site site and across Twitter encouraging users to tweet questions for celebrities that went beyond appearance, and a video the organization posted promoting the campaign was frequently shared across platforms (daralaine 2015). Additionally, Witherspoon (2015) posted an image on yet another social media platform, Instagram, to support and amplify the hashtag. The caption for this image emphasizes her love for the "movement" and states that, while she is "excited to share" fashion details, she would "also love to answer some of these Qs" and then asks fans to share their own ideas. Witherspoon used the intersection of her fame and social media, which combined to give her nearly 2 million Instagram followers at the time of her

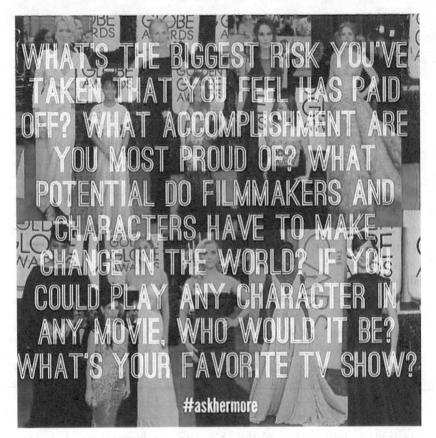

WHAT'S THE BIGGEST RISK YOU'VE TAKEN THAT YOU FEEL HAS PAID OFF? WHAT ACCOMPLISHMENT ARE YOU MOST PROUD OF? WHAT POTENTIAL DO FILMMAKERS AND CHARACTERS HAVE TO MAKE CHANGE IN THE WORLD? IF YOU COULD PLAY ANY CHARACTER IN ANY MOVIE, WHO WOULD IT BE? WHAT'S YOUR FAVORITE TV SHOW?

#askhermore

FIGURE 2.1 Reese Witherspoon's #AskHerMore Instagram.

posting to whom she could publicize this message. Just as with the Smart Girls video, Witherspoon's post was remediated frequently across platforms and garnered nearly 20,000 likes. The suggested questions encourage reporters to move away from appearance and family to focus on actresses' preferences, accomplishments, and goals. Though arguably trite, they are questions that could be answered within the few minutes an actress would spend with a reporter on the red carpet and they achieve the campaign's goal of moving the focus to the actress herself rather than solely her appearance.

Red Carpet Rebellion: #AskHerMore and the Pressures of Celebrity Feminism

Following this publicity, users flooded Twitter with alternative questions for red carpet reporters, an analysis of which reveals the priorities of this particular hashtag campaign and provides insight into the emerging norms and values of popular feminism as articulated through celebrity culture at this historical juncture. Most questions within this sample fell into one of four categories.[2] Those in the first category asked actresses about their understanding, interpretation, and/or portrayal of their character or film. For example, users asked questions such as "Why do you think the #story of the #film you're in is so important? What stories still need to be told?" and "What was your process for becoming that character?" Such questions aimed to get at the actress's process as an artist and as an intellectual participant in her work. Questions in the second category expanded from actresses' immediate work to the larger milieu of the Hollywood community, asking them about their mentors and role models as well as other workers they admire. For example, questions included, "Who has been a mentor to you in your career?" and "Who has inspired you the most this year? Which film did you enjoy most? Who else would you have liked to seen [sic] nominated?" Such questions seek to place the actress within her broader context in Hollywood and to frame that context as one of helpfulness and appreciation. Beyond a focus on the actress as a thoughtful participant in the filmmaking process, these questions aim to understand the entertainment industry as a community of mentorship, inspiration, and admiration.

While such questions focused on the positivity of Hollywood, the third category of questions asked actresses about their impressions of inequality in the industry and/or their role in fighting it. Some addressed the struggle of women in the industry, asking, "What can we do to encourage more female voices in the entertainment industry as a whole?" and the disproportionate struggles of women of color, saying, "What's your advice to the women of color who are discouraged and struggling to make it in the entertainment business?" Such questions acknowledged the power structures within Hollywood that disadvantage women and people of color and asked for the actresses' insight into those dynamics. In doing so, they ask actresses to answer for the inequalities within the industry, presuming that these women care about such issues and are actively working to change them. Finally, questions in the fourth category broadened outside of Hollywood altogether to ask actresses about their work for social justice. For example, users asked, "What social issue would you become involved with if you had unlimited time and money? Why this particular issue?" and "How do u use your celebrity to address the many social justice and inequality issues affecting women and girls today?" Taken together, these questions frame actresses, and ask actresses to frame themselves, as artists and conscientious citizens. They take the expectations of the red carpet as a ritual space of celebrity gossip, commercialism, and aesthetics, where actresses provide sound bites about their films and sartorial choices, and reorient those expectations to include more complex sociocultural issues.

This move reflects shifting expectations of celebrity women, demonstrating that celebrities are increasingly expected to engage in sociopolitical critique and activism. By placing this pressure on celebrity women, who are often on the receiving end of Hollywood's sexism and racism, the questions, and indeed the campaign itself, can further obscure the behind-the-scenes power dynamics of the entertainment industries by focusing on stars who have a limited ability to influence such structural changes. Celebrity women are called to answer for sexist and racist structures on an individual level, demonstrating the entanglements of feminist and postfeminist discourses that Rosalind Gill (2016) identifies as the hallmark of the new visibilities of feminism within popular culture. The campaign focuses more on individual empowerment and surface-level intervention even as it acknowledges that feminism's work is not done.

For many commentators, the results of the campaign on the red carpet were mixed. In the translation from social media campaign to a live televised broadcast, which has different goals and affordances, the intervention was only partially "successful." While I do not have space here to analyze each red carpet interview on E! and ABC, it is worth discussing one in particular. Consistent with her prominence as the face of the campaign, Reese Witherspoon's response to ABC host Robin Roberts's question about her involvement with #AskHerMore was by far the most recirculated interview in the days following the awards show. Of the campaign, Witherspoon said, "This is a movement to, ya know, say we are more than just our dresses." After acknowledging that they appreciate the artists who make their gowns, she says, "This is a group of women, 44 nominees this year, Robin, that are women and we are so happy to be here and talk about the work that we have done." As the most remediated interview related to #AskHerMore, Witherspoon's response does little beyond reaffirming her support of the campaign. This result is thus circular—#AskHerMore was important and successful, transforming the red carpet because it generated responses on that red carpet about its own importance and success. The heavy remediation of Witherspoon's answer highlights the campaign's superficiality.

Loving Those "Feminist Vibes": Praising the Value of #AskHerMore

Despite the apparent superficiality of the #AskHerMore campaign, many members of this networked public lauded it across platforms. Chief among the affirmative responses to the movement, both by news reporters, commentators, and Twitter users who used the hashtag, was the notion that the #AskHerMore campaign was a rebellious feminist statement. Many began with a reiteration of TRP's talking points, emphasizing the devaluation of women as a result of their supposed reduction to fashionistas rather than accomplished career women. For example, a BuzzFeed report stated that the campaign demanded that reporters "#AskHerMore questions of value" (Warren 2015). By framing the issue as one of values—both of the actresses' worth artists and workers as well as, implicitly, the cultural values the questions reflect—such language opens up a space where the intervention is not merely about representation but about what that representation tells us about how our culture values the contributions of women; in the words of TRP allies, the campaign is thus "profoundly subversive." Accordingly, news, commentary, and social media users who agreed with such framing praised #AskHerMore, saying, for example, "It's powerful, it's gutsy, it's attention-grabbing, and it's exactly what we need" (Vaynshteyn 2015). While such hyperbolic language was not consistent across outlets, it is indicative of the perceived efficacy and importance of such social media interventions into the representations and treatment of women in media. This attitude, alongside the attention the campaign received, cast for many a feminist glow over the awards show. Twitter users enthused that "there is a paradigm shift in the air and it smells like progress" and that they were "digging the feminist theme of this year's #Oscars;" similarly, news and commentary outlets praised the "feminist vibes heading into" the Oscar broadcast because of the campaign and concluded that "the 2015 Oscars were a damn good year for feminism" (Ryan 2015; Hodgson 2015). Thus the campaign—which neither called for nor incited systemic/structural changes, at least beyond the confines of the red carpet—became emblematic of "successful" feminism that enacts meaningful change. Its discursive power became both an indicator of and a stand-in for feminist activism (see Zeisler 2016).

While much of the commentary framed the campaign as a culture-changing success, this narrative of success does not consider a different type of value generated by the campaign—the value that jumping on the bandwagon of a popular hashtag can have for social media users in terms of increasing exposure to audiences and user engagement. Outlets such as *UpWorthy*, *People*, and *Elle* magazine, and even brands like Goldie Blox, encouraged users to tweet red carpet questions at them for retweeting to reporters and/or posted links to stories using the hashtag on Twitter. Further, Amy Poehler's Smart Girls, the main Twitter account that spearheaded asking for and retweeting questions, received a huge amount of exposure and engagement by participating in the campaign; in turn, users who tweeted at and were then retweeted by the Smart Girls account also gained exposure and engagement from other users. These actions likely drove some users to these outlets' and organizations' websites, increasing traffic and boosting ad revenue. Their participation in a trending topic with at least a nominal gesture toward the increasingly marketable ideas of feminism helped these outlets and organizations to associate their brands with social consciousness. Both symbolically and materially, these actions added value to these users, outlets, and organizations.

Not only media outlets and other organizations but also many celebrities increased exposure and engagement by participating in the hashtag. Most prominent was Reese Witherspoon, whose Instagram post was heavily recirculated in news and commentary about #AskHerMore as she became the face of the campaign. Most online and legacy news and commentary articles in this sample acknowledged Witherspoon's key role in publicizing the campaign, with some erroneously crediting her with starting it and many lauding her role without any mention of TRP or Smart Girls (e.g., Bender 2015; Boardman 2015; Alter 2015). Other stars chimed in on Twitter, and, as is common with many news and commentary articles, their words were heavily remediated. Most notable were Lena Dunham, Maria Shriver, Shonda Rhimes, and Gloria Steinem, whose voices added another dimension to the discourse and to the campaign; asking female celebrities more diverse and complicated questions is not a "movement" or desire that exists solely on the outside looking in at Hollywood, but also comes from within. Especially when that request comes from someone who will be on the red carpet, like Witherspoon, the campaign shifts from "ask her more" to "ask me more," lending it a greater sense of immediacy. Her voice became principally important in amplifying the campaign, by virtue of her use of social media to publicize it and the platform of her A-list fame. The other celebrities mentioned here also added greater "newsworthiness" to the topic by supporting the hashtag and giving reporters and commentators more content to work with, and Steinem's stamp of approval in particular added a sense of feminist legitimacy. Reciprocally, the newsworthiness of these celebrities' support also increased their exposure to audiences as their words were remediated across outlets.

By using social media platforms to support the hashtag, these celebrities further associated their brands with the increasingly marketable platform of feminism, even if the campaign itself was meek and superficial, increasing the exposure and value of that brand. These rewards can call into question the value of highly visible hashtag campaigns, with feminist critics and scholars such as Zeisler (2016), Gill (2016), and Banet-Weiser (2018) critiquing such popular feminist moves as politically vacuous branding techniques that render such "activist" campaigns more postfeminist than feminist. While these arguments help to explain some of the dynamics surrounding the hashtag, it is important to note that the campaign was not universally lauded. In the next section I analyze the backlash to #AskHerMore to demonstrate how feminist hashtag campaigns can become a site of contestation and negotiation not only around the value of women but also around the value of different forms of feminist intervention.

"Take the Money and Walk": Critiquing #AskHerMore

Not all of the social and legacy media discussion lauded the #AskHerMore campaign as a great feminist success. Many writers, mostly in news and commentary articles that afford more space for expression and discussion than do platforms like Twitter, criticized the campaign for several key reasons. The first is the economic structure of red carpet fashion. Actresses get the dresses for free and often get paid quite handsomely to wear a certain designer's gown; contemporary reports put fees for wearing designer pieces anywhere from $100,000 to $750,000, depending on the star and the designer (Schwiegershausen 2015). Because of these complimentary goods and payments, many commentators critiqued the idea that actresses should not talk about their clothing. Heather Cocks and Jessica Morgan (2015), who together run the popular fashion blog *Go Fug Yourself*, said on Twitter, "#askhermore is great, but it's ALSO okay to ask/say who you're wearing. You got it for free. It's a transaction. Tip your server." In other words, brands dress stars for free or for a fee because the exposure of the red carpet adds value to the brand. Most viewers are not sartorially savvy enough to recognize a designer gown without having the designer identified. Thus #AskHerMore could actually devalue the investment designers make in dressing celebrities for the red carpet.

Other writers added that, contrary to the apparent impetus of #AskHerMore, actresses' careers and their sartorial decisions are related to one another. If designers see that their investments in red carpet gowns become less valuable, that can impact a star's career and earnings in multiple ways. As Bronwyn Cosgrave (2015) pointed out in an article for CNN ahead of the Oscars, the red carpet is a kind of "audition" for more work and for magazine covers. Celebrities, whose star personas have always been deeply intertextual, stand to benefit greatly from this exposure, and an identity that includes "fashionista" can help actresses get more work. Further, multiple voices in online commentary pieces ambivalently praised the increased earning potential of actresses from their red carpet appearances, especially in light of the overall gendered inequalities in Hollywood. For example, Jessica Goldstein (2015) argued that the red carpet is one of the few arenas in Hollywood in which women outearn men, and the sexist, capitalist dynamics that value women's and men's work differently go untouched by #AskHerMore. Thus, these writers and others used the affordances of outlets like *Glamour*, the *New York Times*, and the *Chicago Tribune*, which allow writers to engage in longer-form critiques, to take a more complex and nuanced approach to the campaign. In their estimation, the campaign's apparent frustration with fashion talk on the red carpet is misplaced and in fact harmful to the women who walk it.

Beyond these arguments that the fashion focus on the red carpet is indeed valuable to actresses, many also argued that the campaign was not transformative in any meaningful way. In a piece for the *New York Times*, Cara Buckley (2015) stated that the rapturous coverage of red carpet "rebellions ... goes to show just how low the bar can be for what passes as a gender-equality push in Tinseltown." Others called #AskHerMore forgettable and "ridiculous," arguing that all it succeeded in doing was making the red carpet awkward and lumping the campaign in with "hashtag activism" that "offers little more than symbolic gestures as solutions for endemic social ills, raising awareness and

FIGURE 2.2 Zendaya at the 2015 Academy Awards. (Credit: Walt Disney Television, via Flickr.)

tweets for the fleeting virtual struggle du jour" (Hocking 2015). For commentators like Bree Hocking, the symbolic struggle over representation on the red carpet does nothing to change the culture around female representation.

In addition to these critiques, events on the red carpet also revealed serious problems with #AskHerMore. During an Oscar season fraught with racial tension foregrounded by #OscarsSoWhite, the campaign paid no attention to issues of race, nor did it gesture to the intersectionality of race and gender as it pertains to red carpet fashion. The additional representational burden placed on women of color came into focus when longtime "E! News" and "Fashion Police" contributor Giuliana Rancic commented on actress Zendaya's red carpet look. Zendaya wore a slinky white Vivienne Westwood dress and had her hair styled into beautiful, long, thick dreadlocks. During E!'s "Fashion Police" segment, Rancic described her as follows: "I feel like she smells like patchouli oil . . . maybe weed" (People staff 2015). Rancic's comments were suffused with racist assumptions about African Americans and bias against Black hair textures. Her commentary on Zendaya's red carpet appearance went beyond the supposed sexism and devaluation #AskHerMore was working against, demonstrating that Black women's appearances are evaluated and policed differently than those of white women. When Zendaya and a host of social media users and media outlets called out Rancic, she quickly apologized on Twitter, claiming she was "referring to a bohemian chic look" that had "NOTHING to do with race" (Rancic 2015). This excuse adds another layer of racism onto her words by associating locs with white "bohemian chic" aesthetics instead of the Black communities from which they were appropriated.

Rancic's comments and this controversy's total disconnect from the hashtag or broader discussions of women's representation on the red carpet provide further examples of how safe the #AskHerMore initiative ultimately was, functioning as a surface-level campaign that focused more on the individual "empowerment" of celebrities rather than the interrogation or disruption of gendered or racialized power imbalances in Hollywood or beyond. Moreover, this incident demonstrates how little the campaign engaged with issues such as misogynoir. Overall, it reveals a much more complex set of dynamics around the Oscar red carpet than #AskHerMore sought to address because the campaign did not acknowledge the factor of race. As a result of this lack of intersectionality, the hashtag campaign defaulted to white women who face the supposed "devaluation" of their work because of a focus on their appearance, but it failed to address how that focus on appearance functions differently for different bodies, and how Hollywood and society more broadly differentially value women based on their race.

Calling Out Patricia Arquette and the (White) Actress as Commodity

"Wage Equality Once and for All": The Platform of the Celebrity Feminist Emissary

While #AskHerMore demonstrated that even simplistic media-focused hashtag campaigns can give rise to discussions regarding gender, labor, and race, the controversy over actress Patricia Arquette's comments about wage inequality on and off the Oscar stage provides insight into the role that calling out can play as a strategy for exerting the pressures of the white feminist and intersectional imperatives: both the role that celebrities can play in amplifying critique and their role as the subject of those critiques. In digital contexts, calling out refers to users who "post, tweet, re-post, and comment in public and semi-public social media spaces in order to respond to and remediate racism and misogyny" or other bigoted actions (Nakamura 2015, 107). These responses may counter behavior that occurs on digital platforms or behavior that occurs in other spaces that is then critiqued via social media. Further, these call-outs often flow across platforms, spreading across social and legacy media sites as news outlets report and comment on the controversy. The ways in which outlets remediate social media callouts can have a profound effect in shaping public understandings of the controversy for the many members of the issue public who did not follow the controversy as it unfolded on platforms like Twitter. As such, this section analyzes the contestations as they arose on social media as well as the dominant narratives regarding those contestations in news and commentary pieces.

The Sony hack's revelations regarding wage inequality spawned a great deal of discussion about systemic inequalities within Hollywood, and many celebrities, including Patricia Arquette, weighed in. Arquette had spent decades in the industry as a film and television actress, best known for her starring role alongside Christian Slater in *True Romance* (1993) and her six-year stint as psychic Allison Dubois on NBC's *Medium* (2005–2011). She reached a career high in 2014 with the release of *Boyhood* (2014) from writer-director Richard Linklater. The ambitious film was shot over a twelve-year period and follows the life of a boy named Mason from his childhood to early adulthood. It received critical acclaim and many awards, including for Arquette, who played Mason's mother, Olivia. In an interview with *The Guardian* soon before her Oscar win, Arquette referenced the hack and its broader implications for equality in the United States, saying, "Women in America, we act like we have equality when the truth is we don't. With the Sony hack, it was recognised that those actresses worked every bit as hard, they were just as valuable commodities, they had won awards, they had huge followings and big audiences yet Jennifer [Lawrence] was paid less than the men?" (Iqbal 2015). Arquette's platform as a celebrity and, moreover, as an Oscar nominee, afforded her access to a profile in a prominent outlet like *The Guardian*, which she used to amplify the injustice of wage inequality. Her framing of the issue places actresses' value as "commodities" squarely at the center of the injustice. Her incredulity centers on neoliberal notions of individual, and particularly celebrity, worth: hard work and marketability. This framing reifies actresses and actors as commodities who hold a great deal of value not only for themselves but also for the production

FIGURE 2.3 Patricia Arquette accepting the Oscar for Best Supporting Actress, 2015. (Credit: Walt Disney Television, via Flickr.)

companies that pay them as laborers. As salable products, actresses like Lawrence are high-quality, award-winning, popular commodities that draw in many consumers. By framing wage inequality in this way, Arquette highlights it as the purview of liberal rather than more radical, anticapitalist feminisms. Understandably, considering her positionality as an actress who would benefit from wage equality in Hollywood, her critique is not of the system that renders actresses commodities; rather, she critiques the system for compensating men's work differently. Just as #AskHerMore did not advocate for dismantling the underlying sexism that means men and women are treated differently on the red carpet, Arquette does not advocate dismantling these objectifying and inequitable structures but modifying them so that women and men are equally valuable commodities.

Arquette continued her focus on wage inequality when she won the Academy Award for Best Supporting Actress. As she stood on the Oscar stage and came to the end of her list of thank-yous, she said, "To every woman who gave birth to every taxpayer and citizen of this nation, we have fought for everybody else's equal rights. It's our time to have wage equality once and for all and equal rights for women in the United States of America." Arquette extended her comments from the platform of the celebrity interview to that of the Oscar stage. As with her comments in *The Guardian*, she emphasized working within established power structures, this time of the government, calling for "taxpayers" and "citizens" to band together to support women's equality. In response to her speech, in arguably the moment of the ceremony that generated the most discussion and GIFs, the camera cut to Meryl Streep and Jennifer Lopez, seated next to each other, clapping and shouting their support for Arquette along with thunderous applause from the rest of the crowd. Unlike the jeering that followed Sacheen Littlefeather's politically charged acceptance speech decades earlier, Arquette's words were met with acceptance and praise. Such reactions reflect the growing mainstream acceptance of such views, but not from a postfeminist perspective; Arquette articulated the need for continued work toward gender parity, emphasizing that the project of feminism is not complete.

However, when Arquette went backstage following her win and expanded on this statement for reporters, she eroded much of the goodwill she had earned just moments earlier. Clutching her golden statuette, she reemphasized pay inequalities in the United States. Then, shifting tactics, she said, "It's time for all the women in America and all the men that love women, and all the gay people, and all the people of color that we've all fought for to fight for us now." With this statement, Arquette demonstrated a skewed view of feminist history and made it clear that, when speaking about the category of "women in America," she meant white, heterosexual women. First, her statement ignored the long history of the feminist movement's ostracization of women of color and LGBTQIA women (e.g., hooks 2014; P. H. Collins 1989; Rich 1980; Crenshaw 1991). Further, she rhetorically divided her audience into four groups: women, men who love women, gay people, and people of color. By creating these discursive divisions, she implied that these categories are mutually exclusive. This division frames "women" as straight and white, and "men" as presumably white and definitely heterosexual. Her language silos gay people and people of color separately from "women" and even "men," defining them solely by their difference from straight, white people. Stemming from and contributing to a growing public awareness of the concept of intersectionality, this incident constituted a moment in which the limits of Arquette's expression of feminism—as a movement primarily for white, straight women—became visible and subject to the negotiated pressures of the intersectional imperative. Her comments spawned a wave of supporters and detractors who took to both social and legacy media platforms to debate the merits of calling out celebrities and the role of intersectionality within popular feminism.

"No Good Deed Goes Unpunished": Supporting and Defending Arquette

If contestations over the value of #AskHerMore revealed tensions around what constitutes a worthy feminist intervention, reactions to Arquette's backstage comments demonstrate how challenging the labor of calling out problematic interventions can be, particularly when the subject of that critique is a privileged white woman. While Arquette's comments sparked ire, many members of this networked public supported her, elided her lack of intersectionality, and even vehemently defended her against the "toxic" discourse that called out her misstep. A significant proportion of commentators emphatically lauded her speech; *Mashable* (2015) tweeted "@PattyArquette can have another award for that speech," while outlets like *ThinkProgress* and the *New Yorker* praised Arquette's "feminist bona fides" and gave her speech an "A+" (Steiger 2015; Schulman 2015). These comments—that her feminism is bona fide, A+, and award-winning, serve to legitimize her and her message as prime examples of feminism. This framing discursively constructs her and this version of feminism—liberal white feminism—as not only dominant and appropriate but in fact a stellar exemplar of the movement. Over and over, her speech was called "badass," and with the heavy recirculation of GIFs of Meryl Streep's enthusiastic response included in a majority of news accounts and commentary, one message was abundantly clear: "Meryl Streep's reaction should be your reaction, too" (Lockett 2015). Within most articles and tweets in this dataset, commentators framed support and even adulation as the commonsense response.

Despite myriad criticisms of her backstage comments, many news outlets provided cover for Arquette, failing to comment on or openly excusing her anti-intersectional framing of wage inequality. For example, *Access Hollywood* interviewed Arquette to give her the opportunity to "respond to the haters" but never stated who those "haters" were or why some people were critiquing her words (Feigenbaum 2015). By failing to explain why people criticized her, *Access Hollywood* protected Arquette's legitimacy by delegitimizing those who pushed back on her statement as "haters," which typically describes those who criticize without justification. These discursive moves obscure the nuances of the conversation around Arquette's remarks and position her as the victim of unspecified "haters." These articles simplify the narrative and thus popular understandings of feminism, sugarcoating her lack of intersectionality for a more palatable liberal feminist message.

However, many went beyond covering for Arquette to lambast those who called her out. Examples of this sentiment are plentiful and are suffused with misogynistic language. For example, an article in *The Daily Beast* praised Arquette's "vitally political" speech and maligned "the usual shrill condemnation that awaits anyone who doesn't stick to the received feminist script and also fails to include every other minority-within-a-minority concern in their speeches" (Crocker 2015). Like those who praised Arquette and her speech as prime feminist examples, Lizzie Crocker frames her message as "vital," reifying the importance of white feminist goals and placing Arquette on a pedestal from which shrill, whiny naysayers are trying to take her down. Beyond using sexist language, Crocker's characterization of feminism as homogeneous and militantly policed via "call-out culture" ignores the fact that feminism is multifaceted and multivocal, maligning the role of internal critique within the movement. Other online and print news commentators also criticized "the intersectionality crowd on Twitter," saying that it is "a waste of energy to be sniping at each other" and characterizing those who called out Arquette as "acid" (Nguyen 2015; Maschka 2015; Puente 2015b). This language mirrors that analyzed by other scholars around prior incidents in which women of color feminists took to social media platforms to critique white feminism (see Loza 2014; Risam 2015). The move to shame, silence, and discredit women of color for criticizing white feminists reflects broader racialized power dynamics within the feminist movement that are expressed within popular feminist discourses. Indeed, such responses demonstrate a contestation over who deserves to be subjected to the pressures of the intersectional imperative. The dominant discourse—ultimately that of whiteness—worked to promote and preserve Arquette's status as an ideal feminist, framing her white liberal feminist call for wage equality as more important than her disenfranchisement of Black and LGBTQIA women and demonstrating the prioritization of straight white women's issues over calls for intersectionality.

#AskAWhiteFeminist: Contesting the Labor of Calling Out

As these defensive tweets and articles imply, Arquette's lack of intersectionality moved many on social and legacy media to call her out. In the days following her speech, thousands of social media posts, articles, and television segments critiqued her backstage comments and explained the concept of intersectionality to a wide audience. From women's magazines to cable news to Twitter to YouTube, commentators explained the controversy, saying that Arquette "sparked ire" when her feminist message "jumped the rails entirely by telling gay people and people of color that they needed to start fighting for women" (R. Rose 2015; Harris-Perry 2015). Critics explained that her comments "pretty much alienated women of color, both cis and queer," because she "flattened the fact that people embody multiple identities at once" (GlobalGrindTV 2015; McDonough 2015). Many vehemently disavowed her words as "anti-intersectional . . . cringe-inducing . . . [and] historically negligent," and, as a group of Black women commentators pointed out on *The Larry Wilmore Show*, it was clear that "when [Arquette] says 'women,' she actually means 'white women'" (Zirin 2015; see also Hope 2015). These media outlets and speakers used multiple platforms, both legacy and digital, to call out Arquette's remarks and educate readers and viewers on intersectionality.

But even more than calling out Arquette's lack of intersectionality, many pointed out that such a myopic take on the movement is emblematic of white feminism, or the version of feminism that has historically dominated and takes the issues of white, heterosexual women as the basis of its platform while sidelining women of color and women in the LGBTQIA community. Many of the most widely retweeted articles about Arquette's comments addressed her white feminism. For example, Blue Telusma (2015) writing for *TheGrio*, explicitly

Brittney Cooper ✔
@ProfessorCrunk

···

Want thoughts about Patricia Arquette's fuckery. Don't ask Black feminists to do your labor.
#AskAWhiteFeminist

9:38 AM · Feb 23, 2015 · Twitter Web Client

31 Retweets   **38** Likes

FIGURE 2.4 Brittney Cooper's tweet, 2015.

marked Arquette's words as "racist" and indicative of why many Black women eschew the label of feminist—throughout history, the movement has frequently disavowed them. Because Arquette's comments backstage laid bare racist assumptions, she opened the door for critical voices to explain her words in the context of feminist history and educate readers; thus, for many, such as Vox's Kelsey McKinney (2015), this incident became a moment when "the problem with modern feminism" came starkly to light: the "divide between what straight white women want and what everyone else wants."

Arquette's anti-intersectional comments backstage were undoubtedly problematic and harmful, yet those willing to take on the labor of calling her out produced positive outcomes. These dynamics demonstrate one key way that the intersectional imperative operates through the process of calling out: righteous indignation against bigotry is amplified across social media platforms and remediated across news and commentary outlets so that messages about the importance of wage equality and a feminism that decenters whiteness and heterosexuality circulated throughout media discourse. This contestation is key, but it often comes at the cost of emotional labor to marshal such critiques and deal with other members of an issue public that disagree. The labor that is required for the negotiations of feminism to take place was central to Brittney Cooper's critique of Arquette's backstage remarks.

Cooper, associate professor of women's and gender and Africana studies at Rutgers University and cofounder of the Crunk Feminist Collective, was the most prominent voice in calling out Arquette's white feminism. The morning following the Academy Awards, Cooper took to Twitter to critique Arquette, writing, "Looking 4 ALL the white feminist thinkpieces ripping Patricia Arquette today, my polite way of saying, 'white feminists come get ur girl'" (Cooper 2015c). Several users replied, asking, "What's so bad about [Arquette's remarks]?" and "Because we can't simply be feminists without referencing race?

why not?" To these Cooper responded, "#AskAWhiteFeminist." She continued to use the hashtag, tweeting, "Wonder why WOC give feminist movements
the side eye, don't ask us. Consider Patricia Arquette & then #AskAWhiteFem-
inist" and "Want thoughts about Patricia Arquette's fuckery. Don't ask Black
feminists to do your labor. #AskAWhiteFeminist" (Cooper 2015d, 2015e). A few
days later she expanded her thoughts in an article for Salon (Cooper 2015a) in
which she declared that she was "going on strike" from the labor of calling out
and correcting ignorant white feminists. As Cooper stated, "Asking black
women and other women of color always to explain, show and prove to white
people what is so wrong about what they have said or done, when we have no
guarantees that they will change, shift or grow, is unacceptable. I demand better conditions of work."

Just as members of TRP and Smart Girls did to amplify #AskHerMore,
Cooper used the affordances of different platforms to engage in different types
of critique. On Twitter, she was able to succinctly express her frustration with
the labor often requested of women of color to explain white feminists' lack of
intersectionality. Further, she created the hashtag #AskAWhiteFeminist, which
allowed others on the platform to add their own thoughts and enables all of
those tweets to accumulate. Then, because of the platform available to her as a
professor and a prominent digital feminist and anti-racist voice, she was able
to access a longer-form platform: Salon. Salon afforded her the space to expand
and add nuance to her argument beyond what is possible on Twitter without
creating a massive thread of tweets. Then, she and others were able to circulate
her argument on Salon across social media through the affordance of hyperlinking. Cooper's cross-platform critique of Arquette emphasizes the importance of analyzing how popular feminism is shaped through a negotiative
process that takes place in a wide and intersecting range of digital spaces. Cooper uses her voice across digital platforms to contest the dominant narrative
that emerged following Arquette's speech—that she is a feminist heroine—and
generates a counternarrative (see Foucault Welles and Jackson 2019) that not
only points to Arquette's lack of intersectionality but also critiques the demands
placed on women of color to call out racism.

Cooper's argument effectively turned Arquette's message of unfair labor
compensation around, deploying it as a critique not only of Arquette's message
but also of the networked publics who use platforms like Twitter to demand
the labor of women of color, either explicitly or implicitly. As Lisa Nakamura
(2015) has argued, the labor of calling out racism and misogyny typically falls
on the shoulders of women of color, and this labor is emotionally taxing, deval-
ued, and unpaid. Responses to Cooper's tweets make clear that this labor is
not just implicitly demanded when a woman of color encounters ambient racism and/or misogyny, whether on a social media platform like Twitter or an
architectural platform like the Oscar stage; other members of the networked

public around this incident explicitly demanded that labor, asking Cooper to explain Arquette's mistakes and justify her own anger and frustration. Cooper finds this demand unbearable and thus vows to withhold her labor, directing people to "ask a white feminist." This move transfers the labor from her to white women, those who should be responsible for coming to "get [their] girl," as Cooper tweeted the morning after the Oscars. White women have benefited from the structures of power within feminism that have disadvantaged Black women, and Cooper argues that she should not be asked to do the emotional labor of calling out and explaining white feminists' mistakes.

Sparking a Conversation, Energizing a Movement: Arquette as the Face of the Wage Equality Debate

While much of the discussion analyzed in this chapter has worked to excuse Arquette's lack of intersectionality, Arquette's way of speaking about wage equality shifted after voices like Cooper called her out. Following her speech, Arquette took some ownership for her lack of intersectionality and endeavored to correct her statement. The next day on Twitter, she emphasized that women of color "are the most negatively effected [*sic*] in wage inequality" and said, "Women stand together in this" (Arquette 2015a). This time, her use of "women" seemed to include nonwhite women and acknowledged that women are differentially affected by wage inequality. As with Zendaya and Rancic's use of social media to respond to controversy, Twitter enabled Arquette to use her own voice to speak out and gave a sense of personal responsibility to her response.[3] Months later, in December 2015, she continued to use her voice, this time mediated through the *Hollywood Reporter*, a well-regarded industry publication that lent her voice greater legitimacy and authority. In a guest column, she addressed the aftermath of her speech and said she blamed herself for her "stupid wording" backstage "that made some women feel left out or slighted." She stated that, following her speech, she had "learned a lot more about the feminist movement and how women of color have been left out of the process," and because of this greater understanding, she was "sad that [she] may have added to their feeling of being excluded" (Arquette 2015b). Unlike voices that criticized those who called out Arquette, she explained that this critique moved her to educate herself about the feminist movement's racist history. While this statement lacked a nuanced explanation of her words within the context of feminist history—and, indeed, lacks an apology altogether—she acknowledged her participation in the erasure of women of color and LGBTQIA women. This is not to say that Arquette absolves herself of critique, but rather to acknowledge that the labor of many feminists who called her out moved her discussion of wage equality in a more intersectional direction. Even if only nominally, the often-maligned labor of pushing forth the intersectional imperative made a difference.

Arquette's star power and participation in various events continued to propel the newsworthiness of the wage equality debate into the following year. She played a major role at several Hollywood events during which she gave speeches championing wage equality. And as Arquette endeavored to foreground women of color in her framing of feminism, the mainstream media outlets that praised her and continued to report on her activist efforts paved the way for her prominent role within a newly salient discourse on wage equality that continued, in Hollywood and beyond, throughout 2015 and into the following year. Despite the many voices that rightly critiqued Arquette, she became one of most prominent "face[s] of gender equality in Hollywood," and much of this continued discussion referenced and credited her for bringing the issue such public attention (Conlon 2015). News and commentary outlets, including *Variety*, *Vogue UK*, *Glamour*, and *Elle*, all cited her importance in making "pay disparity for actresses in both TV and film . . . a hot-button issue" (Setoodeh 2015). Indeed, outlets from the *Washington Post* to the *Wall Street Journal* to *Slate*, to name just a few, published detailed articles backed up with data contextualizing and explaining the wage gap, crediting the Sony hack and Arquette for bringing the issue to the fore (Woodruff 2015; McGregor 2015).

But more than a focus on Hollywood, these articles connected the situation in the entertainment industry to that of women more broadly, pointing out that "when it comes to the gender gap in wages, the entertainment industry looks like the rest of us" (Morath 2015). Other pieces discussed the wage gap in general, using statistics and expert economists to back up assertions that the wage gap is gendered as well as racialized (Portlock 2015; Cassese, Barnes, and Branton 2015; DePillis 2015). Even though Arquette's original comments lacked a focus on women of color and gay women, much of the information about the wage gap that sprang up because of the publicity her statements received did provide intersectional context and highlighted how different the wage gap is for different women. All of this information was publicly available prior to Arquette's speech. However, her use of two platforms—her celebrity and the Oscar stage—allowed her to refract the attention audiences paid to her onto the issue of wage inequality and amplified its importance. She transferred some of the newsworthiness afforded to her, as a newly minted Oscar winner, and to the Academy Awards, onto the wage gap. News and commentary outlets then produced content that contextualized her speech, capitalizing on a presumed uptick in interest in the topic.

Further, many directly credited Arquette's speech with aiding in the passage of the California Fair Pay Act. Two days after Arquette's speech, state senator Hannah-Beth Jackson introduced the bill "to feed off the momentum created by Arquette's speech" (Panzar 2015). Jackson had long been working on the bill as part of the California Legislative Women's Caucus and said of Arquette, "Her rallying cry has energized a movement that has long been calling for this," and "credited the news media attention with helping to raise momentum to pass the bill" (Ryzik 2016). Touted as the toughest such law in the country, it requires that male and female employees performing "substantially similar" work be paid equally, whereas the previous law only protected employees who perform exactly the same job. The bill passed, was signed into law by Governor Jerry Brown in October 2015, and went into effect on January 1, 2016.

This legislative achievement demonstrates the complex, problematic, yet potentially substantial possibility of celebrity feminism. By using the platforms of fame and the Oscar stage, Arquette was able to momentarily elevate wage equality within the national discourse, creating a surge of public interest and outcry that lawmakers such as Jackson were able to parlay into the state legislature's interest in the Fair Pay Act. While many scholars critique popular feminism and celebrity feminism for their commercialization and relative toothlessness, the passage of the California Fair Pay Act on the heels of Arquette's speech presents a relatively rare instance wherein celebrity feminism helped to manifest structural changes. Scholars such as Shelley Cobb (2018) have lamented that the efforts of celebrity feminists often obscure and overshadow the long-standing work of scholar-activists like Cooper and legislators like Jackson who put in the hard work while the (usually white) celebrity spokesperson often gets the credit. Moreover, by incorporating this feminist cause into her public persona, Arquette was able to extend the publicity she received for her Oscar win and consequently gain increased positive press, potentially adding to the value of her celebrity brand. These benefits and the ways in which Arquette's prominence obscured the work of others less famous than she undoubtedly hamper and problematize the potential benefits of feminist celebrity emissaries. But moments like this demonstrate that, with the right combination of public attention (complicated and amplified further by the process of calling out), legislative acumen, and fortuitous happenstance, celebrity feminism may help breed concrete change.

Feminist Values: Conclusions on Reforming Celebrity

The #AskHerMore hashtag campaign and Patricia Arquette approached the media ritual of the Academy Awards as a highly public platform on which to intervene in representational and economic gendered inequalities and negotiate the pressures of white feminist and intersectional imperatives. With #AskHerMore, celebrities used the dual platforms of fame and social media to construct the red carpet as a space where audiences could use digital platforms to reshape the values of that media ritual. By encouraging users to use the affordances of social media to call for representational change, the campaign pushed for the red carpet to represent women as valuable for their labor rather than their appearance; however, this intervention ignored the fact that walking the red carpet is a form of labor that can add value both to the celebrity as a commodity and to the designer who dresses her. Further, the campaign failed to engage in this intervention intersectionally, ignoring race and implicitly maintaining a focus on white women. Then during her acceptance speech, Arquette used the dual platforms of fame and the Oscar stage to publicize the gendered pay disparity and agitate for wage equality. But her anti-intersectional comments laid bare the fundamentally white and heteronormative foundations of liberal feminism, ignoring that the labor of straight white women is valued differently from that of women of color and/or LGBTQIA women and sparking a wave of callouts. Despite the nuanced critiques that called out Arquette, the dominant narrative circulated across most legacy media platforms preserved her status as a feminist heroine, emphasizing her determination and legal efficacy.

However, as this chapter illustrates, one of the defining features of popular feminism in the digital age is the way in which the intersections of feminist ideas and digital platforms around issues of celebrity culture afford the possibility of debate and negotiation on a scale that is not possible through legacy media platforms. As such, the often-frenzied pace and content of these debates not only amplifies certain feminist issues, such as wage equality or intersectionality, but also more easily enables that debate, when taken as a whole, to emerge as more complex and nuanced because so many voices have access to platforms from which to speak. Those platforms are by no means created equal. Witherspoon, Arquette, and even Cooper were able to access certain platforms like the Oscar stage or Salon, which most members of these issue publics cannot, or have far larger audiences than the average user on more "democratic" platforms like Instagram or Twitter. These dynamics undoubtedly give more power to celebrities than to average users. However, especially because platforms are so deeply intertextual and content flows easily across their boundaries, more voices can be heard and amplified. Even if they do not become dominant as legacy media overwhelmingly continue to privilege famous voices and those who champion and defend white feminist perspectives, we have seen that they may shift the conversation and build a greater awareness of intersectional feminist issues.

From its inception, the Academy of Motion Picture Arts and Sciences and its award ceremony centered on two key dynamics we see at play in these non-intersectional feminist interventions at the 2015 Oscar ceremony: labor and values. Louis B. Mayer founded the Academy as an elite organization of above-the-line industry players to try to combat the impending unionization of below-the-line workers and created the awards ceremony to present Hollywood as a place of ethics and strong values. At their core, both objectives aim to achieve capitalistic goals, preserving high profits for those controlling the means of production and augmenting public support to ensure the continued financial viability of the entertainment industry. Similarly, while both #AskHerMore and Arquette's call for wage equality were framed (with varying levels of success) as rebellious, culture-changing feminist statements, they too centered on and reified structures of capitalism. Even as the #AskHerMore campaign sought "more positive" representations of actresses by curtailing red carpet reporters' focus on their appearance, it worked to reinscribe them as laborers within a patriarchal capitalist system that it did little to critique. Similarly, Arquette's call for wage equality was explicitly focused on increasing women's value as laborers and, indeed, as commodities. To borrow a phrase from Sarah Banet-Weiser and Laura Portwood-Stacer (2017), these campaigns trafficked in feminism. They reinforced liberal white feminist ideals, treating some symptoms of capitalism but leaving intact its structures, which serve to buttress and support the patriarchal dynamics the campaigns ostensibly aimed to disrupt.

These case studies illustrate both the perils and the possibilities of feminist hashtag activism and callout campaigns as refracted through the lens of celebrity culture. The #AskHerMore campaign and Arquette's acceptance speech constitute part of a larger moment in which feminism was becoming increasingly the purview of celebrity culture and vice versa, with celebrity functioning as a platform on which audiences (through the use of social media platforms like Twitter) and celebrities could engage in feminist intervention. The next chapter will examine another set of case studies that allow us to explore further the co-constitutions of celebrity, feminism, and networked publics, and the ways in which popular feminism is increasingly informed by contestation over intersectionality. Through an analysis of Gloria Steinem's and Madeleine Albright's statements during Hillary Clinton's 2016 presidential primary campaign, I will build on the insights from this chapter about the role of "imperfect" feminist spokeswomen who "misspeak" feminism and the networked publics who call them out. But in chapter 3, we will see how the dynamics change when those spokeswomen are not feminist celebrities but rather celebrity feminists, long-standing "icons" of the feminist movement who are speaking directly about how feminism maps onto political decision-making.

3

Nasty Women, Silly Girls

Feminist Generation Gaps
and Hillary Clinton's 2016
Presidential Campaign

In the previous chapter, I explored several forms of pressure: public pressure on media institutions and rituals like the red carpet broadcast, celebrity pressure in support of structural change such as wage equality legislation, and feminist counterpublics' negotiated pressure on celebrities who do not speak or engage in activism intersectionally. Through hashtag activism and callouts, individuals and groups mobilized the publicness of social media and the newsworthiness of celebrity to enact the discursive pressures of the white feminist and intersectional imperatives around the 2015 Academy Awards. Such pressures motivate a discursive flow across the boundaries of varied yet intersecting sociocultural spaces: feminist theories and activism, celebrity culture, policy making, anti-racism, social media, and Marxist critiques of labor and capitalism. Sometimes this pressure generates progressive momentum across these different spaces as they commingle in provocative and often surprising ways. In this chapter, I will continue to explore the pressures placed around the blurry boundaries of fame and feminism by foregrounding and analyzing the role of anger within feminist activism.

Anger and outrage have informed each of the previous chapters. Outrage at hackers who exploited celebrity women shaped much of the discussion about the celebrity nude photo hack. Frustration and anger motivated audiences and celebrities to agitate for more complex coverage of women on the red carpet, and outrage was a driving force for those who called out Patricia Arquette's lack of intersectionality. The following chapter highlights this recurring theme and interrogates outrage and "angriness" as motivational to many dynamics that inform popular feminism through an analysis of reactions to Gloria Steinem's and Madeleine Albright's controversial statements while campaigning for Hillary Clinton's nomination in 2016. Unlike entertainment celebrities such as Arquette, these women achieved fame by virtue of their feminist activism and political work, and thus their roles within the feminist movement and as some of its public faces hold a different weight. However, like Arquette, Steinem and Albright both caused controversy and were called out for a lack of intersectionality and a failure to fully contend with both the history and the current state of the feminist movement. In this chapter, I more deeply examine intersectional critiques of white feminism and online outrage through a situated analysis of two instances of highly mediated feminist anger directed toward fellow feminists. I pay special attention to how outrage is shaped by and shapes social media logics and, in turn, how those logics in conjunction with sexist narrative frames informed the ways news outlets covered the controversy. And while the events discussed in this chapter took place just two weeks shy of the one-year anniversary of Arquette's speech, the sociopolitical stakes at the time were more fraught and much, much higher.

The Battle for New Hampshire: Gendered Debates and the 2016 Democratic Primary

In February 2016, the U.S. presidential primaries were in full swing. The Republican race was a cacophony of chaos, featuring the largest number of candidates in history, including the erratic Donald Trump. On the left were two Democratic candidates with substantially different platforms. The first was the presumed favorite, Hillary Clinton. The former secretary of state under President Barack Obama, former senator from New York, and former First Lady of the United States boasted an impressive track record in Washington. However, many voters found her controversial for a variety of reasons. Some of these reasons were based on policy, such as her support of American military intervention over the course of her career, while others were based on her personal life, such as her reaction to the infidelity of her husband, Bill Clinton, during his presidency. Critiques of Hillary Clinton abounded and were amplified across the media landscape, many tinged or outright drenched with sexism. Moreover, her more moderate, centrist policies earned her growing critique from the farther left segment of the party, which had been given voice through her rival Senator Bernie Sanders of Vermont. Sanders identifies as a democratic socialist, and his platform was built on a series of progressive policy initiatives such as Medicare for All and free college tuition. As primary season kicked into high gear, Clinton and Sanders had more or less maintained a "civil" competition centered on their political differences, but tension between their supporters was beginning to bubble to the surface, particularly around one issue: gender.

As news outlets breathlessly reported in the lead-up to the New Hampshire primary on February 9, Clinton was losing the young female vote to Sanders. Polls showed her trailing by as many as 26 points overall during the week before the primary, and exit polls eventually showed that Sanders outpaced Clinton among women voters in particular by 11 points (Silver 2016; NBC Newsnight 2016). Among younger female voters, the spread was a chasm: 82 percent of women under age thirty voted for Sanders in New Hampshire (ABC News Analysis Desk 2016). On its face, this was a surprising turn of events: the first female candidate with a likely shot at a presidential run was lagging because young women were unimpressed? Beyond and intersecting with Clinton's dearth of support from young women, another phenomenon placed gender at the center of leftist political analyses: the increasingly virulent sexism and outraged rhetoric from certain segments of Sanders's base. In late 2015, political commentators and journalists began noting that a subset of Sanders supporters were especially active on social media and often aggressively—*very* aggressively—defended their chosen candidate and launched attacks against Clinton and her supporters. Robinson Meyer (2015), writing in *The Atlantic*, dubbed these supporters "Berniebros," highlighting the fact that many of them were male, and caricaturizing them as fiercely loyal, self-righteous, and performatively feminist. This archetype, which came to be more popularly known as the "Bernie Bro," became a shorthand for the most ardent of Sanders supporters who harassed Clinton and her supporters across social media in explicitly misogynistic terms and also spawned much political commentary (e.g., Lind 2016). These two seemingly contradictory phenomena—a groundswell of young female support for Sanders alongside aggressive "Bernie Bros" whose sexist and harassing behavior popularized an image of his supporters as sanctimonious socialist frat boys—highlighted the centrality of gender and outrage in the race for the Democratic nomination.

In response to the unimpressive polls out of New Hampshire, two of Clinton's surrogates spoke out in her favor ahead of the vote. While a veritable laundry list of entertainment celebrities, including stars such as Oprah Winfrey, Beyoncé, Natalie Portman, and Katy Perry, would eventually support and lend their spotlight to Clinton's campaign for the presidency, her campaign chose to feature long-standing celebrity feminists rather than feminist celebrities ahead of this primary. One of those was Gloria Steinem, a storied feminist icon, a journalist, and an activist, who rose to national fame as a leader of the feminist second wave during the 1960s and 1970s. While promoting a new book on February 5, Steinem was asked by talk show host Bill Maher for her thoughts on Clinton's lagging support among young women. After commenting that young women are "very activist" and "more feminist" than ever before, she changed gears by saying, "When you're young, you're thinking: 'Where are the boys? The boys are with Bernie.'" This comment, taken out of context, provoked uproar on social media and beyond from feminists, many of them younger women, and particularly those who supported Sanders. This furor was inadvertently compounded the following day when Madeleine Albright, the first female secretary of state, who served under President Bill Clinton from 1997 to 2001, stumped for Hillary Clinton at a campaign rally in New Hampshire. While discussing Clinton's role over the past several decades in the fight for women's rights and her commitment to further supporting pro-woman policies in the White House, Albright declared, "There's a special place in hell for women who don't help each other!" Albright's oft-repeated quip took on a sinister tone with its proximity to Steinem's remark, and commentators across media platforms began asking: What does it mean to vote as a woman and as a feminist in 2016?

In this chapter I examine the role of intrafeminist anger in political discourses and decision-making, how social media can afford and shape expressions of anger, and the implications of its remediation across legacy media outlets. To do so, I analyze online discourses around Steinem's and Albright's comments, paying special attention to how social media platforms were leveraged to express outrage and exert discursive and political pressure on Steinem, Albright, and Clinton.[1] These moments of outrage threw into stark relief historical tensions between white feminisms and intersectional feminisms, offering insight into intergenerational feminist conflicts. These findings not only help to elucidate the digital negotiations of feminist ideals during the mid-2010s and the place of famous voices within the movement, but also help us understand one piece of the complex dynamics around gender, sex, and the 2016 presidential election. The analysis shows that Steinem's comments reflected and reinvigorated feminist generational conflicts over neoliberal notions of choice while exposing the complications that can arise through celebrity feminism. Further, Albright's critique of young feminists as ahistorical clashed with critics who argued it was indeed Albright's and Clinton's political histories, coupled with their insufficiently intersectional feminism, that moved young feminists to disavow Clinton.

Overall, this chapter demonstrates the ways networked publics mobilized outrage to articulate a new feminist politics of choice, extending the discussion of callouts in the previous chapter to interrogate the role of feminist anger and its political implications more deeply. This feminist politics of choice intersects with and is deeply informed by the broader sociopolitical dynamics of the intersectional imperative. Defined simultaneously in contrast to a construction of second wave feminism as overwhelmingly white and middle-class as well as to postfeminist notions of irrational, individualistic choice, the politics of choice articulated within the discourse around these case studies centers on intersectional collectivity and historically informed rationality. Working within the tension between individuality and collectivity, Sanders-supporting feminists framed their decision-making as an individual, rational choice based on their understanding of how that choice affects others. However, because this definitional work occurred within a moment of outrage, the politics of choice served to emphasize generational differences and elided the continuities between various iterations of feminism.

My analysis begins by exploring the role of anger within social and political activism, particularly the pitfalls and risks that arise when that anger is mediated across social media platforms. In doing so, I demonstrate how the media narrativization of these events as "catfights" drew on sexist, ageist tropes and diminished the events' potential as an intergenerational feminist dialogue. Next I examine how Steinem's remark framed feminist choice and explore how her celebrity feminist authority backfired when she "misspoke" feminism, opening the door for the media to craft an intergenerational catfight. Finally, I analyze Albright's speech, demonstrating that her characterization of young feminists' ahistorical view of the movement was out of step with the discourse from her detractors, whose knowledge of Albright's and Clinton's histories often moved them to repudiate their apparently nonintersectional feminist politics. The chapter concludes by returning explicitly to the role of anger, particularly digitally mediated anger, within feminist discord.

"Famous Feminist Fight!": Exploring Anger, Social Media Conflict, and the Catfight Narrative

Fanning the Flames: Moral Outrage, Political Anger, and Social Media

For decades, sociologists, psychologists, media scholars, feminists, and political theorists have explored the roles of anger and outrage within social and political movements. One of the dominant themes across these bodies of literature is that anger is motivational. When members of an oppressed group and their allies become outraged at injustice, anger can help them push past the anxiety and fear that may accompany the risky actions of speaking or acting against those in power (Castells 2012; Sayers and Jones 2014). The risk-taking behaviors that result from politicized anger can create "polarisation and crisis, and out of crisis comes the potential for change" as dominant power hierarchies may be destabilized (Sayers and Jones 2014, 283). The productive agitation that can stem from outrage may disrupt models of rational deliberative democracy, most notably articulated in Habermas's (2015) classic (and heavily critiqued) conceptualization of an ideal public sphere. However, theorists such as

Chantal Mouffe (2005) argue for agonistic pluralism rather than a consensus-based model of democracy. Agonistic pluralism accepts that passion and disagreement are inevitable within democratic governance and seeks to find ways to channel such conflict productively rather than attempt to resolve it. Such scholars argue for the value of "perpetual provocation" as a way to motivate citizens toward action (McCosker and Johns 2013, 188).

This effort to recover the political power of anger has been especially productive for feminist analysis because of the complex relationships between gender, feminist collective action, and outrage. These relationships are laden with layered power dynamics. First, female anger directly contradicts dominant norms of femininity that prize women's submissiveness and care, and much recent popular feminist scholarship continues to encourage women to accept and channel their anger against racist and patriarchal political forces (Chemaly 2019; Traister 2019; Cooper 2018). Further, anger within the feminist movement has long caused anxiety. Conflict between feminists can provoke critiques that anger is a patriarchal power move that has no place within the women's movement and fears that it will destabilize the collective action that is crucial to activism. However, feminist theorists such as Holmes (2004) and Lorde (1997) point out that such conflict is crucial in working toward more respectful relations with one another that radically consider privilege hierarchies among women. Lorde (1997) in particular spoke at length about her experiences as a Black woman within the feminist movement, telling white feminists to acknowledge their privilege and championing the productive role of outrage, stating, "Anger between peers births change, not destruction, and the discomfort and sense of loss it often causes is not fatal, but a sign of growth" (283). Overall, feminist thinkers have argued for women to use the power of anger to mobilize against inequalities both in society more broadly and within the feminist movement.

However, just as many of the pros regarding anger center on motivation to act despite risk, other scholars argue that those risks are myriad. Beyond the physical, legal, emotional, and psychological risks that may accompany anger channeled into activism, some scholars argue that social media exacerbate outrage and shape it in unproductive ways. Crockett (2017) points out that, in our off-line lives, we rarely encounter incidents that provoke our sense of moral outrage. However, social media increase the number and reach of such incidents and lower the risk threshold for expressing that anger; in other words, it is less risky to angrily tweet at someone than it is to confront them in person, and on Twitter we may come across many people and comments that provoke moral outrage. The omnipresence and ease of anger on social media is further shaped by platforms' algorithms, which tend to amplify highly engaging content, and research shows that inflammatory posts tend to elicit more engagement than other posts. These dynamics moved Crockett (2017) and William J. Brady and

M. J. Crockett (2019) to warn that social media can make moral outrage more constant and less surprising, potentially lessening its impact, and channel it into hot-take hyperbolic responses that, they argue, are politically counterproductive. Marwick (2021) posits the expression "morally motivated networked harassment" as a way to conceptualize the ways that networked audiences target individuals who violate established group norms, emphasizing that such behaviors operate across ideological and political spectra and can be highly problematic. Moreover, research indicates that "viral outrage," or incidents of digital anger that garner much attention and generate the "piling on" effect Marwick describes, can provoke backlash, even when the outrage "seems appropriate and justified in isolation" (Sawaoka and Monin 2018, 1676). Researchers found this to be the case even when the "victim" was a high-status public figure like Steinem, Albright, or Clinton. These findings complicate laudatory theorizations of political anger as motivational by pointing out that some of the risks associated with outrage, particularly on social media, should be considered in order to provoke productively.

Catfight! Narrative Framing of Feminist Conflict in News and Commentary

However, the risks of anger, particularly women's anger, are not relegated only to social media. They exist across media as sexist narratives of the catfight tend to dominate news and entertainment narratives about conflict between women. Both fiction and nonfiction texts often deploy this narrative framework to personify and dramatize female conflicts; in the news, this often means reporters individualize, oversimplify, and bifurcate complex disagreements among women and elevate spokeswomen for each side (Douglas 1995, 225). Moreover, existing issues with oversimplified and overdramatized news frames have been amplified as news has become increasingly dependent on digital platforms for circulation, and social media logics that prize content that encourages audience engagement (and consequently is often controversial) have impacted both online and legacy news and commentary outlets (van Dijck, Poell, and de Waal, 2018, 54).

Predictably, across media platforms, the uproar that resulted after Steinem's and Albright's comments was framed as a woman-on-woman fight. Outraged women used Twitter to lambast their statements, pledging again and again to continue to support Sanders. This anger and conflict were then framed in the news, as the *Today Show* (2016) called it, as a "famous feminist fight," a battle between older celebrity feminists and young, idealistic feminist voters. One widely critiqued example of this narrativization was Alan Rappeport's article for the *New York Times* (2016). The title of that piece, "Female Icons Tell the Young to Get with It," frames the conflict as a "generational clash" in which Steinem and Albright told young voters to "grow up and get with the program" and "scolded" any women who disagreed with them (A1). The dismissive framing of "getting with the program"—presumably some sort of Democratic Party line—reduces the complex struggle over how feminists today are grappling with political issues into a scuffle between younger and older women. His use of the word *scold* in particular draws on sexist connotations of a nagging mother rebuking her daughter, an ageist narrative that diminishes the fierce feminist boundary work that went on among networked feminist publics around this issue to a trivial spat. The article was published online with the title "Gloria Steinem and Madeleine Albright Scold Young Women Backing Bernie Sanders," but after backlash from readers, editors changed "Scold" to "Rebuke."[2] While tamping down on the gendered language slightly, this highly circulated article nevertheless retained the catfight narrative as central.

Several young, white feminist writers with large followings on social media criticized this framing in online commentary pieces, and their critiques echo long-standing feminist concerns that intramovement conflict undermines the united front that is so important for activism. Amanda Marcotte (2016) expressed her frustration with Steinem and Albright for playing into the media's love of a catfight when they "should have known better in the first place" and resisted it. Focusing more on the problems with the media narrative itself, Jessica Valenti (2016) pointed out that working through disagreements within the feminist movement can be healthy and productive, but that productivity is problematic when it takes place in "a media landscape that's allergic to nuance" and oversimplifies "complicated feminist discord." Instead of exploring a nuanced moment of contention within the feminist movement, the catfight narrative allowed journalists and voices on both sides to personalize the argument, turning it into a battle between older and younger feminists, between the establishment and the new guard. This rendered Clinton's campaign highly overdetermined, placing upon her candidacy a difference of opinion within the feminist movement that extends and has implications far beyond her bid for the presidency. However, by personifying this disagreement among feminists and placing that burden on the Clinton campaign, the news media's catfight narrative drew on ageism and rendered the conflict more simplistic, deepening divides within the already fractious left.

The Persona Is Political: Celebrity Feminism, Activist Motivation, and Feminist Political Choice

On February 5, 2016, Gloria Steinem appeared on *Real Time with Bill Maher* to promote her new book, *My Life on the Road*. During the interview, Maher turned the conversation to young women's relationship to feminism. Steinem responded, "I find young women very, very activist" and "way more feminist" than the women of her generation, saying, "We were, like,

FIGURE 3.1 Gloria Steinem appears on *Real Time with Bill Maher* (HBO), 2016.

12 crazy ladies in the beginning, and now it's the majority." She went on to emphasize that "gratitude never radicalized anybody," saying that, just as she was, young women are rightly motivated toward feminism by their anger at their circumstances rather than out of a sense of duty to feminists who came before them. Maher then pointed out that these young women, feminist as they may be, "really don't like Hillary Clinton" and were overwhelmingly supporting Bernie Sanders. In response, Steinem said that "women get more radical as we get older," contrasting this to younger women who are "thinking: 'Where are the boys? The boys are with Bernie.'"

In this short exchange, Steinem proposes a contradictory view of cross-generational feminism, political motivation, and political choice. First, she pushes back on arguments that young women do not understand the importance of feminism, positing that feminist activism has not deteriorated but rather blossomed among young people. Emphasizing its growing acceptance among wider swaths of the younger population, Steinem applauds the anger and determination of young feminists directed toward addressing social injustice. But then she moves from speaking about historical, contextual differences between the feminism of her youth and today's iteration of feminism to specifically discuss the age of the women who make up each generation. This change in focus marks a shift in the tone and content of her remarks as she complicates her statement with further intergenerational comparisons. She asserts that these young women, feminist as they may be, are not as radical as older feminists because such radicalization comes with age as women lose social power. She emphasizes young feminists' lack of radicalism by flippantly alleging that their political choice is motivated not by righteous moral outrage at social injustice but by personal heterosexual desire. Confusingly undermining her prior praise of young feminists, this final quote was decontextualized and remediated across platforms, sparking angry debates about the responsibilities of celebrity feminists and feminist political decision-making.

The following sections explore the anger expressed by feminists and Sanders supporters in response to Steinem's remarks. Overwhelmingly, Steinem's detractors expressed frustration and disappointment that a deeply admired icon for young, radical feminists gave voice to such an unnuanced and offensive categorization of feminist generational difference. Their anger was understandable and justified; however, that anger was problematically shaped by social media and news logics that amplify decontextualized outrage and complicated by a history of feminist hand-wringing over intramovement conflict. While debate and anger are important to the fight for a more progressive and equitable movement, the following analysis demonstrates how complex such work can be.

An Icon Misspeaks: What Is the Responsibility of the Second Wave Celebrity Feminist?

Because of her history as a figurehead of popular feminism, Steinem's power and responsibility as a celebrity feminist were frequent features of the debate around her comments. While many critics acknowledged her history of service to the feminist movement, legacy and social media's tendency toward the sensational sound bite meant that most focused on the offensiveness of her final remark, divorced from its context in the interview and amplified by Steinem's fame and currency as a spokeswoman for feminism. Indeed, Steinem's prominence was the most common topic of social and mass media discussion of her statements. Her privileged status within the feminist movement vis-à-vis her iconicity and celebrity gave her words a special weight that deeply shaped women's anger and disappointment at her words. One highly retweeted example read, "I have been lucky enough to speak to @GloriaSteinem and @madeleine in my life. Today I feel like feminism burnt down. I'm sick. Sad."[3] Comments in response to Steinem's apology, posted to Facebook, echoed this sentiment. Most of those who commented on the post did not accept her apology, and the most upvoted commenter called Steinem "one of [her] heroes" but rebuked her statement, particularly for "how much damage" it has done to the feminist movement (Steinem 2016). Steinem's status as a celebrity feminist, a hero of the feminist movement, gave her an authority that rendered her words powerful, both to shape popular conceptions of feminism and to damage them.

Indeed, nearly a fifth of the most retweeted posts mentioning Steinem in the three days following her remarks critiqued her comment in light of their broader implications for the feminist movement. As Taylor (2017) explains, celebrity feminists are in a special position "to mediate what comes to constitute feminism in the popular imaginary," and few have done so in the United States more prominently than Steinem. Her iconicity lends her power, and when such a powerful figure's words were discordant with what young women framed as shifting modern conceptions of feminism, it created great tension and anger. This anger was amplified by the features and temporality of platforms like Twitter, which afford rapid-fire, at that time 140-character reactions that can foster quick and often highly emotional responses. Further, more inflammatory and/or emotionally intense responses can provoke more engagement and attention from others, not only on social media platforms but also on blogs and other news and commentary sites across the platform ecosystem that report on the controversy. Thus digital platforms' features, algorithms, and economic structures afford and reward highly reactive responses like the aforementioned tweet alleging that Steinem "burned down feminism."

Some tried to combat this view of celebrity feminists' role within feminism; for example, the feminist academic and writer Roxane Gay (2016) tweeted, "I am tired but man. Feminism is not what prominent feminists say or do." Here, Gay tries to downplay the discursive power of figures like Steinem to speak for feminism, implicitly prioritizing the collective over the individual feminist. However, despite protestations from some like Gay, because of the discursive power that figures like Steinem hold and the ways in which Twitter makes nuanced critique more difficult than quick reactions, it was clear across the discourse that this moment caused a reckoning among feminists that, within the popular imaginary, destabilized some aspects of the movement.

In her take on Steinem's comments and her status as an icon for The Cut, Ann Friedman (2016) provided a different perspective on Steinem's value as a feminist figurehead. Friedman explained that one benefit of second wave feminism was that it included "icons, like Steinem, who planned national summits and served as spokeswomen for the movement." However, critics of Steinem and certain factions of second wave feminism more broadly pointed out that, while that coherence allowed for a more legible collectivity, the problem with that collectivity as led by Steinem was that popular understandings of the movement often reflected women like the iconic Steinem herself—pretty, white, heterosexual, and middle-class enough to make the general public pay attention to even radical feminist ideas. In contrast, young feminists who critiqued her statement framed themselves as deeply intersectional, and while many make it clear that they are indebted to the feminists like Steinem who came before them, they are critical of the overwhelmingly white bent of earlier feminism. In this way, Steinem metonymically functioned as a stand-in for second wave feminism, and her controversial statements opened space for a much broader critique of the movement. Such critiques demonstrate a totalized view of the second wave as nonintersectional, informed by the prominence, historically and still today, of women like Steinem, Albright, and Clinton: political and activist celebrities that were and still are amplified by the media and thus come to personify the movement in a particularly white way.

However, the frustration expressed toward Steinem as an icon of the second wave was not the new invention of young feminists; rather, it continued the work of second wave feminist foremothers like Audre Lorde and bell hooks, who called out the problematic statements of those within their ranks to agitate for a more equitable and inclusive movement. While Steinem's celebrity helped to provide critics a platform and a target, the majority of their anger was directed more broadly at concerns about the movement and its limitations: to see and respect differences of opinion and to foreground intersectionality. These dynamics moved Steinem's critics to see their version of feminism as more complex and radical, motivating individual choices with the good of an intersectional collective in mind. As I will explore more deeply in the next section, the tension between individual versus collective political choices is at the heart of the intergenerational conflict Steinem's comments brought to the surface, pushes back against critiques of "choice feminism" that plagued the third wave, and provides insight into the politics of feminist tensions in the 2010s.

I'll Be a Postfeminist in the Postpatriarchy: Steinem and the Problem of Choice

Steinem's comments and the outrage and controversy they inspired map onto critiques of the individualistic, apolitical bent of third wave feminism in ways that are complex, contradictory, and surprising considering previous research on the ways the news media frames feminism. Some key criticisms of third wave feminism, which describes the dominant form of U.S.-based feminism roughly from the mid-1980s to the early 2010s, center on its prioritization of individual choice over collective action and third wave feminists' refusal to police the borders of the label. This focus on individual choice is also a quintessential aspect of postfeminism and neoliberal ideologies, through which choices that are problematic according to many feminist ideals—such as a single-minded prioritization of heterosexual romantic love or pleasurable interaction with the industrial beauty complex—are reinscribed as a sign that the goals of feminism have been achieved. Scholars, activists, and other critics of postfeminist ideologies argue that these dynamics and the importance they place on individual choice have hampered the feminist movement. Our supposedly postfeminist culture takes for granted the movement's gains while repudiating the movement itself, and the third wave is hamstrung by a lack of political potency and coherence.

Ruminations on individual choice and its relationship to feminism and political decision-making were a major theme in responses to Steinem's comments, particularly in longer articles that afforded writers the space to analyze

FIGURE 3.2 People4Bernie tweet, 2016.

the controversy at greater length. Some of these responses echoed the tenets of postfeminist critique and denigrated young feminist activists; for example, in her article for the *Washington Post*, Kathleen Parker (2016) argued that feminists like Steinem helped to usher in their own undoing. She explained, "Through their temerity and hard work, they've created a world in which their original purposes have become obsolete through acceptance," emphasizing that young women take for granted a "go-girl power" view of the world and cannot imagine the battles women like Steinem fought for their rights. She continues, saying that young feminists "really can have it all, including the choice to not vote for a woman just because she's a woman, because, after all, this would be sexist." However, this critique not only ignores Steinem's own statements about young feminists during her interview with Maher but also was contradicted explicitly and vehemently by the majority of responses to Steinem's comments. Parker's arguments demonstrate that postfeminist readings of popular feminism, while they may explain the dynamics at work for some young people, are insufficiently complex to deal with the shape the feminist movement is taking today.

In response to critics like Steinem and Parker, feminists on Twitter took aim at this postfeminist reading of their politics and pushed back. In many of the responses to Steinem's comments, critics ignored her acknowledgment that young women are angry and activist, focusing solely on her comments about young women supporting Sanders because that is "where the boys are" and criticizing the postfeminist notion that young women's choices are led by personal desire rather than feminist political goals. This was particularly evident on Twitter, where many tweets lashed out at Steinem with the hashtag #NotHereForBoys. Approximately 15 percent of the most retweeted posts directed at Steinem in the days following her comments provided policy-based and historically informed reasons for supporting Sanders over Clinton. These reasons included his plans to forgive student debt and to address job and wage disparities, his disavowal of Wall Street, and his allyship with minorities, to name just a few. These Twitter users utilized the platform to speak back to Steinem's dismissal of their political decision-making and counteract a postfeminist media narrative that would frame their political choices as selfish and simplistic rather than collective and nuanced. Their anger at her statements motivated them to affirm and explain their support for Sanders's candidacy and push back on postfeminist critique of their politics.

However, as discussed in more detail earlier in this chapter, the tendency of both social and mass media to favor provocative sound bites that garner attention at the expense of nuance and complexity yielded many arguments that agreed with the broad strokes of Steinem's overall interview but soundly criticized this decontextualized comment. One particularly angry example comes from the *Huffington Post*, where Rebecca Massey (2016) explains, "Plenty of terrible things still happen to women and girls, for no other reason than that they (we!) are women and girls. Do our elders really think we young women are so coddled or so dim that we don't see this?" Her criticism addresses the incident as it was reported and discursively circulated—as an offensive sound bite—rather than in its original context, thus framing Steinem's comments as a postfeminist critique of young women's politics. This tendency to focus on offensive quotes feeds into the intergenerational catfight narrative, pitting younger and older feminists against one another by emphasizing the discontinuities within the movement rather than the points of connection. Thus, even longer-form think pieces like Massey's that helpfully complicate and push back on postfeminist narratives about young women's choices often serve to deepen and reify generational divisions.

A focus on intersectionality, many members of this issue public said, is what drove their choice for Sanders rather than Clinton, not a desire for male attention. The most shared and discussed articles on Twitter took Steinem and, by extension, Clinton to task for their lack of intersectionality and thus their fundamental misunderstanding of "today's" feminism. Sarah Grey's (2016) "Open Letter to Gloria Steinem on Intersectional Feminism" was one of the most frequently retweeted articles about Steinem's comments and centered on her problematically middle-class white presentation of feminism. While grateful to the "amazing" work these women and other second wave feminists have done, critics again flattened the second wave and emphasized that its focus on white, heterosexual, cisgender, middle-class women disenfranchised many women and does not mesh with current ideas of what is radical and progressive. Steinem's continued lack of intersectionality was also called out in another highly tweeted article. Teresa Jusino (2016) adds a critique of the transmisogyny in Steinem's interview. After Steinem's comments about young female Sanders supporters, Maher made a transmisogynistic joke at celebrity Caitlyn Jenner's expense, to which Steinem lightly chuckled and shrugged. For Jusino, this is further proof that Steinem and, by extension, Clinton personify a nonintersectional, outdated version of feminism that has no place in feminisms shaped by the intersectional imperative. While rightfully critiquing Steinem's statements, these articles reflect a tendency within the discourse across social and legacy media to privilege a progress narrative; "modern feminism" has progressed, focusing on current "battles" as a diverse collective that considers multiple axes of oppression, whereas second wave feminists are stuck in the past, insufficiently intersectional, and beholden to individual (white) leaders. As Astrid Henry (2004) argued in her analysis of the tensions between the generations of feminism, feminism is delineated as much by what it is not (supposedly regressive, nonintersectional second wave feminism) as by what it is (modern, diverse, and inclusive).

Overall, many of the conflicts around Steinem's comments ultimately centered on the notion of choice: What heuristics should a feminist use to choose a political candidate? How might that reasoning change with age? How much should iconic figures within the movement influence that choice? And how should feminists choose to express their frustration and even outrage with their fellow feminists? Steinem implied that Clinton was the logical choice for the radical feminist activist, which young women may grow to be but were not yet. However, drawing on third wave ideals of individual choice, critics decried this statement as decidedly sexist and anti-feminist. Emphasizing that second wave feminists like Steinem fought for young women's right to make individual choices, criticism simultaneously acknowledged Steinem's contributions while rebuking her statement.

This complicated stance toward feminist history and neoliberal ideals of individual choice demonstrates that many of these young feminists do not take for granted the gains of feminism. Instead, they framed themselves as crafting their individual political choices with the collective good—and, indeed, an intersectional feminist collective good—in mind. While some of these critiques hinge on simplistic and flattened notions of feminist history, many younger feminists argued that they are more radical than their (white) second wave predecessors, with many arguing that Sanders's policies would best achieve feminist goals that would benefit all women. Overall, it was this collective—the younger, progressive feminists who enacted the pressures of the intersectional imperative on Steinem—who were authorized to speak, whose voices were remediated, and whose views were amplified most prominently across the platform ecosystem. While some defended Steinem, and most applauded her history of fighting for women, many questioned or challenged her authority to speak for feminism. In the process, the media and many of Steinem's critics who spoke across platforms reified and oversimplified the intergenerational catfight narrative of feminism, emphasizing the separation between the generations rather than acknowledging their continuities.

"A Vote for Gal Pals Everywhere": Madeleine Albright, Identity Politics, and the Symbolism of a Female President

The day after the Gloria Steinem debacle, Madeleine Albright, the former secretary of state under Bill Clinton, spoke at a Hillary Clinton rally in Concord, New Hampshire. Directly addressing young female voters, Albright said, "We [older women] can tell our story of how we climbed the ladder, and a lot of you younger women don't think you have to—it's been done. It's not done, and you have to help. Hillary Clinton will always be there for you. And, just remember, there's a special place in hell for women who don't help each other" (Rappeport 2016). Next to her on the stage, Clinton laughed uproariously, and the crowd clapped and cheered in support. However, the response outside of the rally, across media platforms, was far less supportive and

FIGURE 3.3 Hillary Clinton and Madeleine Albright in New Hampshire, 2016. (Credit: Getty Images, Bloomberg Images.)

congratulatory. Particularly in proximity to Steinem's cross-generational comments the day before, Albright too became an "old guard," establishment foil for younger feminists, adding to the already fiery debate about how feminism intersects with age and political choice.

In addition to echoing postfeminist critiques of young women's ignorance about the continued need for feminist action, discussed in the previous section, Albright's argument was based on particularly narrow notions of identity politics. While Albright has repeated this "special place in hell" quip for years and, based on her smiling delivery and the hyperbolic tone of the statement, meant it as a half joke, her frustration with imagined young female voters is clear from the quote's context within her speech. Although she emphasized that Clinton is a champion for women who has worked to overcome sexism, this quote couched that endorsement squarely in the realm of solidarity with fellow members of one's sex. In her response to the media outcry, Albright admitted she made a mistake in her wording but stuck by her assertion that "women have an obligation to help one another" (Albright 2016). She emphasized the importance of female politicians as both symbols of progress and sympathetic policy makers, contending that young women do not have the experience of older generations and may not grasp the importance of figures like Clinton. Near the end of her apology she stated that she welcomed intergenerational dialogue with young feminists. And while some did take her words as an opportunity to discuss generational differences within the feminist movement, overall her comments ignited outrage and criticism on both the left and the right. In contrast to the discourse surrounding Steinem, in which the anger was expressed primarily as frustration and disappointment, the outrage against Albright was more vehement and directed against her personally. Many critics framed her call for female solidarity as working to provide cover for her past atrocities against women, using the opportunity to further assert their policy-based feminist political decision-making. And beyond these legitimate and complex critiques, once again, a flattened, overwhelmingly white image of second wave feminism became a backward boogeyman for "modern" intersectional feminisms to play against, serving as further justification for conservatives to disparage feminism and identity politics.

"I Don't Vote with My Vagina": Critiquing Identity Politics and Challenging Uncritical Female Solidarity

Central to feminist anger against Albright's comments was a rejection of female solidarity as inherently feminist or progressive. In an oft-quoted interview, actress Susan Sarandon declared of a potential female president, "I want the right woman. There are great women that I admire that have headed nations . . . but I don't vote with my vagina, you know?" (BBC NewsNight 2016).[4] This rejection of supposedly uncritical, cisfemale body–based identity politics pervaded the discourse, and many of the most prominent sentiments expressed by frustrated feminists across social and legacy media were given voice in Jessica Williams's (2016) segment on *The Daily Show* called "Breaking Down the Vagina Vote." When host Trevor Noah asked Williams about Sarandon's comment, she sarcastically exclaimed, "I mean, Trevor, what else am I gonna vote with? I *literally* vote with my vagina." Through absurdity, Williams critiqued the idea that assigned sex is central and, indeed, indispensable to women's political choice. She continued, saying that it is "diminishing" both "for women to accuse other women of supporting Hillary only because she's a woman" and "for women to tell other women they're obligated to vote for Hillary because, you know, we all have vaginas." Her critique emphasized the importance of individual choice; women should be able to use whatever heuristic they desire to choose a political candidate. For critics, Albright's apparent implication that a candidate's sex should function as the primary factor was offensive and patronizing. If many critics read Steinem's comments as accusing young women of prioritizing heterosexual desire over rational political choice, Albright's quip was criticized for encouraging young women to eschew that rational political choice in favor of female solidarity. In both cases, younger feminists asserted their will to vote based on policy over heterosexual desire or gender.

And, in a rare moment of agreement in a highly partisan election cycle, conservative voices capitalized on the tensions within the left and also criticized Albright's focus on identity, inflaming divisions and framing her comments as a prescriptive call for conformity. While the vast majority of the most retweeted critiques of Steinem appeared to come from Sanders supporters, far right voices joined the fray regarding Albright. Some of the more frequently retweeted comments regarding Albright in the three days following her comments came from far right conspiracy theorist Paul Joseph Watson and linked to articles from the right-wing news and opinion site founded by Fox News's Tucker Carlson, *The Daily Caller*. These conservative critiques pointed out Albright's past support of American militarism and, notably, used the opportunity to lambast a caricaturized version of identity politics. *New York Post* writer Michael Goodwin (2016) claimed that Steinem and Albright revealed the "dirty secret" of leftist identity politics, their supposed belief that "biology trumps individuality, and those who don't agree are traitors to their gender." This notion—of politicians on the left somehow denying access to the category of "woman" for those who do not share their political views—was echoed by Republican presidential candidate Carly Fiorina. In an interview on the Fox News program *On the Record with Greta Van Susteren* ("Fiorina Slams Hillary's 'Desperate Appeal' to Women" 2016), Fiorina claimed, "Liberal women have long said that unless you agree with them, you don't count. Unless you're liberal and agree with their orthodoxy, then somehow we don't count as women." These comments extend far beyond Albright's call for female solidarity, interpreting that solidarity as an exclusive, partisan club that has the power to decide who counts as a woman. By twisting and exaggerating her statements, voices on the right like Goodwin and Fiorina used Albright's gaffe to deepen partisan divides along gender lines, ignoring how progressive and conservative policies differentially impact women and instead focusing solely on sex. Overall, Albright's comments opened a space for both Democratic and Republican naysayers to critique this narrow view of identity politics, warping her words to argue that she and Clinton were prioritizing sex over policy issues, emphasizing the gap between feminist generations as well as between the right and the left.

The Right Woman: Debating the Symbolic Value of a Female President

Extending criticism of Albright's apparent focus on assigned sex over policy as the appropriate influence of political choice, feminists also grappled with the importance of Clinton's presidency as a symbol. In that same rally in New Hampshire, Albright implied that Sanders, despite his more progressive policy initiatives, was not as radical as Clinton, saying, "People are talking about revolution. What kind of a revolution would it be to have the first woman president of the United States?" The revolution here would stem from the symbolism of having a woman in the highest office in the United States, and this argument became a key point of contention between female voters on the left.

Writing for the *New York Times*, Gail Collins (2016) explained that "the idea of a woman as president is a very important marker" for older women in particular who experienced egregious and explicit barriers to success because of their sex. The representational power that a female president would convey was portrayed as simultaneously a stand-in and a harbinger of increased equality for women. Because a woman would gain access to the most powerful position in American politics, that achievement would symbolize the gains that women have made, even though her exceptional positionality does not necessarily reflect larger gains in equality that extend across women of all ages, races, ethnicities, and sexualities.

While many women agreed that it would be important to see a woman in the White House, voters expressed ambivalence about whether Clinton's symbolic victory would be followed up by progressive actions that would help all women. Often, Sanders supporters acknowledged the symbolic weight of a female president but prioritized Sanders's more progressive policy decisions over that symbolism; for example, actress Emily Ratajkowski (2016) conveyed this prioritization succinctly at a rally for Sanders in New Hampshire, which she shared via Facebook, saying, "I want my first female president to be more than a symbol. I want her to have politics that can revolutionize." Pushing back on Albright's implication that sex is inherently and sufficiently revolutionary, women like Ratajkowski emphasized that their choice is based on Sanders's radical politics, which they see as more beneficial for women and thus more feminist. Just as critics of Steinem often ignored her comments praising young women's activism and pushed back on the notion that Clinton was the logical choice for the radical feminist activist who was not befuddled by heterosexual desire, Albright's critics also ignored her statements in favor of Clinton's history of pro-woman policy decisions by framing her statement as irrational identity politics. Albright's apparent prioritization of symbolism and solidarity over policy again allowed many critics and media outlets to pit second wave feminist ideals against supposedly more progressive, modern, intersectional feminisms.

Ironically, Albright's comments opened space for a critique of gender solidarity to take center stage. While many of Albright's and Clinton's feminist critics would likely agree that sexism directed against Clinton was having a material impact on her campaign, the narrative trajectory that followed this controversy elided that impact and, in many cases, framed the Clinton campaign as the true perpetrators of sexism. Within a media landscape that prizes woman-on-woman conflicts and context-free hot takes, the next sections demonstrate how legitimate critique can be co-opted and how misogynistic, oversimplified media narratives can hamstring and twist potentially productive intrafeminist conflict.

Not All Women: Intersectionality, History, and Feminist Generation Gaps

In addition to questioning Albright's articulation of identity politics, many feminist-identifying Sanders supporters explained that their choice to vote for him was based on the contrast between his more progressive platform and what they viewed as Clinton's and Albright's histories of nonintersectional positions and policies. Often, that criticism implicitly or explicitly turned Albright's contention that women should support other women on its head by pointing out that she and Clinton had supported policies that help certain types of women (i.e., white Western women) while ignoring or even harming others. Of the 295 most retweeted tweets referencing Albright in the three days following her comments, 30 percent of them angrily attacked Albright, saying there was a "special place in hell" for her. Many lambasted her as a hypocrite for her support of military intervention in Palestine that resulted in many civilian casualties or her defense of Bill Clinton against the women who accused him of sexual misconduct. Critics emphasized the whiteness of Clinton and Albright, questioning whether they were "real all[ies]" to "brown and black women [who] face a litany of concerns" (Zimmerman 2016). This anger was common across social media from frustrated women of color, typified by remarks like this tweet: "Dear Madeleine Albright, Oh really? Sincerely, Black women." The implication that all women, including women of color who were harmed by Clinton's policies, had a duty to support her candidacy, evinced for many a self-serving white feminist agenda.

Other journalists and pundits further emphasized the white middle-classness of Albright and Clinton's feminism, characterizing it as outdated because Clinton and Albright's "message of tweaking the current system to open floodgates for more trickle down (which is how she sounds) is not change enough for all the other things we care about" (Nakashima Brock 2016). For feminists who foreground intersecting categories of oppression, the liberal feminism espoused in messages of gender solidarity from politicians who do not seem to fully grasp the importance of race, gender, sexuality, and class as overlapping systems of oppression rang dangerously hollow. Further, while Albright's comments during the rally implied that young feminists who supported Sanders rather than Clinton did so because they were ignorant of history, many comments from her critics worked to demonstrate otherwise. It was many Sanders supporters' specific knowledge of history—namely, Albright's and Clinton's (and, to a lesser extent, Steinem's) history—that turned them away from Clinton and rendered them highly critical of her and Albright.

As mentioned earlier, a large proportion of articles and tweets written by critics cited two key moments from Clinton's and Albright's histories as anti-feminist: their imperialistic tendencies and their attacks on then president

Bill Clinton's sexual harassment victims. One particularly clear and incisive example of this critique came from Sarah Lazare (2016). Citing, as did many other articles and tweets, a 1996 interview with *60 Minutes* in which Albright said that the deaths of half a million children as a result of U.S. sanctions against Iraq were "worth it," Lazare argued, "Feminists should unequivocally declare that Clinton's policies of war and empire that kill, wound and traumatize women around the world are not compatible with feminism." Here Lazare emphasizes that intersectional and global feminisms are incompatible with Clinton's capitalistic and imperialistic policies. Together, Albright's and Clinton's political track records were marshaled as incompatible with intersectional definitions of feminism, and those histories not only did not merit them unqualified feminist support but in fact barred them access to it.

While media narratives still often framed this conflict as an intergenerational spat, it ultimately centered on authenticity: Which feminism is "real" feminism, white feminism or intersectional feminism? Which policies does one have to support, or which policies can one not support, to be "truly," "authentically" feminist? Critics of Albright and Clinton asserted that female solidarity cannot be uncritical, and it can be, as Lorde (1997) asserted, necessary and productive to call out fellow feminists' words and behavior. However, this particular instance provoked bad actors on the right to jump into the fray and amplify tensions, actions that were afforded by platforms like Twitter and a media landscape that prizes conflict to promote engagement. Coupled with Albright's problematic political track record and the more inflammatory nature of her comments, her outraged critics focused much more on destroying her rather than working toward a more equitable and just political and activist platform alongside her. Overall, the dominant discourse around this incident gave voice to younger feminists who enacted the pressures of the intersectional imperative against the white feminist perspectives of Steinem, Albright, and Clinton. In doing so, they expressed their frustration with celebrity feminists and prominent politicians relying on what they saw as outdated narratives and policies that prioritize power over feminist policies.

Nasty Feminists?: Conclusions on Feminist Discord

While multifaceted and complex, discussions around this moment of conflict centered on two key debates between white feminist and intersectional feminist perspectives: how feminist political decisions should be made, and what a progressive feminist political platform looks like. Although her full comments were much more nuanced and respectful, Steinem's words as circulated seemed to accuse young feminists of making political choices based on personal reasons, namely, heterosexual desire, while Albright seemed to assert that young women should vote for Clinton as a show of (white) female solidarity and support for the symbolic victory of a woman in the White House. These two modes of choosing—based on individualistic desire or solidarity under a narrow view of identity politics—drew ire from mostly younger feminists, whose voices were affirmed and amplified across media platforms as they asserted their desire to make political decisions based on candidates' policy initiatives that they believed would most benefit all women. The ways in which they asserted the importance of making this choice individually does not map neatly onto postfeminist critiques. Instead, this feminist politics of choice argues for a marriage between the individual and the collective through political decision-making, voting for either Clinton or Sanders because the voter reasons they would be the best candidate to serve the interests of all women.

The second source of conflict relates to and extends the first: What makes a radical feminist, and what should today's progressive feminist platform be? Steinem located radicalism in the wisdom that comes with age, arguing that as women get older, they recognize their lack of power. Albright echoed this generational divide, accusing young women of ignorance about the continued importance of feminist action, and asserted that true radicalism and revolution come from helping women gain positions of power. Discourse around these comments interpreted Steinem and Albright as saying young women who supported Sanders did not, and perhaps could not, understand or be radical feminists. However, feminist critics of Steinem and Albright, still amplified and overwhelmingly affirmed across media platforms, argued that truly progressive feminism stems from intersectionality and championing policies and politicians whose initiatives will benefit as many women as possible, not just those who are white, middle- or upper-class, heterosexual, cisgender, and Western. In many cases, this positionality relied on narratives of feminist progress that emphasized discontinuities among the generations rather than their consistencies. Through a combination of uninterrogated ageism, antiestablishment sentiment, the increasing prominence of intersectionality as common sense in media discourse, and the overall unpopularity of Clinton as a political candidate, this case study reveals a shift in feminist conflict as articulated through digital platforms and represented in the news. In contrast to prior work on the topic, the pressures of the intersectional imperative gained prominence over Steinem's, Albright's, and Clinton's supposedly more reformist, white feminist platforms.

This moment of feminist outrage and discord could have, and for some participants almost certainly did, spawn productive intergenerational reflections about how feminist politics must change and develop over time while helpfully destabilizing the political power of white feminism. However, in addition to this productivity, the conflict was framed in simplified and sensationalized terms, circulated across media platforms, and placed squarely on Hillary Clinton's shoulders. It added to her campaign's already considerable overdetermination and contributed to the swell of discontent against her as a presidential hopeful, deepening fissions not only within the feminist movement but also among Democrats. And crucial to any analysis of this moment of anger is its entanglement with an increasingly vicious and misogynistic presidential election. While within the smaller context of the Democratic primary between Sanders and Clinton this debate had a particular set of meanings and implications, it happened within the larger context of a political battle between Clinton and Donald Trump. The animus that had been building against Clinton within certain segments of the Democratic Party for years gained traction over the course of the primary, and incidents such as this arguably contributed to it.

This is not to say that those who enacted the pressures of the intersectional imperative against the Clinton campaign were wrong to do so or "toxic"; quite the contrary, their critiques of Steinem, Albright, and Clinton were productive and necessary for a more equitable feminist politics. The problems arose when this conflict was decontextualized from feminist circles, recirculated through misogynistic and ageist media frameworks, and exploited by bad actors who sought to amplify discord among Democratic candidates and supporters. Continual exposure to moral outrage against Clinton helped to motivate a sizable enough number of leftist #NeverHillary voters and/or conscientious objectors to help usher in a Trump presidency. This potential for corrupted translation and the circulation of harmful narratives around popular feminism is another downside to celebrity feminism's visibility. While the attention afforded to famous figures like Steinem, Albright, and Clinton can open a public and accessible way to engage in feminist educational work and productive debate, that publicness also means that, as these debates are circulated across the media landscape, they can have unintended consequences that are difficult to anticipate or control. In this book's conclusion, I will return to explore these issues surrounding feminist outrage, examining what lessons we might learn from these case studies about how to engage the pressures of the intersectional imperative as we work to amplify a more equitable feminist politics.

The political climate around the 2016 election provided myriad opportunities for outrage not only in places we might expect, like a presidential primary, but in places that seem less obvious, like the casting decisions for a modern reboot of a 1980s action-comedy. The next chapter, which explores the misogynistic, racist online harassment of *Ghostbusters* actress Leslie Jones, provides another example of the interplay between national politics, celebrity culture, and feminist engagement. And as we return to the themes of online harassment explored in chapter 1, we will see what happens when that harassment takes on an explicitly political tone, and how digital feminist publics cohere and rally around a celebrity to engage in sociopolitical critique and mobilize for change.

4

Platform Vulnerabilities

Fighting Harassment and
Misogynoir in the Digital
Attack on Leslie Jones

This chapter draws together the dynamics discussed in the three previous chapters, exploring another instance of online harassment that mobilized networked publics around celebrity culture as a platform for feminist intervention. As discussed in chapter 2, the #AskHerMore red carpet campaign sought to critique sexist representations of women in media and agitate for change. And, from a certain perspective, 2015 seemed like a time when those representations were shifting. The rising popularity of feminism throughout 2014 and 2015 had arguably begun to impact some casting and green-lighting decisions, and one shift was particularly prominent: female characters were taking over major action franchises that had previously been led by men. Charlize Theron starred as the enigmatic, powerful Furiosa in *Mad Max: Fury Road*, while Daisy Ridley took the helm of one of the most profitable film franchises in the world with her role as Rey in *Star Wars: The Force Awakens*. Continuing this trend of casting women in roles previously held by men, in October 2015, director Paul Feig announced that he would direct an all-female reboot of the 1984 action-comedy, *Ghostbusters*. Feig was no stranger to directing movies starring women. His previous films *Bridesmaids* (2011), *The Heat* (2013), and *Spy* (2015) had all featured complex, fallible, funny women in the lead roles. However, this reboot came as the political tensions discussed in the previous chapter were coming

FIGURE 4.1 Leslie Jones, Melissa McCarthy, Kristen Wiig, and Kate McKinnon in *Ghostbusters* (2016). (Credit: Columbia Pictures; film still via Movie Stills Database.)

to a head, and the female recasting (and particularly with a Black woman in a lead role) of a beloved classic film targeted at young men within a political climate fraught with tensions around "identity politics" meant that the film touched a highly politicized nerve.

From the moment Feig announced the new *Ghostbusters*, male fans who resented what they believed to be its feminist bent took to social media to attack the film and its cast members, particularly stand-up and improv comedian Leslie Jones. Jones had performed stand-up since her college days in the late 1980s. Her wider acclaim came in 2014 with her appearance in Chris Rock's film *Top Five*, followed by a coveted position as a writer-turned-cast-member on *Saturday Night Live*. Poised for major mainstream success, Jones earned the role of MTA staffer Patty Tolan in Feig's *Ghostbusters*, starring alongside fellow comedians Melissa McCarthy, Kristen Wiig, and Kate McKinnon. While the film as a whole provoked backlash, Jones, the only Black woman among the female leads, received the brunt of this harassment. Even before its release, *Ghostbusters* had become an overdetermined discursive space in which its success or failure became inextricably linked to that of racism and misogyny.

Following the film's premiere in July 2016, Milo Yiannopoulos, the now former editor of the far right news site Breitbart, posted a scathing review that singled out Jones as "the worst of the lot." Yiannopoulos was already a central figure in online tensions between geek masculinity and feminism after stoking the Gamergate controversy, a coordinated online harassment campaign targeted at women in the video game industry, two years earlier. His racist and sexist review of *Ghostbusters* added fuel to the already sizable fire of fanboy hatred for the film, and many set their sights on Jones. Harassers, many of them participants in far right movements online, flooded Jones's Twitter mentions with racist, sexist language and imagery, which Jones screenshotted and shared with her followers to expose the level of vitriol she was facing (Jones 2016). Jones temporarily left Twitter, and the platform eventually banned Yiannopoulos. Then, on August 24, 2016, in a move that was likely an attempt to avenge Yiannopoulos, Jones's personal website was hacked and filled with photos of gorillas, her driver's license and passport, and nude photographs stolen from her iCloud account.

This harassment and the discussions that circulated around it provide a provocative case study for better understanding how digital platforms, specifically Twitter, and celebrity culture become spaces for ideological battles over race, sexuality, and gender. This incident provided an opportunity for networked publics to further define and enact developing conceptions of responsibility and accountability regarding racism and sexism, not only for individuals and groups but also for social media platforms themselves. Prior chapters have examined how the white feminist and intersectional imperatives are shaped and enacted across digital platforms through strategies like callout campaigns and hashtag activism, often as a counterdiscourse to dominant narratives that circulate across the media ecosystem. This chapter explores the discursive contestation over which perspectives are mainstream and which are subversive as it analyzes the links between the far right's rise and the mainstreaming of explicitly racist, misogynistic behaviors. Three strategies emerged as most salient as networked publics coalesced to defend Jones. The first involved supportive affective counterpublics who rallied around Jones alongside indictments of those who attacked her. The second strategy was to publicize the need for increased governance on Twitter to protect users like Jones. The third strategy drew connections between Jones's experiences as a Black woman and the political climate emerging around the rise of Donald Trump and the far right. However, the mainstream circulation of media narratives lauding these defensive strategies opened space for members of the far right to frame themselves as marginalized victims.

Overall, these strategies serve as a bridge between the vulnerabilities of platforms and the vulnerabilities of women of color in digital spaces and beyond as publics mobilized to "patch" perceived lapses in security. In computing, security patches are executable files that are released in response to known weaknesses in a platform to mitigate a threat's ability to exploit that vulnerability. Similar to the way that software engineers use patches to correct security vulnerabilities, the supportive awareness campaigns and calls to action that publics launched online (which stemmed from Jones's own agency in making visible the harassment) attempted to discursively "patch" two perceived vulnerabilities—of Twitter as a platform and of Jones herself. Twitter lacks comprehensive methods to combat harassment, and Jones's race and gender render her particularly vulnerable to abuse. As anti-racist tech scholars such as Safiya Noble (2018) and Ruha Benjamin (2019) have pointed out, racism is encoded into platforms like Twitter via biased algorithms and other discriminatory infrastructures that prioritize white perspectives and ignore or explicitly discriminate against users of color. By condemning the harassers and expressing love for Jones while calling for systemic changes to prevent such harassment in the future, Jones and her supporters attempted to patch these vulnerabilities and mitigate the threat the attackers posed.

However, in response to these "patches," members of the far right condemned both Twitter and mainstream media for marginalizing their conservative voices. As with patches of digital software, an attempt to fix vulnerabilities can sometimes have detrimental effects on the platform's overall functioning; in particular, Benjamin (2019) points out that "tech fixes often hide, speed up, and even deepen discrimination, while appearing to be neutral or benevolent when compared to the racism of a previous era" (4). In this case, this discursive patch resulted in backlash from individuals on the far right. It fed into their performance of victimization, allowing them to flip the discourse and frame themselves as oppressed and disadvantaged, demonizing the intersectional imperative pressures that called for them to be held accountable for their misogynoir as the unfair marginalization of conservative voices. This backlash against the pressures of the white feminist and intersectional imperatives has only expanded in the years since as panics around the power of "wokeness" and "cancel culture" have gained prominence, most notably though not exclusively via conservative supporters of former president Trump. The analysis that follows teases apart the illogical bases of such arguments, providing a detailed corrective that highlights the continuing need for cross-platform accountability practices.

This chapter begins with a timeline of the events that led up to the attack on Jones before presenting the three themes that emerged as most dominant in counterdiscourses around Jones's harassment: messages of support, the need for intervention, and connections between identity politics and national politics. Within this analysis, I provide a critique of the marginalization of Black voices in these discussions as well as an analysis of the far right's harassment behaviors to provide context and depth to the three themes.

Murdering Men's Childhoods: A Timeline of *Ghostbusters* Hate

The controversy around the *Ghostbusters* reboot began when director Paul Feig first announced in late 2014 that he would direct the film. Many male fans of the original film were incensed at the idea of women taking on these iconic roles and found a target for their ire on March 3, 2016, when the first *Ghostbusters* trailer was posted online (Sony Pictures Entertainment 2016). Within days it had become one of the most disliked videos ever posted on YouTube and the most disliked film trailer of all time. This vitriolic reaction was part of a targeted campaign by male fans of the original film who were determined to tear down the new film and its cast, coordinated via the same platforms that were instrumental to the celebrity nude photo hack: 4chan and Reddit.

The ire directed toward the *Ghostbusters* reboot and its female stars is an example of what Jonathan Gray (2019) defines as "competitive anti-fandom," which refers to a fan or group of fans directing their dislike or hatred "at a perceived rival of one's beloved fan object" (26). Studying competitive anti-fandom can provide insight into broader sociocultural dynamics through an analysis of "what perceived threat exists to the beloved object in the first place" (26–27) and what that threat says about the choice of rival. This connection between hate and imagined threats resonates with Sara Ahmed's (2004) work on the cultural politics of emotion. In her chapter on hate, Ahmed explains that hate is generative, transforming bodies into objects that "come to embody the threat of loss" (44). I will examine this threat more deeply in the final sections of this chapter, but for now it is clear that the loss of an exclusively white male cast threatened the perceived sanctity of the original film and, by extension, whiteness and masculinity. As the only Black cast member, Jones was doubly threatening, and her body was singled out as the most indicative of loss and the most worthy of hatred. By the film's release, the buzz almost solely revolved around the ire it raised from vocal, misogynistic, and racist anti-fans. *Ghostbusters* was released on July 15, 2016, to middling to positive critical response (it has a 73 percent rating on Rotten Tomatoes, and it received a B+ on CinemaScore) but a lackluster box office that doomed hopes of a sequel. Three days after its release and following the initial swoop of critical response, Breitbart editor Milo Yiannopoulos (2016) posted his own review.

Before jumping into the review and its fallout, a brief history of Breitbart and Yiannopoulos's tenure there is useful. Steve Bannon, who became the executive chairman of the ultraconservative "news" website in 2012 following the death of its eponymous founder, Andrew Breitbart, hired Yiannopoulos to write for Breitbart's tech section in 2014. Yiannopoulos soon rose to more mainstream prominence that summer when he was instrumental in stoking the Gamergate controversy and the harassment of Zoe Quinn, a female indie game developer. His role in propagating sexist conspiracy theories in the gaming world augmented his burgeoning identity as an anti-feminist right-wing provocateur. He continued to hone this brand over the next several years, leading neatly into his ardent support of Donald Trump's presidential campaign. Consistent with his abhorrence of the rising tide of popular feminism within

FIGURE 4.2 Milo Yiannopoulos reviews *Ghostbusters* for Breitbart, 2016.

mainstream media and his brash, explicitly racist takes on popular and digital cultures, Yiannopoulos's review of *Ghostbusters* was scathingly bigoted and helped ignite a firestorm of abuse targeted at Jones.

Yiannopoulos's review is self-reflexive, reveling in the film's status as an emblem of the fight between his "loyal readership" of ultraconservatives on Breitbart and the "social justice warriors" with whom they have been "warring" since the film was first announced. His review blasts the film not only for its "vacuous and incoherent plot" but, more centrally, for "its style and politics." His review took particular aim at Jones, describing her as "spectacularly unappealing, even relative to the rest of the odious cast," especially for her "flat-as-a-pancake black stylings." He marked her body as a physical and political affront to white conservative male sensibilities, a threat that embodied the potential loss of white supremacy and patriarchal authority. Although Jones had been dealing with Twitter abuse for years, the quantity skyrocketed following

Yiannopoulos's review. On July 19, Jones took a break from the platform, and following the attention the incident received, Twitter CEO Jack Dorsey reached out to her. Then, on July 20, Yiannopoulos was banned from Twitter for life; the next day, Jones returned to the platform.

However, Jones's victimization via digital platforms was not over. On August 24, her personal website was hacked. Hackers posted personal information, including images of her driver's license and passports, nude photos, and images of gorillas. Mirroring the abuse Jones had suffered on Twitter more than a month earlier, the hackers' actions typified misogynoir, which Moya Bailey (2021) defines as the "unique co-constitutive racialized and sexist violence that befalls Black women as a result of their simultaneous and interlocking oppression at the intersection of racial and gender marginalization" (1), particularly in digital spaces. Responses to the photos on Twitter, for example on a Drudge Report link about the hack, were full of horrific misogyny and racism. Users derided her appearance, calling the images "the least viewed nude photos ever" and comparing her to a gorilla (Drudge Report 2016). They transformed her body into an object of hatred and scorn in response to the threat to whiteness, to masculinity, and to far right figures like Yiannopoulos that they projected onto her, attempting to reinstate white male dominance and normative power relations as a corrective to the perceived harm they imagined Jones to embody. The key strategies that emerged in response to the attack—supportive counterpublics, calls for platform-level interventions, and connections to identity and national politics—demonstrate the struggle over not only the purpose and meaning of Twitter but also the values that platforms, and the United States itself, should fight to uphold.

"The Good People of the Internet": Messages of Love and Support from Affective Counterpublics

To combat the misogynoir leveled at Jones, the first strategy used by members of this issue public was to flood social media with messages of support. These messages were found primarily on Twitter and in articles that linked back to prominent tweets, compiling them into messages from "the good people of the Internet" who "love Leslie Jones" (Lapowsky 2016; see also, e.g., Koerner 2016; McIntosh 2016). In the days following the hack, thousands of supporters tweeted and retweeted antagonism for her attackers alongside positive messages to and about Jones using the hashtags #LoveForLeslieJ and #StandWithLeslie. As is often the case with controversies or tragedies that receive widespread media coverage, many of the most prominent tweets were from celebrities with large followings. For example, *Ghostbusters* director Paul Feig (2016) emphasized Jones's value and expressed solidarity, tweeting, "Leslie Jones is one of the

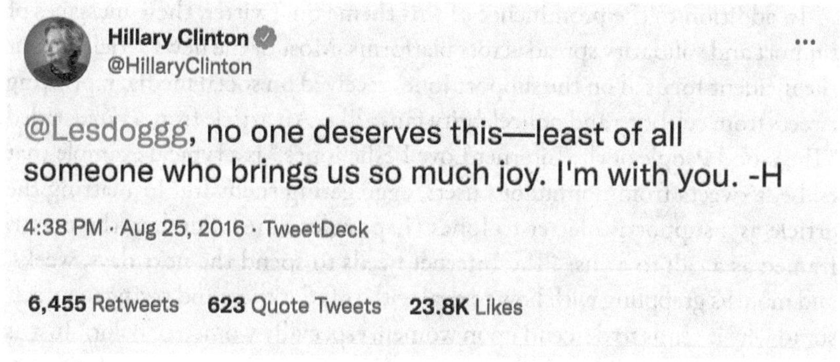

@Lesdoggg, no one deserves this—least of all someone who brings us so much joy. I'm with you. -H

4:38 PM · Aug 25, 2016 · TweetDeck

6,455 Retweets   **623** Quote Tweets   **23.8K** Likes

FIGURE 4.3 Hillary Clinton's tweet, 2016.

greatest people I know. Any personal attacks against her are attacks against us all. #LoveForLeslieJ @Lesdoggg." Other stars, such as writer/director/actress Lena Dunham (2016b) used the attack to drum up love for Jones and call for change, saying, "Let's turn our anger at trolls into love for Leslie Jones and into strategies to protect all the heroines who don't deserve this bullshit." Both Feig and Dunham called for users to support Jones, soundly rejecting her attackers. Moreover, as was common in the online news discourse surrounding the celebrity nude photo hack, Feig, Dunham, and others thematically connected this incident to more widespread issues. Feig attempted to garner empathy by connecting a personal attack against Jones to a wider attack on humanity, while Dunham more specifically likened it to the abuse women suffer, particularly online. She also goes further to argue that this incident should be a springboard for strategies to prevent such attacks in the future.

In addition to entertainment celebrities and fans, some politicians voiced their support for Jones. Following the hack, then presidential candidate Hillary Clinton (2016) tweeted support for Jones. Like Feig and Dunham, Clinton hinted that the attack has implications beyond Jones's personal experiences, implicitly tying it to other instances of online harassment by declaring, "No one deserves this." Further, she ends by connecting her campaign slogan to Jones to express solidarity. More than simply offering support, the use of "I'm with you" discursively ties this conflict between Jones and members of the far right to the struggle between Clinton and Trump for the presidency. Clinton's tweet, and much of the news and commentary about it, drew connections beyond Jones herself, showing that this event is embedded within larger systems of racism, misogyny, and the mainstreaming of far right politics. The vulnerabilities experienced by women of color extend beyond online spaces like Twitter or the iCloud, and the racism that has long structured power relations in the United States is being expanded, deepened, and made more explicit by the current political climate.

In addition to the prominence of this theme on Twitter, these messages of support and solidarity spread across platforms. Most of the news articles about the incident focused on the support Jones received on social media, reprinting tweets from celebrity and noncelebrity fans alike. An article from *Wired*, titled "The Good People of the Internet Love Leslie Jones," is a typical example that embeds tweets from nonfamous users, aggregating them and formatting the article as a supportive letter to Jones (Lapowsky 2016). Further, the post is framed as a call to arms: "The Internet needs to spend the next days, weeks, and months grappling with how to deal with this darkness and trying to understand why it tends to descend upon women, especially women of color." Just as Feig and Dunham did with their tweets, *Wired* connects the abuse Jones suffered to more widespread issues of online abuse, specifically targeted toward women of color, and gestures toward the need for better strategies to combat such behavior.

Members of this issue public who rallied around Jones to provide support and flood social media platforms with positivity functioned as a type of "affective counterpublic" (McCosker 2015). In their analyses of digital feminist activism, Kaitlynn Mendes, Jessica Ringrose, and Jessalynn Keller (2019) explain that feminists cohering on social media platforms to share stories draw on a long history of feminist counterpublics who engage in consciousness-raising. They highlight the affective dimensions of such social media discourse, showing that the activists they interviewed emphasized the emotional and psychological benefits they experienced by engaging in online feminist discourse and sharing their stories as a way to speak back against sexism. But beyond the potential benefits the members of this affective counterpublic experienced by standing up for Jones, they also directed those benefits outward toward her in an attempt to drown out bigotry with kindness. This supportive counterpublic strategy recalls some elements of calling out analyzed in chapter 2. Just as feminists like Brittney Cooper used social media to generate a counternarrative, pushing back on dominant legacy media narratives that upheld white feminism, this supportive counterpublic rallied to counter the far right narrative that would defame and demean Jones.

In her first interview following the incident, Jones appeared on *The Late Show* with Seth Meyers ("Leslie Jones on Her Twitter Trolls" 2016) to speak about the harassment and the support she received. The interview gave Jones an opportunity to address the attack directly, calling the abuse she suffered on Twitter "gross," "mean," and "unnecessary." Further, she highlighted that, if she had said nothing—had not amplified the harassment by virtue of the attention afforded to her as a celebrity—no one would have known about it. After both Jones and Meyers called for increased protections on Twitter, Meyers showed a video fans had posted on YouTube in support of Jones, foregrounding "the outpouring of affection" she received from these sympathetic counterpublics.

FIGURE 4.4 Leslie Jones appears on *Late Night with Seth Meyers* (NBC), 2016.

While they both spent the segment emphasizing the injustice of the abuse and rallying for change, the interview leaves viewers with the message that fans overwhelmingly support Jones, amplifying their corrective narrative. But within this deluge of support, several women of color pointed out that key voices were missing or muted: those of white women. While certain white celebrities who have incorporated feminism into their public personas, such as Lena Dunham, spoke out to support Jones, many remained silent. Kimberly Foster (2016) declared that the Jones harassment is "an opportune time for white feminists to step up," calling out the racist history of the feminist movement. Others, such as Rachael the Lord (2016), specifically called out Jones's white *Ghostbusters* costars Kristen Wiig, Melissa McCarthy, and Kate McKinnon for their failure to offer their support and condemn her attackers. The public silence of these women was surprising, and their failure to rally around Jones and acknowledge the inherent racism of her abuse was a source of frustration for women like Foster, who pointed out these failures as indicative of broader racial inequalities within (white) feminism.

However, when white women and men *did* show support, they were disproportionately praised and amplified across media platforms. The stars and public figures who got the most headlines for speaking out against Jones's harassers were Katy Perry, Dan Aykroyd, and Hillary Clinton. In a televised interview with *ET Canada* that was later posted online, Aykroyd praised Jones's talent as a writer and comedian and called her harassers "insignificant gnats" who "have no lives of their own," positing that they were likely vehemently racist ("Dan Aykroyd Comments" 2016). It is understandable why this clip was newsworthy. Aykroyd, as one of the original *Ghostbusters*, is also one of the men

I stand with @Lesdoggg and all other black women who get harassed on here daily simply bc they exist ✊🏿 #BlackMenSupportLeslie

10:22 AM · Aug 25, 2016 · Twitter for Android

83 Retweets   4 Quote Tweets   206 Likes

FIGURE 4.5 #BlackMenSupportLeslie.

Jones's harassers were supposedly defending. His praise and support of Jones, coupled with his evisceration of her attackers, thus carried a particular weight and relevance, and his language is bombastic and tailor-made for clickbait headlines. However, the amount of press he received dwarfs that of celebrities of color, whose support was often highlighted only on outlets that target Black readers (e.g., "No Jokes" 2016). Indeed, mainstream media's privileging of white voices was epitomized by *Variety*, which invited white actress Lena Dunham (2016) to write a "tribute" to Jones in which she praised her for her resilience following the harassment. Instead of asking a woman of color to write about Jones, *Variety* asked a woman who, for many, typifies the problems with white feminism. Just as legacy media overwhelmingly preserved Patricia Arquette's status as a feminist icon following her lack of intersectionality, much of the mainstream discourse elided the centrality of race and racism by amplifying white supporters.

While white men and women may have received much of the credit for supporting Jones, people of color also rallied around her but received considerably less mainstream attention. For example, activist Blake Simmons started the hashtag #BlackMenSupportLeslie out of a desire to "be there for [Jones] as a Black man to show support" (Davis 2016). Like other supportive messages across platforms, many of the tweets went further and connected Jones's experiences to broader racialized, gendered, and political contexts. Many linked the harassment of Jones to the experiences of Black women online more generally, expressing solidarity with her as a Black woman. Still others drew more explicit connections to racism, declaring support because Jones's "talent and courage is a threat to white supremacy." These tweets echo Bailey's (2021) analysis of Black women's and girls' use of digital technologies to mitigate the damage misogynoir causes and resist it by creating their own digital worlds that foreground and challenge this racialized sexism. However, although this show of solidarity was present on Twitter alongside other hashtags like #StandWith-Leslie and #LoveForLeslieJ, mainstream sources privileged those more general, not explicitly racial, hashtags. In the dataset, only media outlets targeted at Black audiences, such as *BET, Essence*, and *HelloBeautiful*, mentioned #BlackMenSupportLeslie (Diaz 2016; Davis 2016; Kwateng-Clark 2016).[1] Overall, the currency that media outlets afford white voices, even when they speak on issues of racism, demonstrates continued systemic inequalities, even within conversations that seek to call out and disrupt those inequalities. White people, particularly white feminists, are rewarded for their statements with media attention, while people of color are marginalized and often spotlighted only by media specifically for Black audiences. This serves to reinforce the power of white feminism even when the content of white feminists' messages are intersectional in nature. White privilege still affords their words precedence as mainstream media recirculate their words, while Black voices are relegated to "niche" outlets.

This outpouring of love and affirmation attempts to patch Jones's vulnerability as a woman of color. It was her blackness and femaleness that rendered her a target of racists and misogynists who flooded Twitter with abuse. While Twitter provides some methods for blocking or filtering harassment, the platform leaves users vulnerable to attack. In response to this vulnerability, supportive issue publics attempted to assuage the threats posed by attackers, drowning them out with kindness. This discursive patch was, in a way, effective—in the dataset I analyzed, most of the texts were supportive of Jones. Much as security patches work to mitigate the possibility of a threat exploiting a platform's weakness, the issue publics around this event lessened the threat of harassers by overwhelming social media platforms and commentary pieces with love. Further, many of these messages, such as those from Aykroyd, Clinton, and users of #BlackMenSupportLeslie, were not simply supportive but connected this instance of racial and gender politics to both broader issues of misogynoir and national political movements. This theme indicated that the patch was not sufficient to correct systemic inequalities or Twitter's potential as a space of harassment. Therefore, these messages are often explicitly political, providing support to raise awareness and issue a call to action.

"Y'all Need to Get Some Security!": Calls for Intervention on Twitter and Beyond

In addition to support, a second strategy involved pushing for intervention against online hate on Twitter and beyond. Digital platforms themselves became the target of intersectional imperative pressures as members of this issue public rallied around Jones and called for platforms to implement more comprehensive strategies for combating harassment. As Jones mentioned in her interview with Seth Meyers, the type of harassment she suffered is endemic on Twitter yet is often not apparent to the public; unless someone looks at the mentions of a user who is being harassed, such abuse may not show up on their feed. While this abuse is widely understood as part and parcel of life on Twitter, particularly for women of color, the response from Twitter has been much hand-wringing and apologizing followed by scant action (Oluo 2016). In Jones's case, she not only suffered attacks on Twitter, but her iCloud account and personal website were hacked. In response, advocates, fans, and fellow celebrities called for more action from Twitter and beyond.

Because Twitter was the epicenter of the original attack, and because of its history of failing to adequately address abuse, most calls for change targeted that platform specifically. Twitter has frequently found itself at the center of controversies surrounding such regulation, and despite some changes to its policies (typically due to high-profile controversies such as this one), users still have limited agency when it comes to reporting and combating abuse on the platform. Users have several options when it comes to taking action against those who target them: blocking, reporting, setting up content filters or limiting replies. Blocking a user prevents that user from seeing your activity or interacting with you. Reporting a user or tweet allows you to file a complaint with Twitter, and in some instances, the tweet or user will be removed from the platform. Users can also set up content filters that hide tweets that include a set of user-determined keywords, or they can limit who is able to see and/or reply to their tweets. However, these fixes only serve to hide offensive or abusive content for an individual user while allowing the content to remain on the platform; they do not manage or control behavior but simply keep it hidden or out of a user's replies. Filters function as bandages, covering up the sometimes toxic results of Twitter's openness, and leaving it up to users to protect themselves.

Much of the commentary on Jones framed Twitter's response to her experiences as insufficient, likening it to "pour[ing] a cup of water on a dumpster fire" (Beres 2016). As *Vice* writer Sarah Emerson (2016) points out in an article about the harassment Jones faced and abuse on the platform more generally, Twitter's response was lackluster despite recommendations from experts. Consistent with many online platforms, Twitter prides itself on an ethos of "free speech," and CEO Jack Dorsey and his team have been loath to add features that could be viewed as censorship. In a call to investors following the publicity around Jones's experiences, he tempered his promise to find solutions by saying, "We are not, and never will be, a platform that shows people only part of what's happening" (Spangler 2016). The result has been lots of talk and many performative gestures but little substantive change. As Tarleton Gillespie (2018), Adrienne Massanari (2017), and José van Dijck, Thomas Poell, and Martijn de Waal (2018) have noted, this reliance on the language of neutrality serves to distance platforms from their role in shaping public values as they attempt to absolve themselves from the toxicity their platforms afford, host, and often fail to moderate. Some analyses put the lie to Twitter's claims of neutrality, calling its relative inaction an example of "white obliviousness," which *The Root*'s Maiyisha Kai (2016) defines as "an intentional lack of self-awareness subconsciously (or consciously) rooted in maintaining the status quo." Here, Kai draws connections between the governance structures of the platform, such as its policies on moderation, and conservative ideologies. She, like the scholars just mentioned, point out that platforms are not neutral, and in fact their rhetoric of neutrality cloaks their complicity, conscious or not, with bigoted ideologies like white supremacy. As described in the next sections, this baseline of complicity becomes clear when Twitter *does* act against racist, misogynistic harassers like Yiannopoulos, who then cry "Oppression!" and declare Twitter a bastion of censorship.

A key reason this theme had such resonance was because Jones used her platform as a celebrity to argue for change. She continually made statements stressing the need for technological or legal intervention—patches to protect others who are vulnerable on the platform—in her appearances on late-night talk shows, in skits on *Saturday Night Live* (2016), and in her appearance at the Emmy Awards (Grady 2016). Regarding Twitter, Jones explained during her interview with Meyers, "It's like, that's my favorite restaurant. I love the food there. Three people just got shot in front of me. Y'all need to get some security!" Meyers agreed, saying, "They really need to try to start sorting out how to not just protect people like you but the people that don't have this public forum." This exchange highlights several key points. First, Jones emphasizes the violence of the abuse that takes place on the platform. Rather than downplaying its importance, she emphasizes the life-or-death harm that can result from such vulnerabilities. Second, both she and Meyers point out that this abuse is not limited to Jones but is endemic to the platform; Meyers acknowledges that famous users who suffer abuse and garner a lot of press attention may obtain some intervention that is not available to "regular" users. Jones's experience with Twitter harassment points to the double-edged sword of visibility that Sarah Banet-Weiser (2018) identifies in her analysis of popular feminism: the fame and resultant hypervisibility that rendered Jones vulnerable to the type and level of abuse she received also provided her a platform from which to advocate for changes to social media policy. As Bailey (2021) points out, that hypervisibility in media alongside an invisibility when they need "lifesaving help" (6) is amplified even further for Black women. Indeed, both Jones and Meyers used this interview to make it clear that Twitter should be responsible for self-governance and securing the safety of its users rather than leaving this task up to victims.

Moments like this often stir public discourse but yield little meaningful change. While calls for intervention may dominate discussions of online abuse, that prominence usually remains on the level of discourse. The patch provided by the affective counterpublic's supportive messages to mitigate the threat posed by racism and misogyny provides a temporary fix but does nothing to address deeper issues, either on a platform level or in society more broadly. This tension—between highly publicized calls for policy changes versus substantive reforms to address systemic inequality—lies at the center of the Jones attack. Twitter's lukewarm response also provides insight into the different stakes around the public pressures of the intersectional imperative, even as it is amplified by the visibility that celebrity affords. In a previous chapter, public pressure through the practice of calling out motivated Arquette to change the language she used to discuss wage equality and amplified the importance of intersectionality within popular feminism. However, Twitter frames itself as having more to lose by giving in to these pressures. The values of "openness" and "free speech" are and have long been cornerstones to dominant platform governance structures, and other platforms such as Facebook and Reddit have also resisted instituting more aggressive or intentionally equitable moderation policies. Stepping forward as the main platform to push back against right-wing toxicity would place Twitter at the forefront of backlash and accusations of liberal bias, which could jeopardize its bottom line and frighten investors. Coupled with the amount of labor platforms would have to undertake to more comprehensively moderate their content, Twitter's values became clear: it was better to deplatform Yiannopoulos and a few others, addressing the issue as an individual rather than systemic problem, and wait out this moment of outrage.

Misogynoir and MAGA: Connecting the Jones Attack to the Rise of Donald Trump

The final and perhaps most provocative strategy that emerged from the discourse surrounding Jones's harassment took the form of members of the issue public drawing connections between the incident, identity politics, and national politics. Beyond considering the incident in the context of racism and misogyny, online think pieces, newspaper editorials, magazine articles, and social media users forged links between racism and sexism, the rise of the far right, and this instance of misogynoir. Overall, discussions around this incident went beyond the themes that surrounded similar digital attacks such as the celebrity nude photo hack analyzed in chapter 1. While online news coverage of that hack connected the incident to broader issues of what Banet-Weiser (2015) calls "popular misogyny," the issue public that formed around the attack on Leslie Jones pushed a step further, connecting such issues of identity–based harassment to political movements like the far right.

Some of the most prominent discussions of the Jones attack focused on its connection to racism and misogyny. For example, the two most retweeted

KATY PERRY ✓
@katyperry

···

Do not give your eyeballs to this racist, hate-filled, misogynoir crime. | #StandWithLeslie 💜

4:07 PM · Aug 24, 2016 · Twitter for iPhone

9,220 Retweets   **576** Quote Tweets   **26.2K** Likes

FIGURE 4.6 Katy Perry's tweet, 2016.

tweets came from musician Questlove and pop star Katy Perry. Questlove (2016) tweeted that "these acts against leslie jones. . . . are sickening. Its racist & sexist. it's disgusting. this is hate crimes. this aint 'kids joshing round.'" He soundly rebuked the hack and abuse as a hate crime, arguing that the attackers were motivated by racism and sexism. Pushing back against those who downplayed the attack as a juvenile joke, he claimed its seriousness and its interconnection to racial and sexual categories of difference. Jones was the victim of a hate crime, rendered vulnerable to attack because she was Black and a woman, and this fact is "sickening."

Perry, at the time the most followed person on Twitter, had the most retweeted and widely circulated tweet about Jones; while Questlove pinpointed racism and sexism as the cause of the attack, Perry (2016) highlighted the intersectionality of those categories with the term *misogynoir*. By invoking a term that had circulated among feminist academics and activists, Perry added nuance to her critique and brought the word more mainstream acknowledgment; as Caitlin Gibson (2016) notes, Google searches of the term skyrocketed. There is much room to criticize Perry's performance of allyship. She has a history of engaging in cultural appropriation, and the fact that a term coined by a Black feminist scholar, Moya Bailey, attained prominence only after it was used by a white celebrity who did not credit Bailey again demonstrates the inequalities propagated by the overrepresentation of white voices in the media. Perry's shortcomings notwithstanding, the popularity of this tweet demonstrates the growing mainstream prominence of intersectional feminist discourses spreading from academic and activist circles to celebrity culture and beyond.

However, the discussion around the attack went beyond connections with intersectional identities to tie it directly to the rise of the far right, specifically Donald Trump. For example, Ilyse Hogue (2016), president of NARAL Pro-Choice America, concurred with that association, stating, "If u think harassment of @Lesdoggg & rise of @realDonaldTrump r coincidental, u aren't paying attn." Beyond Twitter, the connections also emerged in news commentary, such as a piece by Aja Romano (2016) from Vox, which also provided incisive analysis that used Jones's experiences to help explain the "escalating culture war" of "politicized violence" that the far right is waging online, arguing that the attack on Jones "is indicative of the far right's increasing coalescence as a movement, and its increasing willingness to adopt the language and deploy the measures of extremism." Across the web, members of this issue public foregrounded the interconnectedness of misogynoir and the rise of the far right to this incident, not only embedding it within systems of sexism and racism but also highlighting how prominent and explicit those systems are becoming as leaders like Trump and movements like the far right come to power. Far from relegating this incident to the realm of celebrity, geek, or internet cultures, this strategy demonstrated the increasingly explicit interconnectedness across different sociocultural sites. However, this interconnectedness also informed key strategies by which Yiannopoulos and other members of the far right framed themselves as marginalized victims of liberal political correctness.

"Bitchy Little Tweets": Yiannopoulos, the Far Right, and Online Harassment

On July 20, 2016, Twitter permanently banned Milo Yiannopoulos from the platform, one of several accounts removed for harassment and abuse following the attack on Leslie Jones. Unsurprisingly, Yiannopoulos railed against the ban and used the publicity it received to extend his claims of conservative, white male disenfranchisement. This section examines how Yiannopoulos and other far right commentators such as Alex Jones aimed to discursively invert patriarchal, white supremacist power dynamics to frame themselves as victims of the intersectional imperative. This inversion relies on distortions of the counternarrative strategies discussed in this and other chapters. While networked publics called out Patricia Arquette to critique white feminism and draw attention to the importance of intersectionality, hackers and harassers directly attacked Leslie Jones to humiliate her and viciously attempt to reassert normative power dynamics. Supportive counterpublics rallied around Jones to provide counternarratives of support and kindness while parlaying that support into a call for increased protections against harassment on digital platforms. Yiannopoulos called for far right sympathizers to support him and boycott Twitter, misrepresenting his punishment as evidence of widespread platform-level discrimination against conservative voices. The following analysis provides insight into how these strategic inversions operate across platforms.

Sarah Banet-Weiser (2018) argues that popular misogyny, or the mainstreaming of overtly sexist behaviors exhibited by figures like Yiannopoulos, has risen in tandem with and as a backlash against an increase in popular feminism during the 2010s. As my analysis shows, themes that are consistent with intersectional feminism, such as messages of support, critiques of structural misogyny and racism, and critiques of far right politics, dominated mainstream media coverage of Jones's experiences. As a result, there were plenty of examples that Yiannopoulos and others could point to in support of their feelings of marginalization and victimization. From their perspective, it is not Black women like Jones but rather their own whiteness and masculinity that are vulnerable within the current media landscape. As the pressures of the intersectional imperative discursively circulate across platforms and inform some measures of accountability and responsibility, such as Yiannopoulos's deplatforming, ultraconservative voices can twist that call for accountability into a panic over supposed a "cancel culture" that seeks to unfairly marginalize conservative perspectives.

This adversarial, victimized mentality is maintained by a contradictory attitude toward inequality. For example, when Yiannopoulos was confronted by CNNMoney's (2016) Alison Kosik with a tweet in which he called the cast members of the *Ghostbusters* fat and ugly, he stated that "mainstream" discourses of body positivity and fat acceptance have "started to marginalize traditional beauty standards," explaining that he was coming from a place of "compassion" and concern for the health of women. When Kosik asked Yiannopoulos how his abusive tweet was compassionate, he brushed it off, shrugging and saying, "This is a bitchy little tweet. Who cares?" This example typifies the way in which this perceptual fallacy functions. Yiannopoulos mistakes discursive power (such as the marginally increased presence of body positivity in mainstream media conversations) for structural change. In this case, moderate discursive shifts supersede structural inequalities. However, when confronted with his own language, he disavows the importance of it, writing it off as a "bitchy little tweet" unworthy of outrage. Indeed, in the same interview he goes on to critique those who take trolling too seriously and simultaneously maintains its importance, saying, "So long as there is a politics in this country, as there is, where people can turn victimhood and grievances into a currency, I will continue to be as offensive as possible." Overall, Yiannopoulos, the far right, and indeed the Trump administration selectively chose the relative importance of discourses and structural inequalities, deploying the importance of language and representation when it maintains their perceptual fallacy and underdog mentality but disavowing it when it points to structural inequalities, in this case, between men and women.

Further, Yiannopoulos and others on the far right draw connections from both the intersectional, "woke" feminist ideals they oppose and the "free speech" they champion to struggles over Twitter's identity as a platform, particularly in relation to the harassment of Leslie Jones. The day after Yiannopoulos was banned from Twitter, he appeared on *The Alex Jones Show*, an ultraconservative radio show hosted by temperamental conspiracy theorist and hate-monger Alex Jones. After news of the ban broke, the website InfoWars published an article reporting on and condemning Twitter, arguing that it "has developed a reputation for draconian, onesided and often-unexplained suspensions of conservative users," while "demonstrat[ing] an unashamed bias towards progressive causes" (Thalen 2016). Yiannopoulos echoes this argument in his interview with Alex Jones (The Alex Jones Channel 2016), claiming to be a "free speech martyr" who fell at the hands of a platform that victimizes far right voices. Here we see a reversal of the discourse that dominated in mainstream and social media around Jones's attack; whereas Jones and others were calling for more "security" and safety for users, those on the far right chastised the platform for engaging what they see as highly partisan overpolicing of conservative voices. The platform vulnerability the far right tries to address is not its openness but rather its selective and, from its perspective, biased tamping down of conservative voices.

What emerges as most notable is the way in which the discourse on the far right is almost the exact opposite, a distorted "fun-house" mirror of the popular feminist discourse that dominated social and mainstream media discussions of Leslie Jones and of the lived realities of gender and racial hierarchies (Banet-Weiser 2015). Yiannopoulos's and Alex Jones's counternarrative of the aggrieved white male typifies Sara Ahmed's (2004) analysis of how hate operates; according to Ahmed, hate animates a fantasy in which "the ordinary is in crisis, and the ordinary person [is] the *real victim*" (43). As Bridget Blodgett and Anastasia Salter (2018) point out in their analysis of the role geek masculinity played in the harassment of Leslie Jones, the identity of the harassers is "centered on not having the social capital they feel they deserve" (141). Imagined others—which in this case range from online "social justice warriors" to fictitious female Ghostbusters—are "transformed into 'the hated' through a discourse of pain" as the fantasy of the supposed "real victim" assumes that this "other" has caused them injury (143). In other words, the increasing discursive prominence of popular feminism became indicative of a larger threat to male supremacy. That threat was then projected onto the film and onto Leslie Jones in particular as her blackness made her doubly threatening not only to masculinity but also to whiteness. Constructing Jones as a threat allowed Yiannopoulos and others to attack her as a way to defend against this warped fantasy world. And Twitter's decision to ban Yiannopoulos for defending against this perceived threat added fuel to the far right's sense of persecution by imagining that a range of actors, from Twitter to Leslie Jones and her supporters, constitute an "active hostile force" that needs to be subdued (Blodgett and Salter 2018, 141). Whereas mainstream discourses attempted to patch Jones's vulnerability, constructing her as one of many victims of misogynistic and racist Twitter abuse that spread across platforms, those on the right viewed Twitter as a historically biased platform that disenfranchises conservative voices.

The Consequences of Deplatforming Hate: Conclusions on Digital Accountability

While other instances of online harassment have filtered into and accumulated within the public consciousness, including the celebrity nude photo hack discussed in chapter 1, the hatred toward Leslie Jones surfaced at a cultural and political tipping point. The controversy it engendered spoke to larger political divides within the United States, which amplified its resonance far beyond the confines of celebrity culture. Although these shifts in the American political landscape are ongoing, this case study allows us to better understand the dynamics at play and the significance of digital platforms and celebrity at this cultural moment. The epicenter of the attack was Twitter, and the themes that resonated strongly there filtered across the platform ecosystem. In response to Jones's agency in refusing silence and making visible the harassment she was facing, supportive counterpublics rallied around her, attempting to discursively patch her vulnerability as a woman of color and the vulnerability of Twitter as a platform by offering messages of love and support. In this way, these supportive publics used the incident to, as Zizi Papacharissi (2014) argues, "feel" their way into politics. However, despite the support that circulated across media platforms, mainstream outlets overemphasized white voices and de-emphasized Black voices, demonstrating that racism still impedes the apparently increasing intersectionality of media discourse. The support Jones received across media outlets also highlighted the need to go beyond discursive patches that serve only to combat harassment by drowning it out, as many commenters called for increased governance of harassment on Twitter and embedded the attack on Jones within intersectional, systemic inequalities. Networked publics also connected the attack to national political shifts, providing logistical and analytical connections between this incident and the mainstream ascendancy of far right politics. But the incident also sparked outrage among conservatives who viewed the *Ghostbusters* film and the banning of Yiannopoulos from Twitter as indicative of both a platform-level and a cultural bias against "traditional" values and voices on the right, feeding into an underdog, outsider rhetoric that ultimately helped rally support for far right ideals and, a few months later, a Donald Trump presidency.

Such a concern about backlash may intensify the ambivalence among both the public and the governing boards of social media platforms toward engaging in more intensive moderation and wide-scale banning of figures like Yiannopoulos and Alex Jones. However, the years following this incident provide some insight into the potential outcomes of deplatforming. Yiannopoulos's downfall began in earnest in February 2017. Following his dismissive remarks about child molestation in the Catholic Church and his endorsement of adult sexual relationships with underage boys, Yiannopoulos lost an impending book deal and a prominent speaking engagement at the Conservative Political Action Conference and also resigned from his position at Breitbart under pressure from Alex Marlow, its editor in chief. After years of cosigning or ignoring his inflammatory, bigoted remarks, even most staunch conservatives drew the line at pedophilia. Yiannopoulos had now lost his platform at Breitbart in addition to losing his largest social media audience on Twitter. He launched his own website, Dangerous.com, and relied primarily on Facebook as the mainstream social media platform on which he could cultivate and monetize his base. However, Facebook and Instagram banned Yiannopoulos and Alex Jones from the platform in May 2019, citing them as "dangerous individuals and organizations" that "promote or engage in violence and hate" (Paul and Waterston 2019).

Without access to Twitter, Facebook, or Instagram, Yiannopoulos lost his largest audience bases. On September 9, 2019, a Twitter user posted screenshots of Yiannopoulos's posts on the open source, end-to-end encrypted messaging platform Telegram. Several extreme far right voices, including Yiannopoulos and anti-Muslim conspiracy theorist Laura Loomer, migrated to that platform in 2019 after Facebook and Instagram banned their accounts. However, as Yiannopoulos bemoaned to his scant 19,000 followers, "Everyone is stalling on Telegram. . . . We're all losing interest in it. Microscopic followings like 20k are not going to sustain people like me," complaining that smaller platforms like Telegram do not reach "audiences who buy or commit to anything." He went on to admit that "big tech has us on the ropes here, we aren't working with many options," and with no lucrative platforms, they "are just going to be driven off the internet forever." Like other digital entrepreneurs, Yiannopoulos and his extremist ilk were able to monetize their large followings on common social media platforms via sponsored content, selling merchandise and tickets to their appearances, soliciting donations, and parlaying their audiences into additional opportunities such as book deals. However, because lesser-known platforms like Telegram have a much smaller user base, these monetization strategies do not work. Without income to sustain his brand, Yiannopoulos also shut down one of his last large mouthpieces, his personal website, in October 2019.

Yiannopoulos's downfall demonstrates that the accumulation of scandal and the continual calls for responsibility and accountability around toxic behaviors on and off platforms can eventually have a concerted impact on hateful individuals, albeit one that is absurdly delayed. Moreover, it points to the potential of deplatforming as a strategy to combat toxicity if the majority of the dominant platforms within the ecosystem come together. Yiannopoulos did not implode until Facebook, Instagram, and Twitter all took away his access to his fan base on those platforms. The process was furthered because these platforms also removed far right mouthpieces like Alex Jones and his outlet, InfoWars, in 2018, so figures like Yiannopoulos did not have allies they could run to on major platforms in order to drum up support and outrage as he did in 2016 after his Twitter banning. While this is only a single set of examples that are not universal, they do point to the potential of deplatforming as a strategy to stamp out digital bigotry and push back on toxic technocultures. Indeed, the major platforms' decision to ban Donald Trump following his response to the insurrection at the U.S. Capitol on January 6, 2021, points to the role such strategies may play going forward.

Consistent with the events analyzed in prior chapters, the themes around the attack on Leslie Jones extended beyond her idiosyncratic experience, framing this attack as emblematic of broader, systemic inequalities. Just as online news and commentary about the celebrity nude photo hack emphasized that many women, not just those who are famous, experience similar types of digital sexual harassment, the networked publics who rallied around Jones connected her experiences to those of other women of color. Further, the increased prominence of the intersectional imperative in discourse around Albright's and Steinem's comments was also central to conversations around Jones. While discussions of race were invisible in discourses around the nude photo hack and often overshadowed by defenses of Arquette's white feminism, we can see from these two case studies that discussions of intersectionality were integral and in fact dominant in 2016. However, mainstream discourse still privileged white voices and white-led hashtag campaigns over those of people of color, demonstrating a continued investment in preserving whiteness within mainstream feminist discussions, even those that are ostensibly intersectional.

Because this was a time of such contentious politics, the connections between pop culture and national politics were more prominent and explicit. Whereas discussions of the nude photo hack drew connections to misogyny, the discourse around the attack on Leslie Jones went beyond these broader social structures to draw connections to specific political parties. This was because the publics that participated in the attack were more easily identifiable as a political faction; because the platform on which this event began was an explicitly far right site (Breitbart) it was easier to make the connection. This gave the bifurcation and unequivocal damning of online communities, similar to what we saw in the nude photo hack, an explicitly political target that allowed members of this discursive public not only to make broader statements about social inequalities but also to connect those social inequalities to the platforms of particular political parties. Perhaps what we are seeing here is an increasingly politically minded popular feminism as the lines between entertainment, celebrity, and politics are becoming so obviously blurrier. With a reality television star president whose communications with the public occurred mainly via

Twitter, the dynamics of proximity and intimacy that structure theorizations of celebrity culture are amplified; from this perspective, it is not surprising that celebrity is the platform on which these negotiations of feminism are playing out because other sociopolitical negotiations are, too, on multiple levels. While this phenomenon did not begin with Donald Trump—discussions of charisma have drawn together theorizations of politicians and celebrities for decades—the bombastic, publicity-driven nature of his presidency has amplified the connections between the worlds of celebrity and politics.

5

TIME'S UP

Celebrity Feminism after #MeToo

While the prior two chapters explored the lead-up to the 2016 presidential election through an analysis of Hillary Clinton's campaign and the politicized harassment of Leslie Jones, this final chapter shifts from the before to the after. Late in the evening of November 8, 2016, the world watched as Donald Trump was announced the president-elect of the United States. His supporters exalted in his surprising victory, while much of the rest of the world responded with horror. As Clinton conceded and the reality of the coming four years began to set in, a woman named Teresa Shook created a Facebook event calling for a feminist march on Washington following Trump's inauguration. The event quickly garnered global support and spread beyond DC to cities across the world. Activists Vanessa Wruble, Carmen Perez, Tamika Mallory, and Linda Sarsour and fashion designer Bob Bland worked together to grow a one-off Facebook event page into what would become one of the largest protests in U.S. history: the Women's March (Broomfield 2017; Cauterucci 2016). On January 21, 2017, the day after Trump was sworn in as president, an estimated 5 million protesters worldwide took to the streets to advocate for human rights issues, including women's rights, in the face of the new administration. Among the participants at the march were a host of entertainment celebrities, some of whom were invited to speak. Alongside celebrated activists such as Angela Davis and Gloria Steinem, celebrities such as Scarlett Johansson, America Ferrera,

Ashley Judd, and Janelle Monáe took to the stage to encourage people to turn their devastation into action, fighting for American democracy and the rights of all the nation's citizens.

The Women's March continued as an organizing body for feminist activism but proved to be deeply flawed, reproducing long-standing tensions between white feminism and intersectional, multiracial feminism. Following allegations of racism, anti-Semitism, and overall elitism, several founding members stepped down, and the movement struggled to reconcile and regroup (Stockman 2018). The star-studded Women's March—and the centrality of tensions between the white feminist imperative and the intersectional imperative in its execution— spoke to the rising yet contentious tide of feminist activism galvanized by the traumatic election of President Trump and to the role celebrities played in its reinvigoration. Feminist celebrities and celebrity feminists stood side by side as the public faces of the movement. As 2017 progressed, Trump's presidency proved as devastatingly regressive as many had feared, and resistance to his administration grew. Then in October, within this volatile sociopolitical landscape, two bombshell articles landed within days of one another that formally exposed another powerful, white cishetero businessman with a storied history as a misogynist and bully: Miramax kingpin and decorated film producer, Harvey Weinstein.

Jodi Kantor and Megan Twohey (2017) for the *New York Times* and Ronan Farrow (2017) of the *New Yorker* published a series of articles detailing Weinstein's decades-long reign of terror against women in Hollywood. Actresses such as Mira Sorvino, Asia Argento, and Ashley Judd told harrowing accounts of Weinstein's harassment and assault, and former employees and victims explained how he used his power in the industry to make or break the women he terrorized. Beyond the physical and emotional torment he inflicted on scores of actresses, he spread vicious rumors about those he could not conquer and those who threatened to tell others about their experiences, thus having a direct hand in hamstringing many careers. Consistent throughout these stories was the sense of isolation and powerlessness the women experienced as they grappled with their trauma. Despite survivors' isolation and feelings of shame, rumors about Weinstein swirled around Hollywood for years and became a running joke, with comedians making highly public quips about his bad reputation everywhere from sitcoms like *30 Rock* to the Oscars stage (Yahr 2017). However, the women he victimized were threatened and silenced for speaking publicly, and they resorted to underground gossip networks of friends and coworkers. As discussed in chapter 1, gossip can be a powerful tool for sharing information and establishing community, particularly for women who may lack other recourse; that certainly appears to have been the case for celebrity women who worked together to warn one another and keep each other safe and supported. However, with Weinstein's power in Hollywood waning, the general sense of sociopolitical rupture that came with Trump's election, a groundswell of feminist organizing in response, and the work of these reporters, many women took the opportunity to tell their stories. As Judd said, "Women have been talking about Harvey amongst ourselves for a long time, and it's simply beyond time to have the conversation publicly" (Kantor and Twohey 2017).

Despite the long-standing open secret of Weinstein's abusive behavior, the publication of these allegations sent shockwaves well beyond Hollywood. However, in the days after Twohey and Kantor's story was published on October 5, few celebrities made statements. In a scathing article for the *New York Times*, Brooks Barnes (2017) reported that he had called more than forty Hollywood insiders for comment, but all had refused to speak on the record. Except for a few tweets from stars like Lena Dunham, Brie Larson, and Seth Rogen, celebrities were silent, and Barnes's reporting was damning: "A publicist for an A-list actress said there was no 'upside' for her client to comment, especially since she did not have a movie to promote." His assessment was harsh but typical, pointing out the hypocrisy of supposedly "woke," liberal Hollywood. Actress Rose McGowan (2017), who had long ago accused Weinstein of misconduct and felt herself an industry outcast for it, specifically called out her fellow actresses on Twitter, saying, "Ladies of Hollywood, your silence is deafening." Despite the exploding popularity of feminist branding and, to an extent, activism in celebrity circles, many were hesitant to call out a member of their own community, particularly one who had been such a star-maker.

The tensions between cultivating a feminist persona and performing the role of Hollywood team player came to the fore, and many hesitated as conflicting aspects of their star brands collided. Then, on October 15, actress Alyssa Milano (2017) tweeted a screenshot of text that said, "Me too. Suggested by a friend: 'If all the women who have been sexually harassed or assaulted wrote 'Me too.' as a status, we might give people a sense of the magnitude of this problem." She continued, "If you've been sexually harassed or assaulted write 'me too' as a reply to this tweet" and herself responded, "Me too." Notably, these tweets do not mention Weinstein or even Hollywood; rather, Milano focused more broadly on the widespread issue of sexual violence. In doing so, however, she continued a trend within celebrity feminism and, indeed, white feminism more broadly: eliding the contributions of Black feminists.

Tarana Burke, a Black feminist and anti-racist activist, had been inspired to create Me Too long before the Harvey Weinstein allegations. Spurred by her decades-long work with survivors of sexual assault and her nonprofit program for Black girls aged twelve to eighteen, Just Be, Burke started Me Too in 2006 on MySpace to provide a space for Black girls and women to share their stories of sexual assault, draw attention to its prevalence, and form a community of survivors (Garcia 2017). Milano's co-optation of the phrase as a hashtag emerged within and exemplified a broader feminist conversation already taking place on Twitter in the days after the Weinstein allegations. Twitter had briefly locked actress Rose McGowan out of her account after claiming some of her tweets about Weinstein violated its terms of service for including private, personal information (Ohlheiser 2017). In protest, feminists—largely white feminists, and including fellow celebrities like Alyssa Milano—organized #WomenBoycottTwitter for October 13, 2017. However, activist April Reign, the originator of #OscarsSoWhite mentioned in chapter 2, started #WOCAffirmation in response, pointing out the grave disparities in how white and women of color survivors are treated when they come forward with stories of sexual assault and calling on users to uplift Black women's voices rather than participate in the silence around the boycott. This tension emphasizes that silence can have different meanings for different women. For white women, who have long been at the center of feminist action, the withholding of their voices and, by extension, the value they add to Twitter can seem a powerful tool of protest. However, for women of color who have long been sidelined, ignored, or blamed in conversations around assault, that silence feels not like a protest but rather like a continuation of historical marginalization. Besides the goals of the white feminist imperative and the intersectional imperative being at odds, the optimal strategies to achieve their goals may also be different. These conflicts around silence, visibility, and power would continue to structure celebrities' post-#MeToo strategies.

The story of #MeToo is inextricably shaped by the hypervisibility afforded to celebrities and, in particular, to white celebrities, over and above the work of women of color feminist activists. This discrepancy continues to concern academics and activists who point out that celebrity feminism often prioritizes individual branding over collective action, lacks nuance, and is too deeply entangled with capitalist logics to be truly liberatory. Prior chapters have demonstrated, however, that celebrity feminism does not exist in isolation but in conversation with other feminisms. Through these conversations, and in particular the discursive pressures of the intersectional imperative, popular feminisms have shifted and evolved just as academic and grassroots feminisms shift and evolve. This chapter examines a particularly fascinating moment in that evolution, when celebrities joined together with a diverse group of activists to put their money and their time where their branding was: the creation of the feminist organization TIME'S UP and its public introduction via the 2018 Golden Globes Blackout.[1] While a great deal of digital feminist scholarship explores the ways in which everyday feminist activists utilized and understood #MeToo, there has been less scholarly work on the activism that came in the hashtag's wake as a celebrity phenomenon. In this chapter, I argue that, despite the intersectional goals of the initiative and the steps celebrity organizers took to decenter their fame and uplift activists, the self-promotional, hyperindividualized norms of celebrity culture subverted these aims by amplifying celebrity voices, identities, and self-brands. Moreover, the newsworthiness of (mostly white) stars exacerbated these power imbalances as news and commentary about the Blackout framed white celebrities as saviors at the expense of more nuanced discussions. Overall, the launch of Time's Up and its unraveling in the ensuing years crystallize and lay bare the multilayered problems that can arise when wealthy, powerful, privileged individuals posit solutions for communities to which they may only be tangentially connected—issues that can be amplified and made hypervisible by celebrities' involvement but are often endemic to large-scale, high-profile nonprofit organizations.

Understanding #MeToo as Restorative, Transformative Justice

Before jumping into a more in-depth discussion and analysis of post-#MeToo Hollywood activism, it is important to examine the complexities of #MeToo itself as arguably the most widespread popular feminist movement of the last several decades and the catalyst for the celebrity women's initiative. Much of the recent scholarship on digital feminisms has, necessarily and importantly, focused on the impact that #MeToo and other feminist hashtags centered on sexual assault and trauma have had on everyday feminist activists and the media narratives about them. Many researchers have foregrounded the complex, often contradictory emotional impacts of making and engaging with traumatic disclosures via social media. From their interviews with survivors who interacted with the hashtag #BeenRapedNeverReported, Kaitlynn Mendes, Jessica Ringrose, and Jessalynn Keller (2018) detail the simultaneous catharsis of receiving support for their disclosure and the "emotional 'tax'" (239) of engaging with such devastating content. While interacting with other survivors of sexual assault on social media can provide an exhilarating sense of community (see also Page and Arcy 2019; Jackson et al. 2020), it also requires a great deal of emotional labor to witness painful disclosure after disclosure, which may be retraumatizing. And that is just the trauma that comes from engaging with supportive members of a burgeoning digital community of survivors. As discussed throughout this book, the growing visibility and popularity of feminism, particularly in digital spaces, has fostered a vehement backlash of what Sarah Banet-Weiser (2018) terms "popular misogyny." Users who engage in digital feminist activism, particularly around sexual assault, open themselves up to misogynistic harassment from unsupportive members of the issue public (Mendes, Ringrose, and Keller 2019; Linabary, Corple, and Cooky 2019). These dynamics—the often exhausting but fulfilling work of finding and forming a community of survivors alongside networked misogynistic backlash—shape and constrain everyday experiences of digital feminist awareness-raising and activism like #MeToo.

Moreover, extrajudicial forms of accountability like #MeToo have helped to spawn reflection on and anxieties about various forms of justice—some in good faith, and some focused squarely on protecting perpetrators and, by extension, upholding male supremacy in the face of growing popular feminist critique (e.g., Salter 2013; Pain 2020; Lanius 2019; Mack and McCann 2019). In the introduction I described how panics around "cancel culture," largely stoked by the those on the right, garnered widespread media attention in the wake of #MeToo and continue to inform backlash against progressive movements. However, feminist scholars and activists point out that community-centered networks of support and affirmation for survivors, like those afforded by issue publics that sprang up around #MeToo, provide an alternative to carceral feminist responses to sexual assault that focus on punishing perpetrators (Page and Arcy 2019). Once a term relegated to discussions of punitive feminist responses to sexual assault, today the term *carceral feminism* more generally describes "decades of feminist anti-violence collaboration with the carceral state or that part of the government most associated with the institutions of police, prosecution, courts, and the system of jails, prisons, probation, and parole" (Kim 2018, 220). Mimi Kim (2020) provides an illuminating history of the alignment of feminist anti-violence efforts alongside the growth of the criminal justice system throughout the 1970s and explores key critiques of that alignment—namely, that the carceral state disproportionately harms communities of color and has historically supported perpetrators of sexual violence while doubting and retraumatizing survivors. Ultimately, criticisms of carceral feminisms echo Audre Lorde's argument that "the master's tools will never dismantle the master's house." A white supremacist, patriarchal carceral state cannot provide liberation and justice for survivors of white supremacist and/ or patriarchal violence.

Instead, many critics of carceral feminism advocate for restorative justice, which focuses on the harm that violence causes not merely to victims and perpetrators but also to communities more broadly. Their goal is the "healthy reintegration of all parties back into the community" and/or transformative justice, which contends that the individuals and communities impacted by violence, particularly marginalized communities, understand best how to seek intervention, accountability, prevention, and transformation and should be empowered to do so (Kim 2018, 225–226). So, while critics of #MeToo rail against perpetrators losing work or facing other extrajudicial consequences without "due process," many feminist scholars and academics praised #MeToo for centering survivors rather than perpetrators and focusing on healing and restoration, often outside of a carceral framework (Page and Arcy 2019).

This transformative, restorative community-building was a key feature of #MeToo, inherent in the name Burke chose for her movement: an individual, me, joining a group of survivors who have experienced sexual violence, too.

#MeToo demonstrates a blending of individual and collective experiences, of personal trauma made public, centered around shared experience and a sense of belonging. However, as soon as #MeToo emerged as a global phenomenon, cultural critics and journalists began asking, "What now?" Was #MeToo a moment or a movement? What, if any, substantive change would grow out of it, or was it a flash-in-the-pan hashtag movement that would fade as quickly as it emerged? As accusations across a range of industries, entertainment and beyond, continued to flood public discourse in the weeks and months following Milano's tweet, it seemed that #MeToo may in fact mark some shift in public awareness of and response to sexual assault and harassment. Then, after nearly three months, celebrity feminists banded together to announce their plan to build on the momentum of #MeToo: the Time's Up initiative.

Dear Sisters: Launching TIME'S UP

On January 1, 2018, a full-page open letter appeared in both the *New York Times* and *La Opinión*, a Spanish-language newspaper.[2] With words nested around a large headline that read, "Dear Sisters," more than 300 women in the entertainment industry addressed the activists of the Alianza Nacional de Campesinas (Heil 2018). Weeks earlier, cofounder Monica Ramírez had written her own open letter on behalf of women farmworkers expressing solidarity and support for women in Hollywood coming forward about their experiences with harassment and assault. The letter was a controversial one; one of Ramírez's allies suggested that she should critique celebrities and industry insiders for ignoring the plight of farmworkers, but she instead offered support, saying the Hollywood stars "'were women workers, too'" (Tobar 2018). The letter attracted the attention of a group of celebrity women, including Reese Witherspoon, Kerry Washington, Shonda Rhimes, Natalie Portman, America Ferrera, and Amber Tamblyn, who were already in talks with one another about post-#MeToo steps. These actresses had originally envisioned an initiative that would focus on ending harassment in the entertainment industry; however, upon seeing Ramírez's letter, they shifted their sights beyond the confines of Hollywood. They teamed up with a diverse group of feminist, anti-racist, and labor activists—including Ramírez—and formed a foundation that aimed for a more expansive and intersectional form of celebrity feminism: Time's Up, whose inaugural goal was a legal defense fund to provide subsidized counsel for those who have faced harassment and discrimination in the workplace across industries (Buckley 2018).

The genesis of Time's Up demonstrates the tensions, potentials, and pitfalls of a form of celebrity feminism that is adapting to the ambient pressures of the intersectional imperative while constrained by the myopia of hyperprivileged white feminism. Ramírez's engagement with the celebrity women is

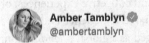

Amber Tamblyn ✓
@ambertamblyn

Got 3 copies of our letter in @nytimes today. One for
me, one for my mom and one for my daughter to read
someday. Emotional. Proud. Happy. Fueled. Ready.
Timesupnow.com #TIMESUP

Dear Sisters,

In Solidarity,

👤 The New York Times and 2 others

FIGURE 5.1 Amber Tamblyn's tweet, 2018.

illustrative. Ramírez and the Alianza recognized the connections between the
plights of female farmworkers and celebrities as women oppressed by patriarchal capitalism, not the celebrities who have much more structural power via
their economic privilege and, in many cases, white privilege. Moreover, it was
Ramírez who elected to engage in the emotional and actual labor of reaching
across the privilege gap to extend her support rather than to call out celebrities
for their overly narrow focus and their ignorance of less privileged women's
experiences. Prior chapters have demonstrated that women of color who call
out white feminists are often labeled toxic and further marginalized from
activist discussions. Ramírez's decision here engages in the emotional labor of

magnanimity to avoid that pitfall, meeting her celebrity counterparts more than halfway. The celebrity women's response, considering the overwhelming performativity and inaction of much celebrity feminism over the last decade, was undoubtedly shaped by increasingly mainstream conversations about and pressures toward intersectionality that have swelled alongside the growing popularity of (white) feminism. And unlike prior prominent celebrity feminist moments that elided or erased the work of women of color feminists, like Patricia Arquette's speech or Alyssa Milano's unintentional co-optation of #MeToo, with Time's Up, celebrities recognized that they did not have the knowledge or skills necessary to engage in substantive feminist work and called on established activists for their assistance. This choice presents a trade-off: while it allows activists a prominent and well-funded platform and acknowledges their expertise, it simultaneously relies on them to shape the work while the celebrities will almost certainly get most of the credit. One example that illustrates the role celebrity news and gossip logics played in the mediation of the Time's Up initiative is a *Today Show* (2018) interview with actress America Ferrera and Ramírez a few days after the legal defense fund was announced.

First, it is notable that Ferrera was chosen as the celebrity spokeswoman for the initiative, and that she elected to have Ramírez alongside her rather than another celebrity. Ferrera has long been outspokenly involved in feminist and Latinx activism, and by foregrounding her along with another Latinx activist, the Time's Up rollout clearly demonstrates the celebrity women's desire to present intersectionality as central to its goals and foreground connection with women farmworkers. This goal is emphasized by Ferrera's consistent focus on the legal defense fund's goal of aiding all marginalized people in fighting against harassment. Moreover, during the interview, Ramírez pushes back on the framing of Hollywood women as more powerful than women in lower-wage positions such as farmworkers because of their privilege. While she acknowledges the privilege afforded by their fame and wealth, she affirms that farmworker women are powerful and touts their experience and expertise at organizing against sexual harassment in the workplace, expressing a desire to share that expertise with celebrity women. Overall, this interview emphasizes the intersectional goals of the initiative, its collaboration with and appreciation of women of color activists, and its focus on sustained action toward systemic change.

However, interviewers Hoda Kotb and Savannah Guthrie ask Ferrera twice as many questions as they ask Ramírez, deferring to Ferrera to explain Time's Up while asking Ramírez to react and respond to these explanations. As a result, Ferrera speaks twice as much as Ramírez (119 seconds vs. 60 seconds). Finally, the segment wraps up with a celebration of Ferrera's newly announced pregnancy. When Guthrie congratulates her, Ferrera smiles and immediately attempts to redirect focus back to Time's Up, saying, "Thank you. All the more

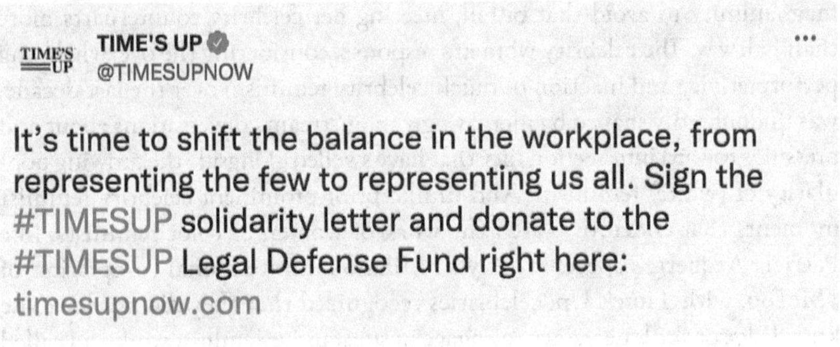

TIME'S UP ✔
@TIMESUPNOW

⋯

It's time to shift the balance in the workplace, from representing the few to representing us all. Sign the #TIMESUP solidarity letter and donate to the #TIMESUP Legal Defense Fund right here:
timesupnow.com

FIGURE 5.2 One of the inaugural tweets from the TIME'S UP launch on January 1, 2018.

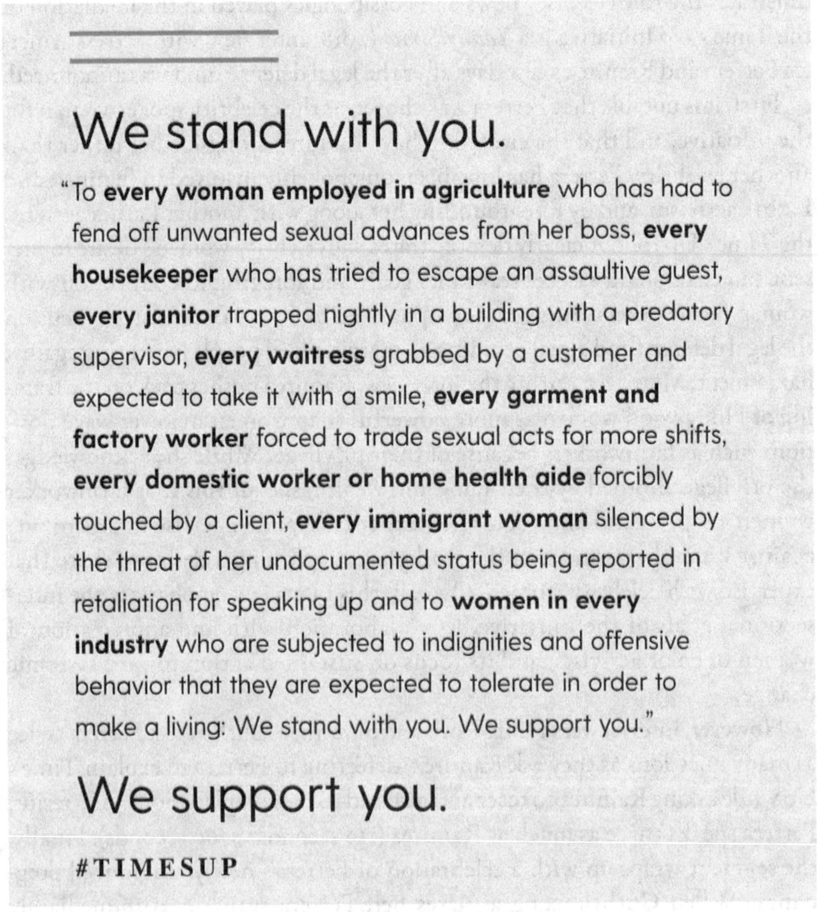

We stand with you.

"To **every woman employed in agriculture** who has had to fend off unwanted sexual advances from her boss, **every housekeeper** who has tried to escape an assaultive guest, **every janitor** trapped nightly in a building with a predatory supervisor, **every waitress** grabbed by a customer and expected to take it with a smile, **every garment and factory worker** forced to trade sexual acts for more shifts, **every domestic worker or home health aide** forcibly touched by a client, **every immigrant woman** silenced by the threat of her undocumented status being reported in retaliation for speaking up and to **women in every industry** who are subjected to indignities and offensive behavior that they are expected to tolerate in order to make a living: We stand with you. We support you."

We support you.

#TIMESUP

FIGURE 5.3 TIME'S UP statement posted to Twitter alongside the tweet in figure 5.2, 2018.

reason to get back to work and fix what needs to get fixed, right?" But her attempt fails as Kotb exclaims, "You're beaming!" and Guthrie asks, "Do you know if you're having a boy or a girl?" Ferrera demurs, saying, "I might, but I'm not telling!" as Kotb and Guthrie laugh. Not only does the interview emphasize Ferrera's role over Ramírez's, but this ending reinstitutes the norms of celebrity gossip: it amplifies an individualized focus on celebrity's private lives, with a particular emphasis on traditionally feminine domains such as relationships and children (McDonnell 2014). Rather than leaving the viewer with information about how to contribute to the legal defense fund, further details about Ramírez's work, or the future plans around Time's Up, the interview ends by reemphasizing interest in Ferrera's personal life and reconstituting her identity as a mother-to-be.

These tensions between labor, privilege, gossip, and visibility were simultaneously addressed and expanded by celebrities' announcement that they would publicize Time's Up by wearing all black to the 2018 Golden Globes ceremony. They also announced that nearly a dozen actresses planned to bring activists as their dates, providing them a platform on the red carpet to amplify their work. The launch of the Time's Up initiative was a moment that, on its face, attempted to marry style and substance. The Blackout's goal was to symbolically prioritize intersectional collectivity over individuality, to redirect attention and financial gain to activism rather than (or perhaps in addition to) stars' fame and bank accounts, and to make visible the work of established activists by using the spotlight afforded to celebrities to foreground a feminist initiative whose goal was systemic change via legal intervention. But what role can celebrities play in supporting solutions for communities of which they are not a part, particularly when their vision of justice centers on helping survivors navigate a complex legal system that has historically harmed them and communities of color? The Time's Up initiative and, in particular, its introduction to the public via the Golden Globes Blackout demonstrate the complexity of a popular feminism that goes beyond branding to action as it is refracted through celebrity culture.

In the pages that follow, I analyze two facets of celebrity and activist publicization of Time's Up at the Golden Globes: celebrities' red carpet interviews alongside their activist dates, and reporting and commentary on the event and the legal defense fund. After exploring the publicity push around the Golden Globes, I step back and analyze Time's Up itself, considering the organization's goals while interrogating the numerous scandals that have plagued it in the years since the Blackout, which led to its eventual demise. The chapter ends with reflections on the limits of the hypervisibility celebrity feminism provides in negotiating the tension between white feminist and intersectional imperatives.

A Red Carpet Like No Other: Serious Banter, Competing Logics, and the Struggle for Control on the Golden Globes Red Carpet

Celebrities' publicization of Time's Up on the red carpet, many of them alongside their activist dates, showcased a power struggle to realize the Blackout's purported goal—to divert attention from celebrities and toward survivors and action—as celebrity journalists, celebrities, and activists navigated this hypermediated and celebritized space. Working within the substantial limitations of celebrity journalism and the social situation of the red carpet (see Lawson and Draper 2021), celebrities and their activist dates worked to varying degrees to wrest control and visibility away from red carpet reporters and celebrities and on to Time's Up and the other organizations the activists represented. First and foremost, celebrities' decision to wear black reflected their goal to push back on the competitive individuality of the red carpet and sartorially project solidarity, providing less fashion-related fodder for postshow commentary and encouraging reporters to ask them instead about their choice to support Time's Up. This power struggle, uneven though it was, demonstrated ruptures in the celebrity and media logics that curtail celebrity activism, particularly on the carpet, as some celebrities and activists hesitated or outright refused to "play the game" and engage in standard red carpet banter. The result was an uneasy mix of glossy smiles, clumsy activist-focused Q&As, and, as the goal stated, a few subversive moments that did indeed make for a red carpet like no other.

One example of this tempered rupture came from an interview with Tarana Burke and actress Michelle Williams. On the E! Red Carpet & Award Shows (2018), Ryan Seacrest first introduced Burke, signaling his attempt to reframe the conversation away from his celebrity guest and to her activist date, ostensibly respecting her position in this moment. However, he immediately pivoted to Williams and asked why she and Burke were attending together, giving her control and authorizing her to speak for both of them just as Guthrie and Kotb did for Ferrera on *The Today Show*. Williams said, "You know why we're here? We're here because of Tarana. You might think we're here because I'm nominated for something, but that's not the case. We're here because Tarana started a movement." Despite Seacrest's focus on Williams, she worked to direct him back to Burke. Seacrest then asked Burke what the resurgence of Me Too has meant to her. After she discussed how the movement has grown and how humbling it is, expressing gratitude for the opportunity to talk about her work on behalf of Black girls and women, Seacrest again shifted back to Williams for more standard red carpet banter. "I know it's about the message," he said, "but I wanted to congratulate you for your work," going on to praise her performance in *All the Money in the World*. She waved away the compliment with her hand and a "pfft," and as he went on she smiled blithely while shaking her head "no" the whole time. "Well, thank you, I appreciate it," she said through pinched

America Ferrera ✔
@AmericaFerrera

BECAUSE EVERY WOMAN, EVERYWHERE, HAS
POWER AND A VOICE.
BECAUSE EVERY WOMAN, EVERYWHERE, DESERVES
SAFETY AND DIGNITY.

Why do you wear black? And I wanna see a pic of you
in black! Tweet at me please!

#WHYWEWEARBLACK #TIMESUP

FIGURE 5.4 America Ferrera's tweet, 2018.

WHY I WEAR
BLACK TODAY

For **equity** and **parity** across all industries.
For **safety** among every worker
in every occupation. For **inclusion** of all
women and marginalized people.

#TimesUp

FIGURE 5.5 TIME'S UP statement regarding the Blackout that was shared by many
celebrities, including Ferrera alongside the tweet in figure 5.4, 2018.

lips when he had finished, "but really the most important thing is I thought I would have to raise my daughter to learn how to protect herself in a dangerous world, and I think because of the work that Tarana has done, and the work that I'm learning how to do, we actually have the opportunity to hand our children a different world." She refused to engage in typical red carpet talk and shifted the conversation to Burke's accomplishments, emphasizing her activist expertise and achievement over and above Williams's own. More than blending celebrity and activism, Williams slipped out of celebrity-focused questions and refocused attention on Burke and Time's Up, exercising control over the interview and working to achieve the Blackout's goal.

While Williams subtly and smilingly refused to play the celebrity game, an *Access* (2018b) interview with Black–Puerto Rican activist, journalist, politician, and media-maker Rosa Clemente and actress Susan Sarandon presented a more overt example of rupture. Upon walking up to reporters, Sarandon immediately introduced Clemente and talked about her work on behalf of Puerto Rico. Reporter Kit Hoover then excitedly turned to Clemente and asked if she was so excited to get a call from "the great Susan Sarandon" to walk the red carpet with her. Clemente responded, "No, actually, Tarana Burke, the founder of Me Too was a friend of mine for over twenty years. I'm an organizer. I've been doing work for a long time. I know Susan, we're Green Party folks, she supported me when I ran a long time ago." Clemente pushed back on both celebrity control and centrality, emphasizing Burke's organizational power in putting the red carpet event together and reframing Sarandon's role as a political activist rather than a star. Clemente continued to refuse to play the celebrity-focused red carpet game when Hoover interrupted her discussion of the continued devastation in Puerto Rico following Hurricane Maria to ask, "JLo's there right now, right?" Clemente paused and said, "I don't know about that," then smoothly continued to list the challenges facing Puerto Ricans in the wake of the storm. Hoover's question reveals the power of celebritized red carpet norms: the relative simplicity, familiarity, and glamour of celebrity more intuitively gels with the fast pace and visual focus of the red carpet. The gravity of celebrity culture, the dense center of the red carpet broadcast, exerts a strong pull, particularly for red carpet reporters like Hoover whose work focuses entirely on celebrity. But Clemente, farther outside of celebrity's sway, resisted and reframed the discussion away from Sarandon-the-actress to Sarandon-the-activist, from giddiness at celebrity attention to the outcome of a network of longtime organizers, from Jennifer Lopez's presence in Puerto Rico to Clemente's own ongoing work. The activists are much better equipped to achieve the goals of the Blackout and the launch of Time's Up, although the efficacy of their presence is consistently hemmed in by the attention afforded to their celebrity dates and, more specifically, the celebrity-focused discourse steered by red carpet reporters.

Beyond these more spectacular moments, the majority of red carpet interviews touched on the Blackout and the launch of Time's Up, if only briefly, and the buzzword of the night was clear: *solidarity*. The Blackout itself was meant to sartorially signal such solidarity as one marker of symbolic collective action. And, as indicated by the broad focus of the legal defense fund, that solidarity was intended to extend beyond the red carpet. As Weinstein survivor Ashley Judd told *Access* (2018b), "We know that sexual harassment and hostile workplaces are very grave injustices experienced by the majority of women in the workplace and also some men." She put forth the legal defense fund as a way that celebrities, alongside their activist partners, aimed to express their solidarity with fellow workers as "a beacon of hope across all industries." To underscore that sense of solidarity and to emphasize collaborative effort over individual agency, celebrity women framed Time's Up as "leaderless" and downplayed their centrality, often uplifting their activist colleagues. One example is a backstage interview from *Access* (2018a) with Reese Witherspoon, Nicole Kidman, Zoë Kravitz, Laura Dern, and Shailene Woodley following their win for the HBO series *Big Little Lies*. While talking about the inspirational power of women and artists, a reporter asked Witherspoon if she was the "ringleader" for Time's Up. Witherspoon shrieked, "No!" while her colleagues jumped in to emphasize how much effort she put in organizing the initiative. Kravitz stepped forward and said, "She won't say it, but she's been working very hard," and Witherspoon immediately shifted to praise activists who have done this hard work for years, emphasizing that "they wake up and do this every day" and stating that the celebrities "are standing in the path" these activists have created. Even if Witherspoon's reaction was disingenuous (by all accounts, she and other stars were integral to Time's Up's launch), it is important to note that many celebrities intentionally downplayed their roles and emphasized the activists they worked with, pushing back on individualized narratives of celebrity-as-savior. However, as we will see in the next section, not all news and commentary on Time's Up followed their leads.

Further, not all red carpet interviews demonstrated such a concerted effort to decenter celebrities or to direct attention toward Time's Up and/or longtime activists. Most discussions of Time's Up on the red carpet consisted of perfunctory praise of survivors' "bravery" and calls to stand together that were often overwhelmed by typical banter about nominations and appearance. As I will discuss in the next sections, many outlets reamed red carpet reporters and celebrities alike for their superficial engagement with issues of gender discrimination and sexual assault, and much of the footage consisted of performatively self-serving mentions of Time's Up, milquetoast declarations that "things need to change," and no follow-up on the red carpet itself or in the following months (e.g., Bryant 2018). However, the preceding examples demonstrate that some celebrities, through their sartorial statements and their inclusion of activist voices, endeavored to shift the focus onto Time's Up and their activist dates. In doing so, they and the activists strategically pushed back on the intensively individualized norms of the celebrity-focused red carpet while simultaneously working with those norms as a way of garnering the spotlight. But despite their best efforts, celebrities, and in particular white celebrities, still received most of the attention and accolades from red carpet reporters. That trend would continue after the red carpet.

"A Watchable Revolution": News and Commentary on the Blackout

Girl Power: Postfeminist Entanglements and a "Toothless Tiger"

The publicization of Time's Up at the Golden Globes resulted in a massive surge in interest in the organization. Although the initiative had been publicized via the "Dear Sisters" open letter and celebrities' social media since January 1, 2018, Google trends data show only small bumps in searches for "Time's Up" in the week before the Globes but a tenfold spike on January 8, the day after the awards show, when the term hit its peak. Moreover, Forbes reported that such attention translated into donations: the Time's Up legal defense fund raised $20 million in the month after the Golden Globes ceremony (Robehmed 2018). In the aggregate these figures of money and attention show that the Blackout was relatively successful in directing audiences to the goal of supporting survivors with legal counsel. But like the red carpet interviews, coverage of and commentary on the event presented an uneasy blend of celebrity gossip and activism; of postfeminist and feminist discourses; of intersectional and white feminist perspectives; and of an overall shift in tone and content that was uneven, short-lived, and often perfunctory despite the goals of the Blackout. While some stars and activists were able to exercise more control over their narratives during red carpet interviews, they had much more limited sway over news and commentary about Time's Up. Because the individualized, capitalist-driven logics of celebrity culture are powerful forces and celebrities are reliant on them for amplification, the arm-wrestling match begun on the red carpet swung heavily in reporters' favor after the Globes ended.

Some of the articles in the dataset were quintessentially postfeminist, espousing the same type of "girl power," commodity-focused rhetoric that has marked popular feminist media cultures for decades. For example, one article in *People* magazine offered "Girl Power Pieces to Rock in Support of the TIME'S UP Movement," listing a slew of apparel and accessories described as the "best girl-power styles to rock in support of women's social, cultural and political rights" (K. Phillips 2018). This classic example of commodity activism provides consumers with a seemingly easy fix to complex social problems like sexism in a way that is wholly compatible with capitalism: the purchase of some traditionally feminine clothing or jewelry items that espouse feminism stands in for more substantial and transformative feminist action (Banet-Weiser 2012). Still others emphasized women's desire to focus on more traditional and feminine aspects of the red carpet. After noting that the Globes would be the first awards show since "heroic women in Hollywood came forward to share their harrowing stories of sexual assault within the industry," Kaleigh Fasanella (2018) for *Allure* said, "But just because we've all got a very serious subject on the brain tonight, doesn't mean we don't also care about the red carpet beauty prep from our favorite celebs," following this declaration with embedded social media posts from celebrities as they got ready for the awards show. While *People* and *Allure* also published in-depth articles about how to support Time's Up and background on the activists, the presence of these articles demonstrates the power postfeminist logics still hold over popular feminist discourses.

Articles as blatantly postfeminist as those just mentioned were in the minority, but like many red carpet interviews, others engaged in business as usual with a veneer of difference, covering stylists' behind-the-scenes scramble to find black dresses for their celebrity clients at the last minute once the Blackout was announced (e.g., Moore 2017) and evaluating fashion choices with a particular focus on who was able to stand out despite the all-black mandate (e.g., Charuza 2018). As discussed in chapter 2, feminist politics and a desire to know more about the artistry involved in dressing celebrities for a red carpet are not mutually exclusive. But as with the #AskHerMore campaign, the goal of the Blackout was specifically to deindividualize the celebrities, to decenter the emphasis on fashion, and to focus on their activist goals. Articles such as those mentioned here run counter to this goal and demonstrate how the drama of celebrity gossip and the norms of competitive red carpet fashion remained alive and well despite celebrities' ostensible efforts to tamp them down.

But how disruptive were those efforts to begin with? In one of the most scathing reviews of the Blackout, Rhonda Garelick (2018), writing for The Cut, called the demonstration a "toothless tiger," pointing out that wearing black is in no way revolutionary and the gowns were still beautiful designer pieces. She sums up her thoughts in the article's subtitle: "The Women of Hollywood Were Never Going to Deny Us the Pleasure of Their Beauty." From this perspective, black dresses and activist dates aside, celebrities' decision to walk the red carpet in glamorous gowns, hair, and makeup demonstrated an allegiance to celebritized norms of self-presentation and the incorporation of "beautiful" and "fashionable" into their celebrity brands. This allegiance opened the door to coverage that did not adhere to their stated goals, undermining their efforts. Such a perspective pushes back on the notion that celebrities can have their cake and eat it, too, remaining beautiful and enviable while engaging in substantive activism. For Garelick, playing ball enough to

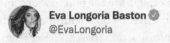

FIGURE 5.6 Eva Longoria's tweet, 2018.

sustain the glamorous spotlight of celebrity is too limiting; more radical disruptions are necessary.

Who Gets the Glory? Praising Celebrity Feminists

Despite such critiques, most articles discussing the Blackout applauded the effort and blended discussions of celebrity culture and fashion with activism in a more elegant and supportive way than those just mentioned. This coverage is perhaps best summed up by Hank Stuever (2018), reporting on the event for the *Washington Post*, who deemed the Golden Globes "a watchable revolution," arguing that it was "less an awards show and more a prolonged statement of cultural correction" that "nevertheless managed to keep things fairly entertaining in the midst of revolution." This blend of entertainment and activism extended to the coverage of the event, which was dominated by the traditional post–red carpet "listicle" (a glorified list in the form of an article) format of glamorous photos, but this time often complemented by or framed with quotes from actresses about Time's Up, links to the organization's donation page, and information on the activists who joined them (e.g., Hardy 2018; Macmillan 2018). Several articles mixed appearance and activism more explicitly by connecting actresses' fashion and styling choices to feminism with varying levels of success, calling the abundance of red lipstick "a timeless symbol of empowerment" and connecting stars' looks to the suffragette movement (e.g., L. Valenti 2018; Ruffo 2018). While the stars might not have denied us their beauty, many articles framed that beauty within a broader context of their goals, praising the Blackout as relatively successful in forcing conversations about sexual assault and harassment on the red carpet and admiring the effort, as imperfect as it was.

Some outlets sought to shift their coverage of the Golden Globes more substantively in line with the actresses' and activists' goals. *Teen Vogue* and The Cut, for example, issued statements letting readers know that their coverage of the event would focus not on evaluating fashion but rather on efforts to support survivors of sexual harassment and assault (@TeenVogue 2018; Petrarca 2018). *The Atlantic* pointedly pushed back on traditional red carpet coverage with a red carpet listicle that excluded photos. Instead, the list answered the age-old question of "what she wore" for each actress and activist with one of their red carpet quotes explaining why they were wearing black and providing information about Time's Up and other activist initiatives (Garber 2018). Moreover, both the *New York Times* and the *Washington Post* framed their laudatory coverage of the Blackout as a critique of legislators' inaction on gender inequity, sexual harassment, and sexual assault (Bruni 2018; Phillips 2018). In both tone and content, these articles acknowledged the changes the actresses attempted to make and shifted their coverage accordingly, and some writers even argued that these celebrities' efforts and rhetoric were more impactful than those of elected officials. While the outcome of the Blackout was uneven at best, in some cases it was able to shift the conversation, if only in the short term, and further establish celebrities as activist forces to be reckoned with. Particularly at a time when U.S. politics resembled a dark three-ring circus, and when the worlds of entertainment and politics had long been filtering into one another, it was unsurprising that some celebrities and entertainment outlets were primed to be the faces of the resistance.

However, across all the coverage, the most detailed, nuanced, and intersectional discussions of gender inequality, sexual harassment, and sexual assault—and Hollywood's efforts to change them—came not from journalists or commentators but from celebrities themselves. For example, stars like Amber Tamblyn (2018), Uzo Aduba, and Tessa Thompson penned essays and gave interviews ahead of the Globes to explain the Blackout and Time's Up, and many articles reprinted celebrities' comments both before and on the red car-pet (Pinson 2018). Nearly all explicit mentions of the intersections of gender, race, and class and the ways women of color and/or poorer women are differ-ently and disproportionately disadvantaged came from celebrities' quotes; the articles themselves were mostly devoid of such intersectional framing or analy-sis (e.g., Gonzales 2018; Frey 2018). This dynamic again demonstrates celebri-ties' power, though limited, to shape conversations around their activism. The attention afforded to them and their statements allowed them, with enough preparation and knowledge, to infiltrate discussions of celebrity with more complex discussions of gender and racial injustice, pushing the intersectional imperative even when the journalists and commentators who covered them neglected to do so.

But celebrities' power to garner and redirect attention was further hemmed in by journalists' overwhelming focus on white celebrities at the expense of celebrities of color and noncelebrity activists. Only 26 out of the 241 articles (10.7 percent) that made up my dataset included names of women of color in their headlines, while 70 (29 percent) name-checked white stars only. As described in the preceding chapters, media amplify white stars, even if the stars themselves attempt to foreground women of color celebrities and activ-ists. Moreover, very few of the articles offered activists the latitude to discuss their work with Time's Up independent of their celebrity counterparts. For example, activists Ai-Jen Poo and Monica Ramírez spoke to BuzzFeed News following the Golden Globes about Time's Up, although the focus of the con-versation remained primarily on the ways in which celebrities were learning and growing in their activism (Lange 2018). Overall, despite their efforts to foreground actresses and activists of color and to incorporate substantive, inter-sectional discussions of systemic issues facing women across industries, pre-dictably, stories of white celebrities as benevolent saviors overwhelmingly dominated the coverage of and commentary on Time's Up.

One omission is particularly glaring. On the morning of the Golden Globes, Tarana Burke posted a statement on Facebook collectively penned by the activists attending the award show. Because Burke has since deleted her Facebook account, her original post is available only via internet archives. The statement appeared only once in my dataset, in a tweet from actress Kerry Washington (2018), although short excerpts appeared in a few arti-cles, such as Camryn Rabideau's (2018) piece in *In Style* magazine. Ahead of the interviews on the red carpet itself, Burke's post was the clearest and most substantive articulation of the Blackout's goals from the activists' perspec-tive, and it is effectively absent from the archive of the event. But if you want to watch Rosario Dawson's statement on Instagram about the message behind the Blackout or another Instagram video in which actresses Reese Wither-spoon, Brie Larson, Rashida Jones, Kerry Washington, Tessa Thompson, and

Tracee Ellis Ross giddily thank those who donated to Time's Up, have no fear: those posts appear dozens of times in the dataset, remediated ad nauseum as some of the most frequently circulated texts related to the Blackout and the launch of Time's Up. Because Burke's statement is so difficult to find, I include her post in its entirety here:

January 7, 2018

Statement from Gender and Racial Justice Activists on their Attendance at the Golden Globes Alongside Actresses

Los Angeles, CA—Tonight, advocates and activists for gender and racial justice, Tarana Burke, Marai Larasi, Rosa Clemente, Ai-jen Poo, Mónica Ramírez, Calina Lawrence, Billie Jean King and Saru Jayaraman, will join actresses Michelle Williams, Emma Watson, Susan Sarandon, Meryl Streep, Laura Dern, Shailene Woodley, Amy Poehler and Emma Stone at the 2018 Golden Globes in a show of support for victims of sexual harassment and assault. Collectively, the advocates have released the following statement ahead of the event:

"As longtime organizers, activists and advocates for racial and gender justice, it gives us enormous pride to stand with the members of the TIMES UP campaign who have stood up and spoken out in this groundbreaking historical moment. We have each dedicated our lives to doing work that supports the least visible, most marginalized women in our diverse contexts. We do this work as participants in movements that seek to affirm the dignity and humanity of every person.

"Too much of the recent press attention has been focused on perpetrators and does not adequately address the systematic nature of violence including the importance of race, ethnicity and economic status in sexual violence and other forms of violence against women. Our goal in attending the Golden Globes is to shift the focus back to survivors and on systemic, lasting solutions. Each of us will be highlighting legislative, community-level and interpersonal solutions that contribute to ending violence against women in all our communities. It is our hope that in doing so, we will also help to broaden conversations about the connection to power, privilege and other systemic inequalities.

"Many of us identify as survivors of sexual harassment, assault and violence ourselves and we believe we are nearing a tipping point in transforming the culture of violence in the countries where we live and work. It's a moment to transform both the written and unwritten rules that devalue the lives and experiences of women. We believe that people of all genders and ages should live free of violence against us. And, we believe that women of color, and women who have faced generations of exclusion—indigenous, Black, Brown and Asian women, farmworkers and domestic workers, disabled women, undocumented and queer and trans women—should be at the center of our solutions. This moment in time calls for us to use the power of our collective voices to find solutions that leave no woman behind.

"This past year was a powerful one in the fight for gender equity and against sexual violence against women—from the Women's March to the re-emergence of 'me too' as a viral hashtag that brought more than ten years of survivor-centered work to the mainstream. There is still much work to do, and many hands required to do it. We want to encourage all women—from those who live in the shadows to those who live in the spotlight, from all walks of life, and across generations—to continue to step forward and know that they will be supported when they do.

"The #TIMESUP initiative joins an ever-growing collective of organizations, movements, and leaders working to end gender-based violence. We look forward to partnering with them and others to organize, support all survivors, and find solutions that ensure a future where all women and all people can live and work with dignity."

The activists' words here present clear and specific goals: to challenge press narratives that focus on perpetrators and refocus those narratives on survivors with the goal of creating systemic changes to cultures of gender oppression and sexual violence that center intersections of race, ethnicity, and class and women who are the most marginalized. The activists use the language of transformative and restorative justice, emphasizing that they will highlight not only broader legislative solutions but also "community-level and interpersonal solutions." This statement reflects their knowledge and experience as activists and presents their promotion of Time's Up not as a spectacular, new phenomenon but as a continuation of their decades of work on behalf of marginalized people, an opportunity to present that work on a huge scale because of the spotlight afforded by "me too" and its newfound ties to Hollywood. Far from a cutesy "getting ready" selfie captioned "#TimesUp" from a celebrity attendee, this statement provides an in-depth explanation of the activists' attendance at the Globes and the goals behind Time's Up. But it is also less digestible and sexy than that selfie, and its absence from the archive demonstrates just how outsized the newsworthiness of celebrities continues to be despite the ostensible goal of the Blackout. Intersectional language from glamorous stars may filter more easily into mainstream news and commentary, but more radical and transformative intersectional activism that focuses specifically on marginalized communities makes for a less sexy—and more disruptive—media narrative.

Overall, reactions to the Golden Globes Blackout and the launch of Time's Up allow us to map some pros and cons of a "watchable revolution," an evening gown–clad, celebrity-initiated attempt at systemic change to gendered inequities. First, the Golden Globes launch afforded Time's Up a good deal of positive attention, and more than simply raising awareness, that attention translated into massive donations for the burgeoning organization. As has often been the case with celebrity feminism, the stars' beauty and charisma were a Trojan horse for often intersectional and sometimes confrontational discussions of sexual assault and harassment. However, celebrities did not boycott the event. They did not refuse to participate in a celebration of the industry that so publicly harmed them and their colleagues. They did not dress down, attending in street clothes as a more pronounced rejection of Hollywood's expectations of women. They did not refuse to speak to reporters. It is impossible to say whether these alternatives may have more profoundly shifted conversations around celebrity feminism well after the awards show ended. However, the participants' choice to remain loyal to celebritized norms of self-presentation on the red carpet arguably cut down on the bite, rendering what was already an overwhelmingly reformist effort less revolutionary, comforting audiences with the assurance that celebrities' glamour was here to stay, and more easily allowing those who wanted to merely nod at or outright ignore their message to do so.

Beyond the Blackout: The Rise and Fall of TIME'S UP

Between 2018–2021, Time's Up grew and expanded into one of the most recognizable charities for the promotion of workplace equality in the West before imploding due to a series of scandals and mismanagement. The following section highlights the goals of the organization and analyzes what its scandals and eventual demise can teach us about the limitations of a celebrity-focused non-profit with deep pockets and complicated loyalties. From its early days, Time's Up was divided into three entities. The first was its inaugural legal defense fund, housed in the National Women's Law Center. According to the Time's Up annual report for 2020, the legal defense fund has supported 4,800 workers with legal representation, 33 percent of whom are Black, indigenous, and other people of color and 75 percent of whom are low income. Time's Up also touted that, in cases where a decision was reached, 90 percent of cases were decided in the victim's favor (Tchen 2020). Moreover, the organization reports providing media assistance to more than 300 cases of workplace sexual harassment and discrimination. While the legal defense fund was relatively straightforward in its goals and deliverables, the two other arms of the organization were more opaque: the Time's Up Foundation, the central 501(c)(3) nonprofit whose main output was research on and programmatic support for workplace leaders (including those in the entertainment industry) for implementing solutions to inequality and harassment; and Time's Up Now, Inc., a 501(c)(4) that makes up the nonpartisan, not-for-profit advocacy and political lobbying aspect of the organization. Financial disclosures and spending reports from the Time's Up Foundation and Time's Up Now have raised eyebrows. It was widely reported that, in its first year, Time's Up raised around $3.7 million, $1.4 million of which went to salaries while only around $312,000 went to the legal defense fund (Vincent and Froelich 2020).

More acute scandals also plagued the organization during its fledgling ascent. It declined to help Tara Reade, the former staffer who accused Joe Biden of sexual assault over a decade earlier, during Biden's 2020 bid for the Democratic presidential nomination, and Time's Up executives continued to financially support Biden's campaign throughout the period of the accusations (Kantor et al. 2021). Dr. Esther Choo, a professor of emergency medicine at Oregon Health and Science University and a cofounder and board member of the health care arm of Time's Up Now, failed to adequately report an allegation of sexual harassment to the proper administrators in March 2021, allegedly telling the victim that reporting sexual harassment was "never worth it. Never." These allegations spawned a mass exodus of board members from the health care initiative as the organization issued public statements supporting Dr. Choo (Keegan 2021). It became increasingly unclear where the organization's priorities were: with the political figures it championed and the powerful people who made up its own ranks, or with the survivors it was charged with supporting.

The organization's suspicious loyalties were further on display during another scandal that highlights the pitfalls of media hypervisibility, fame, wealth, and power for nonprofit organizations. In June 2020, Oprah Winfrey abruptly pulled out of a documentary film project called *On the Record*, for which she was executive producer. The film centers on accusations of sexual assault and harassment against music mogul Russell Simmons, telling the stories of more than twenty women who accused him of misconduct. Even though the allegations against Simmons had been published and extensively vetted by numerous publications in the months prior to the film's release, Winfrey stated she felt the film lacked proper context and cited vague "inconsistencies" in the women's stories. Her withdrawal reportedly came after another Time's Up supporter, Ava DuVernay, excoriated the film at a private screening. Then, despite previous statements of support from Time's Up for the survivors depicted in the film, the organization refused to lend its endorsement ahead of the film's premiere at Sundance, leading to rampant accusations that this decision demonstrated a conflict of interest following the exit of a major donor, Winfrey, from the project. According to the *Hollywood Reporter*, following the film's much-lauded debut at Sundance, "a whisper campaign had begun to scuttle efforts to find a distributor. One A-list actress and Time's Up backer, in town meeting with distributors, continued to malign *On the Record* to top buyers, citing vague problems. None of the major buyers bit" until HBO Max agreed to distribute it (Keegan and Siegel 2020). This story is a murky and disturbing tale that eerily mimics accounts of Harvey Weinstein's efforts to ruin the careers of women who pushed back on his abusive behavior. While Winfrey and those close to her have refused to go on the record to detail the concerns that sparked her withdrawal, it seems likely that her and DuVernay's close ties to Time's Up influenced the organization's decision not to publicly support the project, sparking concern about the undue influence Hollywood power players have over it. Ironically, such scandals demonstrate that Time's Up is complicit in reproducing the very dynamics it was designed to combat.

Then, in August 2021, a bombshell dropped that damaged the organization so severely that Time's Up effectively dissolved. Earlier that year, eleven women came forward to accuse Andrew Cuomo, then governor of New York, of sexual harassment and assault. These allegations precipitated an investigation by the state attorney general, who published the results of that investigation on August 3 (A. L. Clark et al. 2021). Beyond corroborating these women's stories, the report alleged that Roberta Kaplan, a lawyer and Time's Up chair, had advised Cuomo in his administration's attempts to discredit Lindsey Boylan, one of the many women who accused him of sexual misconduct. Kaplan and "the head of Times [sic] Up," presumably then CEO Tina Tchen, approved a letter Cuomo and his advisers had written defending him. The letter "denied the legitimacy of Boylan's allegations, impugned her credibility, and attacked her claims as politically motivated," and Time's Up leaders only made the slight suggestion that Cuomo remove certain details about Boylan's "interactions with male colleagues" (A. L. Clark et al. 2021, 108–109) that would presumably portray her as flirtatious in the workplace. More damning still, the report detailed that other Cuomo advisers balked at the letter and found many allegations unverifiable; Kaplan and (presumably) Tchen were some of the few who had given it the green light.

In response, a group of sexual assault survivors wrote an open letter to the organization, stating that Time's Up "has abandoned the very people it was supposed to champion" (Turkos 2021). Both Kaplan and Tchen resigned, followed by the dismantling of the group's advisory board and the exodus of all celebrity members besides Ashley Judd (Maddaus 2021). A damning internal report, released in November 2021, highlighted the organization's poor management and, in particular, its prioritization of visibility and branding over action (Brown 2021). Following their release of the report, Time's Up announced that it would let all current employees go in order to make way for a "reset"; however, as of June 2022, the organization has made no statements regarding its future. These scandals point to broader issues around power, which survivors receive support, and which abusers' actions are swept under the rug. Over and over, the Time's Up leadership demonstrated a commitment to alleged and confirmed abusers who have power and connections—the very cronyism and insider power plays the organization was ostensibly founded to disrupt. Those issues were magnified by a celebrity-focused commitment to image

over sustained action and, combined with the shaky foundation of mismanagement, Time's Up crumbled under its own weight.

An Organization of Wealthy and Privileged People: Conclusions on TIME'S UP

Following the *Hollywood Reporter*'s publication of the allegations regarding
Time's Up withdrawing support from the film *On the Record*, staffers reportedly went to Tchen with their concerns that the organization was too indebted
to the powerful people who supported it to adequately help survivors (Shugerman 2021). In a response that, in hindsight, almost certainly reveals more of
the rot at the core than she intended, Tchen told them, "We have always been
an organization of wealthy and powerful people. . . . That is what Time's Up
is. That is what distinguishes Time's Up from a lot of organizations. It's why
we got the attention we did. It's why we have the power and influence that we
do." This statement perfectly encapsulates the ambivalence of the organization
and, indeed, of celebrity feminism more broadly. The launch of Time's Up at
the 2018 Golden Globes and the issues that plagued it in the years since center
on power, labor, and visibility. Weinstein's power in Hollywood allowed him
to harass and assault women with impunity for years, harming their mental and
physical well-being along with their careers and silencing them. #MeToo provided survivors in Hollywood and beyond the power to make visible their experiences, engaging in the emotional labor of speaking and listening to one
another; however, the stories of white, powerful women were amplified far more
than those of women of color, the women Tarana Burke intended to uplift years
before the Weinstein allegations. Celebrities joined with established activists,
using the power of their fame to draw attention to Time's Up, but that fame
simultaneously hampered their success.

When it comes to celebrity feminist initiatives like the Golden Globes Blackout and Time's Up, the central questions become: Who does the work? What
kind of work do they choose, and where do their loyalties lie? How do they and
other interlocutors explain that work to the public? And who gets the credit?
Overwhelmingly, the glamour and newsworthiness of celebrities, particularly
white celebrities, inextricably shaped conversations around the Blackout and
Time's Up, earning them individualized accolades even when they endeavored
to uplift established activists and foreground intersectional solidarity. Celebrities' words, their power, and their labor were prioritized, amplified, and lauded
over and above those of the activists whose experience supposedly formed the
foundation of Time's Up.

The work of Time's Up and the ways in which celebrities communicated that
work to audiences demonstrate the struggle between competing logics: celebritized media logics of branding and spectacular individuality versus activist

logics of solidarity and collective action. The power struggle between these competing logics was on display as some celebrities and activists pushed back on the typical red carpet norms. That conflict in and of itself was newsworthy as stars like Michelle Williams and Reese Witherspoon and activists like Rosa Clemente and Tarana Burke disrupted entertainment reporters' by-the-book behavior and wrestled to assert values of solidarity over stardom. However, these stars used the logics of celebrity to amplify that message, arguably hampering it by playing into celebrity norms with their glamour and their red carpet appearances. While this calculated risk potentially allowed their message to filter into mainstream cultural conversations more easily, earning Time's Up attention and donations, it also opened the door for the pull of celebrity discursive norms to exert their pressure, particularly across news and commentary on the event. While celebrities often spoke eloquently and with nuance about intersectional gendered violence when allowed the space to do so in op-eds and interviews, the overall shifts in the coverage of the Golden Globes, when they happened, were short-lived rather than systemic, responding to the particular event but overall not substantially changing. The Blackout represented a moment, not a movement in terms of shifts in coverage. While the goals of Time's Up were systemic, the Blackout was not, and its momentariness, alongside celebrities' failure to continue to promote it heavily in the coming months and years, meant that any changes in coverage and approaches to awards shows and/or the coverage of celebrity activism were momentary as well. This was a temporary disruption that ultimately faded, to be replaced in the press by coverage of scandal after scandal within Time's Up itself.

Between 2018 and 2021, many of the founding celebrities remained figureheads and major donors of Time's Up, serving on the advisory board alongside academics, activists, and attorneys, and women who are leaders in their fields, like Dr. Esther Choo and Roberta Kaplan, spearheaded its various initiatives. However, the scandals that have emerged from within the organization demonstrate that issues of power and privilege extend well beyond Hollywood and raise broader questions about the efficacy of large-scale nonprofits. Major organizations such as Time's Up bring with them money and prestige, and the truly harmful scandals recounted in this chapter point toward an aversion to radically transformative solutions to gender and racial injustice. If the system benefits you, why would you fight for systemic change? As one Time's Up employee told leadership in June 2020, according to notes obtained by the *New York Times*, "We are not close to the women we want to help"; but the heads of the organization are indeed very close to the wealthy and powerful (Kantor et al. 2021). Despite the high-minded rhetoric, the slick marketing, and a few initiatives that have had a marked impact, Time's Up shows the cracks in a foundation that is centered on proximity to power rather than community-specific solutions.

Moreover, the legal defense fund, widely lauded as the one truly positive outcome of Time's Up, continues the trend of viewing gender violence as a problem that must be prosecuted, alongside a concurrent expansion of the justice system in the United States. While well-intentioned, its solutions are punitive, focused on the perpetrator and seeking retribution rather than on the victim. At its foundation, the legal defense fund is built on a mainstream (read: white), legally focused notion of justice that exists in a continuum of punitive strategies. Such strategies are a part of the largely unquestioned ideological norm of how to deal with gendered violence or discrimination, a seemingly obvious answer to the "So what now?" question that emerged following #MeToo. Supporting survivors and cultivating a community around them was not enough; for many, the way to make #MeToo a "movement not a moment" was to seek punitive justice.

The legal defense fund may be a good solution with positive outcomes for some survivors; undoubtedly, many women who wanted to seek legal action but otherwise would not have been able to do so have found support and a sense of justice from it. My goal is not to discount those outcomes. However, it is worth asking how and why the courts are often a universal go-to solution for such issues. Moreover, problems with proximity to power and the pull to support powerful men are not unique to Hollywood or to large nonprofits with well-connected leadership; they are endemic to a culture that supports white supremacist patriarchal hierarchies more broadly. Time's Up, while worthy of sound critique and clearly in need of serious redirection, is not unique, nor do the struggles it faces emerge from nowhere. As with so many aspects of celebrity feminism, Time's Up magnifies and makes hypervisible existing issues within and outside of feminism, and to enact the transformations necessary to adequately agitate for a more just and equitable world, we need to grapple with those issues. The publicness of celebrity can allow for those debates to take place, laying them bare and open to critique. But we must question how much more the wealthy and powerful can do for progressive movements beyond making mistakes the rest of us can (hopefully) learn from.

Conclusion

Celebrity Feminist Futures

As I was writing this book, theorizing and mapping the ways that networked publics negotiate feminist politics by debating the actions of and exerting pressure on celebrities, a distorted version of the topic emerged as a lightning rod at the nexus of entertainment and politics. Digital publics, particularly Black Twitter users, had long used social media platforms to call out racism, misogyny, and other forms of bigotry (for more detail, see Nakamura 2015; M. D. Clark 2020; Brock 2020). But in the wake of public accusations around #MeToo, callouts and other digital accountability practices gained more widespread attention. Many activists and academics praised such practices for providing a platform to those who had often been silenced and lacked access to traditional forms of justice. But others—primarily though not exclusively on the political right—decried the end of due process via the court of public opinion. Throughout 2018 and 2019, social media users continued to call out harmful actions and actors, and by the end of 2019, the controversy around these practices had a name: "cancel culture" (cue dramatic music and panicked screams from the rich and problematic). The concept of "canceling" someone began in the mid-2010s among Black Twitter users as a sarcastic way to indicate the public withdrawal of support or, as Nicole Halliday puts it, "a cultural boycott" (Kurtzleben 2021). However, the term was co-opted and twisted by far right, then mainstream, media and politicians as a way to disparage the "woke mob" of social media users who seek to destroy those who cross them—often the wealthy and powerful. Their arguments centered around "free speech," but their use of that term greatly expanded its meaning from the freedom to speak without risk of governmental retaliation, censorship, or litigation to the freedom to speak and act with impunity. The backlash against the perceived power restructuring that digital accountability practices like those guided by the intersectional imperative wrought is severe and ongoing as those who are on top fear their dominance may be in jeopardy.

However, these concerns are overblown and obscure the negotiative work that networked publics do. Take, for example, Harry Potter author J. K. Rowling, one of the most widely discussed examples of a "canceled" celebrity during this wave of public anxiety. In 2019, Rowling announced her support of an anti-trans businesswoman named Maya Forstater, who had lost her job with the Center for Global Development after posting transphobic tweets. Then, in the summer of 2020, Rowling fully leaned in to anti-trans politics in the name of feminism with a series of Twitter threads and eventually a scorched-earth essay on her website, repeating a host of harmful and discredited arguments. She insisted that acknowledging trans women as women undermined the importance of cis women's experiences of misogyny, a common refrain of trans-exclusionary feminist thought, and discredited and pathologized young people's desire to transition (Rowling 2020).

The backlash against Rowling's articulations of transphobic feminism was swift, with social media users, journalists, commentators, and even the stars of the Harry Potter movies speaking out against her statements and rightfully naming them as transphobic and harmful. Critics of digital accountability practices bemoaned the cancelation of a beloved children's author who spoke out about the importance of "biological" sex, and Rowling was one of the many signatories on the anti–cancel culture *Harper's Bazaar* letter mentioned in the introduction to this book. To be sure, the righteous critique of Rowling, particularly on social media, was loud and newsworthy. But what does it mean to be "canceled," really? The term implies that such public critique results in ostracization and the loss of work opportunities, power, and/or social capital. However, Rowling continues to be wildly successful. The third film installment of her series *Fantastic Beasts and Where to Find Them* was released in 2022 and netted $376 million in box office revenue. The Harry Potter books, films, and theme park remain beloved and profitable. And in 2021, months after the backlash against Rowling began, executives at HBO Max reportedly met to discuss the possibility of a live-action series based on Harry Potter (Goldberg 2021). Rowling joins a host of other "canceled" celebrities whose careers survive and thrive.

I am loath to get down in the muck and engage with arguments around cancel culture as they are overwhelmingly in bad faith, misrepresenting and demonizing the complex types of digital labor and discursive negotiation I discuss in this book. As I describe in chapter 4, based on my analysis of Milo Yiannopoulos and his role in the harassment of Leslie Jones, panics around the increasing visibility of more progressive racial and gender politics and the discursive power of networked publics obscure how intact white cis male authority largely remains, drawing attention away from the flood of regressive policies enacted across the country and toward Twitter. This is not to say that those discursive forces are meaningless; the publicness, the visibility, and the relative ease with which everyday people can point out problematic behaviors and negotiate changing social values have helped to guide substantial sociopolitical shifts in the United States and beyond. However, this backlash raises real questions about the transformative power of digital activism around popular culture and public figures. In the following pages, I will tie the argumentative threads of the book together and explore where they leave us, with insight and suggestions for how to navigate both the promises and the pitfalls of digital popular feminism moving forward.

Transforming and Negotiating Popular Feminism

In this book, I have examined how popular feminism's evolution during the 2010s has been deeply informed by celebrity culture, social media, and the intersections of these two mediated spaces. The preceding chapters have provided an empirical analysis of some processes by which these changes have occurred. *Transformation* happens as ideas, positions, and ways of engaging with feminism *filter* in and out of popular culture. For example, the aversion to identifying with feminism has largely filtered out of mainstream entertainment celebrity culture, and celebrities' alignment with feminism has allowed them to become some of the best-known faces of the movement. The popularity of feminism, the relative ease with which particular definitions of the movement have filtered into celebrity culture, and the conversations networked publics have about it have transformed both the movement and celebrity culture. That transformation speaks to the power of accumulation. Certain ideas and positions gain momentum as they *accumulate* across the popular media landscape, and that momentum can help to restructure dominant expectations. As more celebrities identify as feminists, and increasingly as they highlight the importance of intersectional feminisms, dominant understandings of feminism have shifted. And the infrastructure of social media platforms and the newsworthiness of celebrities can *amplify* particular ideas, positions, and understandings, helping them to loom large in our collective consciousness. However, the amplification that helps to promote the popularity of feminism is often shaped by logics that remain tied to traditional power structures. What gets amplified? Overwhelmingly, less radical feminisms rise to the fore of mainstream media conversations. Who gets amplified? Celebrities, and particularly white celebrities, gain attention over and above other activists or policy makers. And how are those celebrities amplified? The logics that inform news framing and social media discussions about celebrity and feminism often foreground simplified narratives, particularly conflicts, as most newsworthy, hampering the nuances of feminist discussion.

Moreover, these transformations require pressure and *negotiation*. In particular, this book has documented the ideological struggle between two sets of discursive pressures regarding the direction of popular feminism: the white feminist imperative and the intersectional imperative. Those who exert the pressures of the white feminist imperative frame "women" as a universal category, agitating for reform and gender equality in ways that often ignore or outright reject intersecting categories of identity like race or sexuality. The white feminist imperative is a powerful force in shaping dominant conceptions of feminism across the media landscape because it is less subversive of existing hierarchies and thus filters into mainstream discourses with less friction. However, it is increasingly challenged by the pressures of the intersectional imperative, which foregrounds the mutual transformation of, in particular, racism and sexism for women of color. Those who push forward the intersectional imperative often contest simplified notions of gender solidarity and agitate for a more radical restructuring of power hierarchies both within the feminist movement and more broadly. The growing prominence of intersectional pressures, however, risks softening its political edges, turning it into more of a buzzword than a political mandate as white feminists may deploy it as a cover without ceding space and power to women of color. These developments are ongoing, and this analytical framework can help to make sense of both intrafeminist debates and contestations between feminist and misogynistic publics moving forward.

These transformative and negotiative dynamics provide a framework for mapping entanglements of anti-feminist sentiment, postfeminism, white feminism, and intersectional feminism in and around popular culture. Most important, they foreground the ways that popular feminism is in conversation with other feminisms and how those conversations are shaped by digital platforms. Just as the research design of the project highlights the mutually transformative cross-platform flow of discourses, so its central argument highlights the flow of feminist ideas and goals across the permeable boundaries of popular culture and feminisms. More than merely judging particular articulations of popular feminism as right or wrong, these concepts provide a vocabulary for analyzing the broader debates that occur at the intersection of celebrity and feminism (which ideas have filtered in or out, which pressures have shaped an expression of feminist thought, how those ideas build on prior articulations of feminism and accumulate) and for exploring the politics by which media forces— particularly celebrity and social media—amplify and frame various feminisms. Moreover, this framework encourages scholars and other readers to keep in mind the contested continuity of the feminist movement. Rather than framing each new "wave" of activist thought as entirely new and unique, the processes of filtration, accumulation, and amplification can provide a way to speak about the similarities and differences across generations.

While my analyses are grounded in the study of celebrity, these transformative and negotiative processes can provide a foundation for analyzing discourse on social media beyond celebrity culture, particularly that which is related to identity, politics, and social justice. For example, discussions around hashtags like #BlackLivesMatter and #StopAsianHate similarly flow across digital platforms and other mediated spaces, building on the accumulated momentum of prior anti-racist movements both digital and otherwise, using particular incidents to draw attention to systemic oppression and transforming public discourse at the same time as the movements themselves are transformed via those digital conversations. Such negotiations also exert pressure on and work to transform other facets of the media landscape, pressuring news outlets, television, and film for more accurate, diverse, and equitable representation. Moreover, those pressures are interconnected to a wave of progressive politicians, many of them women of color, who are heeding the calls of their constituents and agitating for policies that prioritize the needs of marginalized people. By focusing on the deep connections between social media, popular culture, social justice, and politics, this book encourages a more holistic analysis of the interconnectedness of different cultural spaces, positioning debates over popular culture as part of a much larger matrix of sociopolitical negotiations that are transforming the United States.

Challenging White Feminism

The book also makes more specific contributions to our understanding of celebrity and feminism in the digital age beyond this more broadly applicable framework. Crucially, I demonstrate how a focus on intersectionality has spurred contestations of feminist perspectives that privilege so-called white and establishment feminisms on a wide scale. From the racist, sexist harassment of stars like Leslie Jones to myopic statements from public figures like Patricia Arquette, Gloria Steinem, and Madeleine Albright, networked publics, journalists, and other commentators can use controversies surrounding the rich and famous as a sort of parable. These stories, alongside countless others that grace the pages of celebrity gossip outlets on a daily basis, can lay bare broader issues within Western culture, both within and outside of the feminist movement, particularly regarding the importance of a feminism that prioritizes intersectionality. The contestation around narrative framings of and appropriate responses to these celebrity stories speaks to the role pop culture narratives can play in negotiating norms and values, even as those negotiations are deeply shaped (and often hampered) by the logics of social media platforms and newsworthiness.

Solidarity and Sisterhood

Within these contested challenges to white feminism, the book also maps the renegotiation of the roles of individual choice and solidarity within popular feminism. The role of individuality around celebrity and feminism presents one of the most complex entanglements of feminist and postfeminist logics I discuss. Celebrities, whose fame is predicated on their spectacular individuality, often struggle to balance their roles as icons with the "sisterhood" of feminism, whether through their own statements and actions or through others' preoccupation with their stardom. Individually focused narratives often emerge around celebrities even as they try to push back on that aspect of their fame. Further problematizing claims of solidarity is the prominence of white feminist perspectives that universalize the experiences and goals of white women while sidelining those of women of color (see Kendall 2020). Mainstream media narratives also tend to reinforce images of feminist solidarity as overwhelmingly a space of white, privileged women.

However, more and more celebrities, social media users, and news and commentary outlets are using celebrity stories as a springboard for broader conversations about gender, race, sexuality, and class. Throughout this book, I have demonstrated that incidents of harassment, vulnerability, marginalization, and oppression within celebrity culture often open discussions about how issues like doxxing, hacking, trolling, wage inequality, racism, and sexual harassment and assault can impact the lives of all women, not just the famous. Some of these negotiations not only take place on social media platforms but also target those platforms as objects of critique, mobilizing discussions of the vulnerabilities of platforms and the vulnerabilities of women, particularly Black women, in digital spaces, as networked publics work to "patch" perceived lapses in both platform and ideological security. Ultimately, within these murky blends of feminism and postfeminism, I point to the emergence of a feminist politics of choice that focuses not on individual striving for the sake of one's own success within white capitalist patriarchal structures but rather on intentional, thoughtful individual striving for the good of intersectional feminist collectives. From the young feminist voters who pushed back on white Western imperialism as anti-feminist to the celebrities who banded together to form Time's Up, many popular feminist discourses focused on the individual's responsibility to their feminist sisters, and a responsibility to engage in activism and politics in a way that (at least ostensibly) centers the experiences of women of color.

How Far Can Visibility Take Us?

In her incisive critique of popular feminism, Sarah Banet-Weiser (2018) focuses on what we gain and lose from the spectacular visibility of feminism. While feminism has become "popular" and hypervisible across the media landscape, Banet-Weiser points out that visibility exists in a capitalist context in which some feminisms—and some women who come to embody feminism—become "luminous . . . while others are obscured or eclipsed" (31). Similarly, many themes of this book center on the limits of celebrity feminist visibility, exploring fame as a double-edged sword that cuts success with vulnerability and arguably good intentions with the shortsightedness of privilege. However, while celebrities' visibility can make them the target of harassment or garner them (especially white celebrities) accolades for their activism over and above others, that visibility also invites comments and discussion from a range of feminist voices. Even when celebrities engage in problematic forms of feminism and/or when news and commentary outlets participate in obscuring more radical and intersectional feminisms, the publicness of celebrity and social media opens space for a wide range of individuals with varied perspectives to come together and negotiate their responses. That negotiation, enabled by the visibility of both stars and online discourse, forms the foundation of my arguments regarding the transformative power of popular culture for the feminist movement. This is not to say that all perspectives are equally visible; certainly, in many circles, white liberal feminist ideas remain supreme. However, as more diverse publics, including academics and activists, gather together to contest the limitations and harm of white feminism, popular feminism may transform in a more equitable direction.

However, this raises questions not only about the limits of visibility but also about the limits of the negotiation that visibility affords. How far can the discursive fanfare that bubbles up around celebrity stories get us in terms pushing the feminist movement forward? Ideally, these conversations can provide an educational opportunity, displaying a range of often contentious feminist opinions alongside one another, allowing members of these issue publics to deepen their understanding of feminist complexity if they dig into the controversy. I have seen such an impact firsthand with my students, whose everyday engagements with celebrity culture have provided an approachable way to engage with feminist critique. However, we need to make sure that celebrity feminisms remain in conversation with other feminisms, forming one part of the overall matrix of feminist thought rather than standing in for the whole of the movement. Through those negotiations, celebrity feminism can continue to function as more than a gateway (Hobson 2017).

Navigating a Digital World of Feminist Outrage

The undercurrent of this book, and indeed the underlying force of social movements, is righteous anger. In different ways, each chapter examines frustration and indignation as motivating forces to support victims, to pressure platforms and media outlets to change, and to support candidates and causes that might help make the world a more equitable place. While there has always been a great deal of injustice worthy of ire, that injustice has never been so visible, nor has our ability to speak out against it. So what lessons might we take from the argument this book presents regarding digital negotiations and pressure, and indeed of anger as a motivating force for feminism and other social justice movements? Whether we like it or not, digital platforms have changed and will continue to change how many users experience and engage with conflict, which may inspire moral outrage and politically charged anger. As outlined in chapter 3, prior research has found that our online encounters with content that provokes moral outrage are more frequent, the immediate risk of reacting in anger to that content is lower, and those who "pile on" to the target of that anger may experience backlash out of reactive sympathy. Moreover, these digital conflicts do not occur in a vacuum but are often accompanied by news and commentary regarding the inflammatory incident that summarize and circulate the outrage beyond its origins on social media. News and commentary, in turn, increasingly rely on social media platforms for circulation and often reflect social media logics—inflammatory content receives more engagement, more clicks, and more revenue. From the direst perspective, the confluence of these phenomena creates a perfect storm of toxicity and half-baked malice that threaten the very foundations of a rational deliberative democracy by transforming the public sphere into a dumpster fire. These concerns are valid and of paramount importance both for engaged citizens and for scholars concerned with online toxicity and inequality.

However, as discussed throughout this book, productive anger can be crucial to politics and social activism. It can be motivational, encouraging citizens to join forces and mobilize against oppression and injustice. And even within social justice movements, anger at fellow activists can cause crisis and polarization that can hopefully lead to more equal distributions of power. Anger has been particularly important for the women's movement as women have learned to harness their rage into political action, and women of color have also used anger at their marginalization within feminism to agitate for a more intersectional approach to gender equality. If we are too quick to dismiss the positive potential of anger because of the current sociotechnical environment and media landscape, we risk reproducing the status quo by tone-policing or even silencing important voices in the name of "civility."

Before drawing conclusions regarding anger as a motivating force for digital feminist strategies, I want to return briefly to Mary Holmes's (2004) analysis of intrafeminist "angriness." She argues that angriness is not generalizable as either emancipatory or counterproductive. Each instance must be contextualized and understood on its own terms, and its progressive potential lies in its uptake. She argues that angriness "is likely to be constructive if based on a complex understanding of power relations and a willingness to challenge discursive constructions which might view anger as displaying a lack of care" (224). This means that the conflict that results from anger must be understood not in isolation but as a particular instantiation of broader inequalities. She emphasizes the need to reorient our interpretation of anger. In certain cases, it may stem not from a lack of care but from its abundance—an overwhelming sense of care for those who are marginalized and oppressed. This reorientation toward anger can help us to see that "responsibility, not blame" is key to productive anger, as is "a willingness to redress material inequalities" as its result (224). To borrow language from Chantal Mouffe (2005), the goal should not be to destroy an enemy but rather to work with an adversary toward more respectful relations, which Holmes (2004) explains "is likely to require a sense of process" rather than a singular solution (224).

Within a fraught sociopolitical climate made more complex by the dynamics of digital platforms, how are we to navigate such moments of anger and moral outrage? While there is no one-size-fits-all framework for navigating feminist anger, I propose the following guidelines as a starting point when encountering anger-inducing content or others responding to such content in anger: (1) Recognize that we see more anger-inducing content than people have in the past because of social media platforms. Balance self-care with righteous indignation and carefully consider context when electing to engage. (2) Consider a particular instance of anger within its historical and ideological context. Do not isolate it as a single incident but endeavor to understand it within that broader context. Ask what systems of inequality this incident is a part of rather than immediately taking offense or being dismissive. (3) Accept that anger can be an integral part of the political process. Consider how calls for "civility" often tacitly seek to perpetuate the status quo and silence or disparage marginalized voices, and ask if this may be the case in the given incident. (4) When the anger is between people who are on the same side and who can make a good faith effort to learn and change, seek to agitate for more respectful relations rather than destroy a target. View anger, whether you are angry or someone is angry at you, as an important part of the process while striving for equity and exerting the necessary pressures to push society in a more equitable direction. Ijeoma Oluo sums up this attitude beautifully in her book *So You Want to Talk about Race* (2018). She explains, "You have to get over the fear of facing the worst in yourself. You should instead fear unexamined racism. Fear the thought that right now, you could be contributing to the oppression of others and you don't know it. But do not fear those who bring that oppression to light. Do not fear the opportunity to do better" (224). We must recognize that growing and learning will often be uncomfortable, but we must accept that discomfort as a necessary part of change.

To be clear, these are not suggestions for how to engage with trolls, harassers, or other bad actors; these recommendations are meant to help guide online interactions with those who purport to be on your side but should be held accountable for their actions. However, these strategies are not easy, and they will not always be possible. First, it is clear that these strategies require a great deal of emotional labor and knowledge building. Further, this framework, along with much prior literature on social and political outrage, fundamentally assumes that "good" anger must be productive. But can we find value in other forms of anger that do not necessarily seek to be productive in the same ways? For example, what about the use of anger to let off steam with an inflammatory tweet or comment? On top of all the work marginalized people, particularly people of color, must do to simply exist in the world, let alone agitate for change, is such careful consideration of anger-inducing content fair to ask for? Or do such frameworks risk becoming a more performatively "woke" version of tone-policing? In other words, how can we find and even value ways to scream into the social media void and be unapologetic and unfiltered in our anger? While the answers to these questions are beyond the bounds of this book, scholars should continue to question our assumptions about outrage.

As we look toward the future of the feminist movement, there are no easy solutions to the problems we face. The hypervisibility of white feminism and white feminists relies on a complex apparatus of digital amplification and logics of newsworthiness that will require radical sociopolitical changes to unseat. Moreover, the backlash against progressive social justice movements and politics has only intensified since 2014. Online and off-line, right-wing ideologues challenge feminist and anti-racist movements with harassment, violence, lies, and legislation aimed at reinforcing white supremacist patriarchal dominance. Engaging in the types of negotiations this book discusses and exerting pressure to move the United States in a more equitable direction is arguably as dangerous, frustrating, and important as it has ever been. We must continue to exert those pressures despite, and indeed because of, the challenges facing intersectional feminisms, and work to accumulate enough momentum to generate radical, sustainable change.

Acknowledgments

I am deeply grateful to all the people who helped make this book a reality. First and foremost, I want to thank my mentors from my time in the University of Michigan's Department of Communication and Media. To Robin Means Coleman, whose invaluable instruction in qualitative research methods has been and will continue to be foundational to every project I do, including this one. To Lisa Nakamura, whose Digital Media Theory class was the most intimidating and illuminating course I have ever taken and whose feedback on various chapters of this project has made it so much richer. To Megan Ankerson, whose enthusiasm and support made writing early versions of the book a more joyful process. To Katherine Sender, whose unfailing generosity and mentorship have made me a more thoughtful scholar and instructor. To Susan Douglas, whose expertise in matters of feminist media history and celebrity culture made me want to go to graduate school in the first place, and whose funny, brilliant writing style I aspire to. And finally, to Aswin Punathambekar, who patiently endured more than one of my panicked meltdowns and whose guidance and mentorship during grad school and beyond have meant more than I can say.

I also want to thank the friends, colleagues, and students who have supported me over the years. I am grateful to my mentors at the University of Central Oklahoma, particularly Matt Hollrah and John Springer. Your guidance inspired me to continue my career as a teacher-scholar. I want to thank Stephanie Fillip and Jake Williams for their friendship and for listening to me rattle on ad nauseum about the latest celebrity scandals. I am also grateful to all my students, especially those in my feminist media studies classes, whose humor and insights continually provided me fresh perspectives on my work. To Jimmy Draper and Jamie Moshin for being such supportive friends and collaborators. To Amelia Couture Bue for always being there, and for talking through all the theoretical and methodological quagmires I found myself in while writing this book. And to Annemarie Navar-Gill: every time I read through these chapters, I hear echoes of our myriad conversations about feminism and pop culture over cocktails and coffee. Our time together as cohortmates shaped this book as much as any other force, and I am so grateful for that. Finally to my colleagues at Emmanuel College, whose support and kindness has been a joy.

Prior versions of some chapters have appeared in *Feminist Media Studies* and *Information, Communication, and Society*. I want to sincerely thank the editors and reviewers whose generous and generative feedback transformed not only those articles but also the direction of this book. I also want to extend my sincere gratitude to those who reviewed this manuscript. Your insights have improved the book immensely, and I appreciate the time and energy you devoted to helping make this book a much smarter one (during a pandemic, no less). And, of course, I want to thank all of the wonderful folks at Rutgers University Press, especially Nicole Solano, for their enthusiasm and support throughout this process. Thank you for making this such an exciting and smooth experience.

Last but certainly not least, I want to thank my family. Thank you to my parents, Steve and Marquita Lawson: your unconditional love and support of my goals are the main reasons this book exists. You always encouraged me not only as your daughter but as a writer, and I do not think I would have had the confidence in myself to pursue this if it were not for you. I love you both so much. Finally, thank you, Ben. You are the most supportive partner (and most exacting peer reviewer) I could ever hope for, and you make everything better.

Notes

Introduction

1   This definition combines many of the insights Graeme Turner (2010) shares in "Approaching Celebrity Studies," an excellent introductory text for readers who want to learn more about academic approaches to celebrity.

2   The dataset for this book includes 11,408 tweets, 580 online news and commentary articles, 302 articles from top U.S. newspapers, 161 television/YouTube videos, 240 magazine articles, and 111 miscellaneous objects (such as radio broadcasts or Facebook or Instagram posts that were highly circulated around an incident).

Chapter 1   Hacking Celebrity

1   Bryan Hamade was not the leader of the nude photo hacking ring and was never formally charged. In May 2016, a thirty-six-year-old Pennsylvania man named Ryan Collins pled guilty to federal hacking charges and admitted to engaging in a two-year-long phishing scam to gain access to the celebrities' photos (Yuhas 2016). Collins was sentenced to eighteen months in federal prison. Four other men (Edward Majerczyk, Emilio Herrera, George Garofano, and Christopher Brannan) have also been charged with various crimes related to the hack (Weiner 2018).

Chapter 2   Staging Feminism

1   The dataset analyzed in this chapter includes 1,500 randomly sampled tweets that mention Patricia Arquette on the day of and two days after her acceptance speech; 2,500 randomly sampled tweets, including #AskHerMore, as well as the 300 most retweeted tweets using the hashtag; 168 online news and commentary articles; 31 legacy news articles; 37 celebrity, fashion, and women's magazine articles; and 38 YouTube clips, which include snippets of network and cable news programs reporting on the events.

2   The questions in this section are drawn from a random sample of 2,500 tweets tagged #AskHerMore, as well as the 300 most retweeted tweets with the hashtag

between February 20 and 23, 2015. To preserve the anonymity of these users, I have not included their handles.

3 Authenticity is incredibly difficult if not impossible to determine on celebrities' social media accounts. However, Arquette's tweets demonstrate some of the hallmarks of authenticity described by Marwick and boyd (2011), namely, some grammatical and punctuation errors. Overall, what is key to this argument is that her comments give the appearance of authenticity, whether or not others (such as managers or PR professionals) had input into her statement.

Chapter 3   Nasty Women, Silly Girls

1 The dataset for this chapter consists of the 590 most retweeted tweets that mentioned Steinem or Albright in the three days following their comments; 45 articles from legacy news outlets; 111 news and commentary pieces from top online sources; 33 articles from top U.S. magazines; and 15 clips from cable and broadcast news programs

2 This change is not noted in the article, but the original title is still viewable through the Internet Archive: https://web.archive.org/web/20160207220355 /http://www.nytimes.com/2016/02/08/us/politics/gloria-steinem-madeleine -albright-hillary-clinton-bernie-sanders.html?_r=0.

3 To preserve anonymity, I have omitted Twitter handles here and throughout.

4 After Clinton won the Democratic nomination, Sarandon voted for Jill Stein in the 2016 presidential election. She has faced a great deal of criticism for her white privilege and overall shortsightedness following the election for implying that Hillary Clinton would have been at least as "dangerous" a president as Donald Trump (Brockes 2017).

Chapter 4   Platform Vulnerabilities

1 In total, the dataset consists of 2,864 media objects. It includes 2,500 tweets containing the terms "Leslie Jones," "@lesdoggg" (Jones's Twitter handle), and "#StandWithLeslie" on August 24 and 25, the day of and following the hack of her personal website. These tweets include a random sample of 2,100 tweets as well as the 400 most retweeted tweets. The rest of the data was drawn from other media objects that were linked on Twitter, as well as searches of the top American newspapers (165 articles), articles from top and Black-owned online news and commentary sites (119 articles), magazine articles (43), and television/YouTube clips (37 videos).

Chapter 5   TIME'S UP

1 Official statements from the organization typically stylize TIME'S UP with all caps; however, for a more natural reading experience, I will use title case through-out the book.

2 The dataset for this chapter consists of 33 newspaper articles, 63 magazine articles, 34 articles from online news and commentary outlets, and approximately 4.5 hours of red carpet coverage. The articles were categorized by their main topic (evaluation, fashion, activism, recap, critique, social media, justification for

Blackout) and then theoretically sampled from 243 total articles in order to make the dataset manageable. I also collected and coded 208 social media posts from celebrities publicizing the Blackout on Instagram and Twitter. An in-depth analysis of those posts does not appear in this chapter, but insights from that analysis informed my conclusions.

References

ABC News Analysis Desk. 2016. "New Hampshire Primary Exit Poll Analysis: How Trump and Sanders Won." ABC News. https://abcnews.go.com/PollingUnit /voted-live-hampshire-primary-exit-poll-analysis/story?id=36805930.

Access. 2018a. "Reese Witherspoon Brought to Tears over Daughter Ava's Instagram Post before 2018 Golden Globes." https://www.youtube.com/watch?v= _ajlcBj1SwU.

———. 2018b. "Salma Hayek & Ashley Judd Talk Raising "A Beacon of Hope" with Time's Up Movement | Access." https://www.youtube.com/watch?v =uwk8jbI9zrA.

———. 2018c. "Susan Sarandon & Rosa Clemente on Raising Awareness for Puerto Rico at the Golden Globes | Access." https://www.youtube.com/watch?v =7DdSSjp4Z8k.

Ahmed, Sara. 2004. *The Cultural Politics of Emotion.* New York: Routledge.

Albright, Madeleine. 2016. "Madeleine Albright: My Undiplomatic Moment." *New York Times,* February 12. https://www.nytimes.com/2016/02/13/opinion /madeleine-albright-my-undiplomatic-moment.html.

The Alex Jones Channel. 2016. "Milo on Why He Was Banned from Twitter." https://www.youtube.com/watch?v=P2BqHT0211Q.

Alter, Charlotte. 2015. "Reese Witherspoon Slams Sexist Red Carpet Questions." *Time,* February 22. https://time.com/3718008/oscars-2015-askhermore-reese -witherspoon/.

Amit, Reut. 2014. "That Type of Girl Deserves It." Gawker, September 27. https:// www.gawker.com/that-type-of-girl-deserves-it-1639772694.

Arquette, Patricia. 2015a. "Guess Which Women Are the Most Negatively . . ." Twitter. February 23. https://twitter.com/PattyArquette/status /569940008708276224.

———. 2015b. "Patricia Arquette: What Happened after My Oscar Speech on Pay Inequality (Guest Column)." *Hollywood Reporter,* December 9. https://www .hollywoodreporter.com/tv/tv-news/patricia-arquette-what-happened-my-845822/.

Baer, Hester. 2016. "Redoing Feminism: Digital Activism, Body Politics, and Neoliberalism." *Feminist Media Studies* 16 (1): 17–34. https://doi.org/10.1080 /14680777.2015.1093070.

Bailey, Moya. 2021. *Misogynoir Transformed: Black Women's Digital Resistance*. New York: NYU Press.

Bajwa, Novpreet. 2015. "The Problems with UN's New Campaign He for She: The UN's Campaign May Reinforce the Very Inequality . . ." *Legendary Women* (blog), January 19. https://medium.com/legendary-women/the-problems-with-uns-new-campaign-he -for-she-the-uns-campaign-may-reinforce-the-very-inequality-e5c4ebe83432.

Banet-Weiser, Sarah. 2012. *Authentic^{TM}: The Politics of Ambivalence in a Brand Culture*. New York: NYU Press.

———. 2015. "Popular Misogyny: A Zeitgeist." Culture Digitally (blog). January 21. http://culturedigitally.org/2015/01/popular-misogyny-a-zeitgeist/.

———. 2018. *Empowered: Popular Feminism and Popular Misogyny*. Durham, NC: Duke University Press.

Banet-Weiser, Sarah, and Kate M. Miltner. 2016. "#MasculinitySoFragile: Culture, Structure, and Networked Misogyny." *Feminist Media Studies* 16 (1): 171–174.

Banet-Weiser, Sarah, and Laura Portwood-Stacer. 2017. "The Traffic in Feminism: An Introduction to the Commentary and Criticism on Popular Feminism." *Feminist Media Studies* 17 (5): 884–888.

Barnes, Brooks. 2017. "Harvey Weinstein Is the (Whispered) Talk of Hollywood." *New York Times*, October 8. https://www.nytimes.com/2017/10/08/business /media/harvey-weinstein-harassment-hollywood.html.

Barrow, Jo. 2014. "Ricky Gervais Just Said Celebrities Shouldn't Keep Naked Photos If They Don't Want to Get Hacked." BuzzFeed News, September 1. https://www .buzzfeednews.com/article/jobarrow/ricky-gervais-shocker.

Baumeister, Roy F., Liqing Zhang, and Kathleen D. Vohs. 2004. "Gossip as Cultural Learning." *Review of General Psychology* 8 (2): 111–121. https://doi.org/10.1037/1089 -2680.8.2.111.

Baumgardner, Jennifer, and Amy Richards. 2000. *Manifesta: Young Women, Feminism, and the Future*. New York: Farrar, Straus and Giroux.

BBC Newsnight. 2016. "'I Don't Vote with My Vagina': Susan Sarandon on Not Backing Hillary Clinton—BBC Newsnight." https://www.youtube.com/watch?v =4LoGej6BqMc.

Beck, Debra Baker. 1998. "The 'F' Word: How the Media Frame Feminism." *National Women's Studies Association Journal* 10 (1): 139–153.

Bedhead. 2014. "Jennifer Lawrence and Other Celebs Targeted in Alleged Photo Leak." *Celebitchy* (blog), September 1. https://www.celebitchy.com/384550/jennifer _lawrence_other_celebs_targeted_in_alleged_photo_leak_nf/.

———. 2016. "Chris Martin Is 'Very Supportive' over Jennifer Lawrence's Stolen Photos." *Celebitchy* (blog), March 10. https://www.celebitchy.com/384550/jennifer _lawrence_other_celebs_targeted_in_alleged_photo_leak_nf/.

Bender, Kelly. 2015. "Oscars 2015: Reese Witherspoon Wants Red Carpet Reporters to #AskHerMore." *People*. https://people.com/awards/oscars-2015-reese-witherspoon -wants-red-carpet-reporters-to-askhermore/.

Benjamin, Ruha. 2019. *Race after Technology: Abolitionist Tools for the New Jim Code*. Medford, MA: Polity Press.

Beres, Damon. 2016. "Twitter's Defense of 'Ghostbusters' Star Isn't Good Enough." HuffPost, July 20. https://www.huffpost.com/entry/twitter-leslie-jones-milo -yiannopoulos_n_578f78fee4b0f180da63b014.

Berman, Judy. 2013. "'I'm a White Girl': Why 'Girls' Won't Ever Overcome Its Racial Problem." *The Atlantic*, January 22. https://www.theatlantic.com/entertainment

/archive/2013/01/im-a-white-girl-why-girls-wont-ever-overcome-its-racial-problem /267345/.

Bernstein, Michael S., Andrés Monroy-Hernández, Drew Harry, Paul André, Katrina Panovich, and Gregory G. Vargas. 2011. "4chan and/b: An Analysis of Anonymity and Ephemerality in a Large Online Community." In *International Conference on Web and Social Media,* 50–57. http://www.aaai.org/ocs/index/ICWSM /ICWSM11/%20paper/viewFile/2873/4398.

Biddle, Sam. 2014a. "How Nude-Trading Predators Are Exploiting Whisper Right Now." Gawker, October 6. https://www.gawker.com/how-nude-trading-predators -are-exploiting-whisper-right-1643079536.

———. 2014b. "Which Celebrity Nudes Are Leaking Next?" Gawker, September 22. https://www.gawker.com/which-celebrity-nudes-are-leaking-next-1637818385.

———. 2015. "Feds Seized Chicago Man's Computers in Celeb Nude Leak Investigation." *Gawker,* June 9. https://www.gawker.com/feds-seized-chicago-mans -computers-in-celeb-nude-leak-i-1709153721.

———. 2016. "Feds Raided Another Chicago Home in Nude Celeb Hack Investigation, Still No Charges Pressed." Gawker, January 15. https://www.gawker.com/feds -raided-another-chicago-home-in-nude-celeb-hack-inv-1753200305.

Bird, S. Elizabeth. 1992. *For Enquiring Minds: A Cultural Study of Supermarket Tabloids.* Knoxville: University of Tennessee Press.

Blodgett, Bridget, and Anastasia Salter. 2018. "Ghostbusters Is for Boys: Understanding Geek Masculinity's Role in the Alt-Right." *Communication Culture & Critique* 11 (1): 133–146.

Bonilla, Yarimar, and Jonathan Rosa. 2015. "#Ferguson: Digital Protest, Hashtag Ethnography, and the Racial Politics of Social Media in the United States." *American Ethnologist* 42: 4–17. http://onlinelibrary.wiley.com.proxy.lib.umich.edu /doi/10.1111/amet.12112/full.

Boot, William. 2014. "Exclusive: Sony Hack Reveals Jennifer Lawrence Is Paid Less Than Her Male Co-stars." *The Daily Beast,* December 12. https://www .thedailybeast.com/articles/2014/12/12/exclusive-sony-hack-reveals-jennifer -lawrence-is-paid-less-than-her-male-co-stars.

Brady, Anita. 2016. "Taking Time between G-String Changes to Educate Ourselves: Sinéad O'Connor, Miley Cyrus, and Celebrity Feminism." *Feminist Media Studies* 16 (3): 429–444.

Brady, William J., and M. J. Crockett. 2019. "How Effective Is Online Outrage?" *Trends in Cognitive Sciences* 23 (2): 79–80. https://doi.org/10.1016/j.tics.2018.11.004.

Braithwaite, Andrea. 2016. "It's about Ethics in Games Journalism? Gamergaters and Geek Masculinity." *Social Media + Society* 2 (4). https://doi:10.1177 /2056305116672484.

Brock, André, Jr. 2020. *Distributed Blackness: African American Cybercultures.* New York: NYU Press.

Brockes, Emma. 2017. "Susan Sarandon: 'I Thought Hillary Was Very Dangerous. If She'd Won, We'd Be at War.'" *The Guardian,* November 26. https://www .theguardian.com/film/2017/nov/26/susan-sarandon-i-thought-hillary-was-very -dangerous-if-shed-won-wed-be-at-war.

Broomfield, Matt. 2017. "2 Charts Which Show Just How Huge the Women's Marches against Trump Were." *Independent,* January 23. https://www.independent .co.uk/news/world/americas/womens-march-anti-donald-trump-womens-rights -largest-protest-demonstration-us-history-political-scientists-a7541081.html.

Brown, Leilani. 2021. "Phase 1 Report for TIME'S UP." TIME'S UP Foundation. November 19. https://timesupfoundation.org/leilani-brown-phase-1-report-for-times-up/.

Bruni, Frank. 2018. "At the Golden Globes, Hollywood Does What Washington Won't."*New York Times*, January 8. https://www.nytimes.com/2018/01/08/opinion/golden-globes-washington-women.html.

Bryant, Kenzie. 2018. "Golden Globes 2018: #MeToo, Time's Up, and the E! Red Carpet." *Vanity Fair Blogs* (blog), January 7. https://www.vanityfair.com/style/2018/01/golden-globes-2018-e-red-carpet-giuliana-rancic-ryan-seacrest.

Buckley, Cara. 2015. "On the Red Carpet, a Revolt Builds over the Pageantry." *New York Times*, February 4. https://www.nytimes.com/2015/02/05/movies/awardsseason/on-the-red-carpet-a-revolt-builds-over-the-pageantry.html.

———. 2018. "Powerful Hollywood Women Unveil Anti-harassment Action Plan." *New York Times*, January 1. https://www.nytimes.com/2018/01/01/movies/times-up-hollywood-women-sexual-harassment.html.

Burdick, John. 1990. "Gossip and Secrecy: Women's Articulation of Domestic Conflict in Three Religions of Urban Brazil." *Sociology of Religion* 51 (2): 153–170. https://doi.org/10.2307/3710812.

Burgess, Jean, and Ariadna Matamoros-Fernández. 2016. "Mapping Sociocultural Controversies across Digital Media Platforms: One Week Of #Gamergate on Twitter, YouTube, and Tumblr." *Communication Research and Practice* 2 (1): 79–96.

Cassese, Erin, Tiffany Barnes, and Reginal Branton. 2015. "What Patricia Arquette Got Wrong at the Oscars." *Washington Post*, February 25. https://www.washingtonpost.com/news/monkey-cage/wp/2015/02/25/what-patricia-arquette-got-wrong-at-the-oscars/.

Castells, Manuel. 2012. *Networks of Outrage and Hope: Social Movements in the Internet Age*. Malden, MA: Polity Press.

Cauterucci, Christina. 2016. "Getting the Women's March on Washington on the Road." *Slate*, November 23. https://slate.com/human-interest/2016/11/the-womens-march-on-washington-faces-uncertain-logistics-on-inauguration-weekend.html.

Celebitchy. 2014. "Cele|bitchy | Apple on the Hack: 'Our Systems Weren't Breached, This Was a Targeted Attack.'" *Celebitchy* (blog), September 8. https://www.celebitchy.com/384940/apple_on_the_hack_our_systems_werent_breached_this_was_a_targeted_attack/.

Charuza, Nikita. 2018. "These Showstopping Dresses from the Golden Globes Will Make You Stand Up and Cheer." POPSUGAR Fashion, January 9. https://www.popsugar.com/node/44470329.

Chemaly, Soraya. 2019. *Rage Becomes Her: The Power of Women's Anger*. Repr. ed. New York: Atria Books.

Clark, Anne L., Yannick Grant, Joon H. Kim, Jennifer Kennedy Park, Abena Mainoo, and Rahul Mukhi. 2021. "Report of Investigation into Allegations of Sexual Harassment by Governor Andrew M. Cuomo." https://ag.ny.gov/sites/default/files/2021.08.03_nyag_-_investigative_report.pdf.

Clark, Meredith D. 2020. "DRAG THEM: A Brief Etymology of So-Called 'Cancel Culture.'" *Communication and the Public*, October. https://doi.org/10.1177/2057047320961562.

Clinton, Hillary (@HillaryClinton). 2016. "@Lesdoggg, no one deserves . . ." Twitter, August 25. https://twitter.com/hillaryclinton/status/768910514688815105.

CNNMoney. 2016. *Milo Yiannopoulos Defends His Offensive Tweets*. July 27. https://www.cnn.com/videos/cnnmoney/2016/07/27/milo-yiannopoulos-twitter-leslie-jones-cnnmoney.cnn.

Cobb, Shelley. 2018. "The Geena Davis Problem: The Postfeminist Politics of Celebrity Gender-Equality Activists in Film and Television." Paper presented at the Society for Cinema and Media Studies Annual Conference, Toronto, ON, March 16.

Cochrane, Kira. 2013. "The Fourth Wave of Feminism: Meet the Rebel Women." *The Guardian*, December 10. https://www.theguardian.com/world/2013/dec/10/fourth-wave-feminism-rebel-women.

Cocks, Heather, and Jessica Morgan. 2015. "#askhermore Is Great, but It's ALSO Okay to Ask/Say Who You're Wearing. You Got It for Free. It's a Transaction. Tip Your Server. -H #Oscars." Twitter, February 22. https://twitter.com/fuggirls/status/569662448917094401.

Coleman, Gabriella. 2014. *Hacker, Hoaxer, Whistleblower, Spy: The Many Faces of Anonymous*. New York: Verso Books.

Collins, Gail. 2016. "Hillary, Bernie and History: A Commentary." *New York Times*, February 11. 31.

Collins, Patricia Hill. 1989. "The Social Construction of Invisibility: Black Women's Poverty in Social Problems Discourse." *Perspectives on Social Problems* 1:77–93.

Combahee River Collective. 1982. "A Black Feminist Statement." https://we.riseup.net/assets/43875/versions/1/combahee%25250river.pdf.

Conaboy, Kelly. 2014. "Ten Celebrity Photos I Wish Hackers Would Leak." Gawker, September 5. https://www.gawker.com/ten-celebrity-photos-i-wish-hackers-would-leak-1630549016.

Conlon, Scarlett. 2015. "Patricia Explains Her Speech." *Vogue UK*. http://www.vogue.co.uk/article/patricia-arquette-outlines-gender-pay-gap-oscar-speech.

Cooper, Brittney. 2015a. "Black America's Hidden Tax: Why This Feminist of Color Is Going on Strike." Salon, February 25. https://www.salon.com/2015/02/25/black_americas_hidden_tax_why_this_feminist_of_color_is_going_on_strike/.

———. 2015b. "@GregAlexander8 You Assume . . ." Twitter, February 23. https://twitter.com/ProfessorCrunk/status/569869217983537152.

———. 2015c. "Looking 4 ALL the White Feminist . . ." Twitter, February 23. https://twitter.com/ProfessorCrunk/status/569859649836584962.

———. 2015d. "Want Thoughts about Patricia . . ." Tweet. @ProfessorCrunk (blog), February 23. https://twitter.com/ProfessorCrunk/status/569868890802663424.

———. 2015e. "Wonder Why WOC Give Feminist . . ." Twitter, February 23. https://twitter.com/ProfessorCrunk/status/569868471456174080.

———. 2018. *Eloquent Rage: A Black Feminist Discovers Her Superpower*. New York: St. Martin's Press.

Cosgrave, Bronwyn. 2006. *Made for Each Other: Fashion and the Academy Awards*. New York: Bloomsbury USA.

———. 2015. "Why There Won't Be a Red Carpet Rebellion." CNN, February 21. https://www.cnn.com/2015/02/21/opinion/cosgrave-red-carpet-fashions/index.html.

Cote, Amanda C. 2020. *Gaming Sexism: Gender and Identity in the Era of Casual Video Games*. New York: NYU Press.

Crenshaw, Kimberlé. 1991. "Mapping the Margins: Intersectionality, Identity Politics, and Violence against Women of Color." *Stanford Law Review* 43: 1241–1299.

Crocker, Lizzie. 2015. "Why Are Feminists Attacking Patricia Arquette?" *The Daily Beast*, February 23. https://www.thedailybeast.com/articles/2015/02/23/why-are-feminists-attacking-patricia-arquette.

Crockett, M. J. 2017. "Moral Outrage in the Digital Age." *Nature Human Behaviour* 1 (11): 769–771. https://doi.org/10.1038/s41562-017-0213-3.

Cush, Andy. 2014. "Horny Redditors Donate Thousands to Cancer Research in J-Law's Honor." Gawker, September 2. https://www.gawker.com/horny-redditors-donate-thousands-to-cancer-research-in-1629516635.

"Dan Aykroyd Comments on Leslie Jones." 2016. *ET Canada* (blog). https://etcanada.com/video/728102467972/dan-aykroyd-comments-on-leslie-jones/.

Daniels, Jessie. 2009. *Cyber Racism: White Supremacy Online and the New Attack on Civil Rights*. Lanham, MD: Rowman & Littlefield.

———. 2015. "Interview with Mikki Kendall about White Women, Feminism and Race." *Racism Review: Scholarship and Activism toward Racial Justice*. June 1. http://www.racismreview.com/blog/2015/06/01/interview-with-mikki-kendall-about-white-women-feminism-and-race/.

———. 2013. "Race and Racism in Internet Studies: A Review and Critique." *New Media and Society* 15 (5): 695–719. https://doi.org/10.1177/1461444812462849.

daralaine. 2015. "#AskHerMore Starring Heather Morris." https://www.youtube.com/watch?v=WZ74D-lYuQI.

Davis, Rachaell. 2016. "Creator of #BlackMenSupportLeslie Hashtag Encourages Black Men to Rally behind Black Women." *Essence* (blog). August 28. https://www.essence.com/news/blackmensupportleslie-hashtag-creator-speaks/.

DePillis, Lydia. 2015. "Patricia Arquette Gets It: The Real Gender Wage Gap Is for Moms." *Washington Post*, February 23. https://www.washingtonpost.com/news/wonk/wp/2015/02/23/patricia-arquette-gets-it-the-real-gender-wage-gap-is-for-moms/.

Diaz, Evelyn. 2016. "Amazing: Black Men Prove They Have Leslie Jones's Back on Twitter." BET, August 29. https://www.bet.com/celebrities/news/2016/08/29/black-men-support-leslie-jones.html?cid=facebook.

Donahue, Rosemary. 2017. "Shailene Woodley Is a Feminist Now, But Seems Confused About What That Means." *Allure*, August 22. https://www.allure.com/story/shailene-woodley-confused-feminist.

Douglas, Susan Jeanne. 1995. *Where the Girls Are: Growing Up Female with the Mass Media*. New York: Three Rivers Press.

Drudge Report. 2016. "'GHOSTBUSTERS' Actress Site Hacked; Nude Photos Posted . . . Http://Bit.Ly/2bGfirP." Twitter, August 24. https://twitter.com/DRUDGE_REPORT/status/768487220332290048.

Dunham, Lena. 2016a. "Lena Dunham: How Leslie Jones Triumphed over Internet Trolls." *Variety* (blog), September 27. https://variety.com/2016/tv/news/lena-dunham-leslie-jones-racism-sexism-internet-trolls-snl-1201870102/.

———. 2016b. "Let's Turn Our Anger . . ." Twitter. Accessed June 18, 2018. https://twitter.com/lenadunham/status/768559977518727168.

Dyer, Richard. 1986. *Heavenly Bodies: Film Stars and Society*. New York: St. Martin's Press.

E! Red Carpet & Award Shows. 2018. "Michelle Williams Talks "#MeToo" at 2018 Golden Globes." https://www.youtube.com/watch?v=C-0-D17zx78.

Emerson, Sarah. 2016. "Here's Twitter's Response to the Racist Harassment of Leslie Jones." Motherboard. July 19. https://motherboard.vice.com/en_us/article/pgkz37/heres-twitters-response-to-the-racist-harassment-of-leslie-jones.

Erevelles, Nirmala, and Andrea Minear. 2010. "Unspeakable Offenses: Untangling Race and Disability in Discourses of Intersectionality." *Journal of Literary & Cultural Disability Studies* 4 (2): 127–46.

Farrow, Ronan. 2017. "From Aggressive Overtures to Sexual Assault: Harvey Weinstein's Accusers Tell Their Stories." *New Yorker*, October 10. https://www.newyorker.com/news/news-desk/from-aggressive-overtures-to-sexual-assault-harvey-weinsteins-accusers-tell-their-stories.

Fasanella, Kaleigh. 2018. "The Best Getting-Ready Selfies from the 2018 Golden Globes." *Allure*, January 7. https://www.allure.com/gallery/golden-globes-selfies-celebrities-getting-ready.

Feig, Paul. 2016. "Leslie Jones is one . . ." July 18. Twitter. https://twitter.com/paulfeig/status/755169545501876225.

Feigenbaum, Paige. 2015. "Patricia Arquette Explains 'Surprising' Oscars Speech Backlash | Access Online." *Access*. https://www.accessonline.com/articles/patricia-arquette-explains-surprising-oscars-speech-backlash-158121.

Filipovic, Jill. 2014. "Emma Watson Named Feminist Celebrity of the Year." *Cosmopolitan*, December 19. https://www.cosmopolitan.com/entertainment/news/a34421/ms-foundation-feminist-celebrity-2014/.

"Fiorina Slams Hillary's 'Desperate Appeal' to Women." 2016. *On the Record with Greta Van Susteren*. Fox News, February 8.

Foster, Kimberly. 2016. "White Feminists Need to Get in Formation for Leslie Jones." Shine, August 31. http://shine.forharriet.com/2016/08/white-feminists-need-to-get-in.html.

Foucault Welles, Brooke, and Sarah Jackson. 2019. "The Battle for #Baltimore: Networked Counterpublics and the Contested Framing of Urban Unrest." *International Journal of Communication* 13: 1699–1719.

"The 14th Academy Awards Memorable Moments." 2014. August 27. https://www.oscars.org/oscars/ceremonies/1942/memorable-moments.

Frey, Kaitlyn. 2018. "Connie Britton Defends $380 'Poverty Is Sexist' Golden Globes Sweater after Twitter Backlash." *People*, January 10. https://people.com/style/connie-britton-defends-globes-sweater/.

Friedan, Betty. 2010. *The Feminine Mystique*. New York: W. W. Norton.

Friedman, Ann. 2016. "Stop Pitting Women against Each Other over Hillary Clinton." The Cut, February 9. https://www.thecut.com/2016/02/lets-stop-the-feminist-war-over-hillary-clinton.html.

Gamson, Joshua. 1994. *Claims to Fame: Celebrity in Contemporary America*. Berkeley: University of California Press.

———. 2001. "Jessica Hahn, Media Whore: Sex Scandals and Female Publicity." *Critical Studies in Media Communication* 18 (2): 157–173.

Garber, Megan. 2018. "2018: The Golden Globes' Year of (Literal) Fashion Statements." *The Atlantic*, January 8. https://www.theatlantic.com/entertainment/archive/2018/01/the-best-golden-globes-looks/549917/.

Garcia, Sandra E. 2017. "The Woman Who Created #MeToo Long before Hashtags." *New York Times*, October 20. https://www.nytimes.com/2017/10/20/us/me-too-movement-tarana-burke.html.

Garelick, Rhonda. 2018. "The Red-Carpet Funeral That Wasn't." The Cut, January 8. https://www.thecut.com/2018/01/golden-globes-2018-wear-black-red-carpet.html.

Gay, Roxane. 2014a. "Beyoncé's Control of Her Own Image Belies the Bell Hooks 'Slave' Critique." *The Guardian*, May 12. https://www.theguardian.com /commentisfree/2014/may/12/beyonce-bell-hooks-slave-terrrorist.

———. 2014b. "Emma Watson? Jennifer Lawrence? These Aren't the Feminists You're Looking For." *The Guardian*, October 10. https://www.theguardian.com /commentisfree/2014/oct/10/-sp-jennifer-lawrence-emma-watson-feminists -celebrity.

——— (@rgay). 2016. February 7. "I am tired but man . . ." Twitter, February 7. https://twitter.com/rgay/status/696397830647189504.

Gibson, Caitlin. 2016. "Katy Perry Tweets Support for Leslie Jones—and Now Everyone Is Googling 'Misogynoir.'" *Washington Post*, August 25. https://www .washingtonpost.com/news/arts-and-entertainment/wp/2016/08/25/katy-perry-tweeted -support-for-leslie-jones-and-introduced-misogynoir-to-white-mainstream-america /?utm_term=.009b7bf7bd5a.

Gill, Rosalind. 2007. *Gender and the Media*. Malden, MA: Polity Press.

———. 2009. "Mediated Intimacy and Postfeminism: A Discourse Analytic Examination of Sex and Relationships Advice in a Women's Magazine." *Discourse and Communication* 3 (4): 345–369.

———. 2016. "Post-postfeminism? New Feminist Visibilities in Postfeminist Times." *Feminist Media Studies* 16 (4): 610–630.

Gillespie, Tarleton. 2010. "The Politics of 'Platforms.'" *New Media and Society* 12 (3): 347–364. https://doi.org/10.1177/1461444809342738.

———. 2018. *Custodians of the Internet: Platforms, Content Moderation, and the Hidden Decisions That Shape Social Media*. New Haven, CT: Yale University Press.

GlobalGrindTV. 2015. "The Retweet: What We (and Patricia Arquette) Missed at the Oscars—INTERSECTIONALITY." https://www.youtube.com/watch?v =Y5bxDjkYdac.

Gluckman, Max. 1963. "Papers in Honor of Melville J. Herskovits: Gossip and Scandal." *Current Anthropology* 4 (3): 307–316. https://doi.org/10.1086/200378.

Goldberg, Lesley. 2021. "'Harry Potter' Live-Action TV Series in Early Development at HBO Max (Exclusive)." *Hollywood Reporter* (blog), January 25. https://www .hollywoodreporter.com/tv/tv-news/harry-potter-live-action-tv-series-in-early -development-at-hbo-max-exclusive-4121063/.

Goldstein, Jessica M. 2015. "Take the Money and Walk: Why Women Shouldn't Abandon the Red Carpet." *ThinkProgress* (blog), February 6. https://archive .thinkprogress.org/take-the-money-and-walk-why-women-shouldnt-abandon-the -red-carpet-ec4ad7eb714c/.

Gonzales, Erica. 2018. "Women Open Up about Wearing Black on the Golden Globes Red Carpet." *Harper's Bazaar*, January 8. https://www.harpersbazaar.com /celebrity/red-carpet-dresses/a14773793/celebrities-wearing-black-golden-globes -quotes-2018/.

Goodwin, Michael. 2016. "Hill's Bully Mammoths." *New York Post*, February 10, 11.

Grady, Constance. 2016. "Watch Leslie Jones Fire Back at the Trolls Who Hacked Her Twitter Account." Vox, September 18. https://www.vox.com/2016/9/18/12964740 /emmys-2016-leslie-jones-trolls-twitter-accounting.

Graefer, Anne. 2014. "White Stars and Orange Celebrities: The Affective Production of Whiteness in Humorous Celebrity-Gossip Blogs." *Celebrity Studies* 5 (1–2): 107–122. https://doi.org/10.1080/19392397.2013.798913.

Gray, Jonathan. 2019. "How Do I Dislike Thee? Let Me Count the Ways." In *Anti-fandom: Dislike and Hate in the Digital Age*, edited by Melissa A. Click, 25–41. New York: NYU Press.

Greenfield, Cathy, and Peter Williams. 1991. "The Uses of Gossip: Women's Writing, Soaps and Everyday Exchange." *Hecate* 17 (1): 124.

Grey, Sarah. 2016. "An Open Letter to Gloria Steinem on Intersectional Feminism." Medium, December 23. https://medium.com/the-establishment/an-open-letter-to -gloria-steinem-on-intersectional-feminism-f245248967fa.

Habermas, Jürgen. 2015. *The Structural Transformation of the Public Sphere: An Inquiry into a Category of Bourgeois Society*. Hoboken: John Wiley.

Hardy, Condé. 2018. "Every Celebrity Protesting Sexual Assault on the Golden Globes Carpet." *Teen Vogue*, January 8. https://www.teenvogue.com/gallery/golden-globes -2018-black-dress-sexual-assault-protest.

Harris-Perry, Melissa. 2015. "Arquette's Comments Launch Feminist Debate." https://www.msnbc.com/melissa-harris-perry/watch/arquettes-comments-launch -feminist-debate-405907011736.

Heil, Emily. 2018. "Hollywood Women Launch Anti-harassment Campaign Aimed at Helping Blue-Collar Workers, Too." *Washington Post*, January 2. https://www .washingtonpost.com/news/reliable-source/wp/2018/01/02/hollywood-women -launch-anti-harassment-campaign-aimed-at-helping-blue-collar-workers-too/.

Henry, Astrid. 2004. *Not My Mother's Sister: Generational Conflict and Third-Wave Feminism*. Bloomington: Indiana University Press.

Hermes, Joke. 1995. *Reading Women's Magazines: An Analysis of Everyday Media Use*. Cambridge: Polity.

Hess, Amanda. 2014a. "'Don't Take Nude Selfies,' Shrug It Off, and Other Gross Advice for Hacked Celebs." *Slate*, September 2. https://slate.com/human-interest /2014/09/jennifer-lawrence-and-other-celebrity-hacking-victims-should-not-have -to-play-it-cool.html.

———. 2014b. "Inside AnonIB, Where Hacking Is a Sport and Women's Bodies Are the Prize." *Slate*, September 3. https://slate.com/human-interest/2014/09/anonib -nude-photo-site-where-hackers-and-users-treat-women-as-property.html.

Hilton, Perez. 2014a. "Jennifer Lawrence & Kate Upton's Major Celeb Nude Leak Gets the FBI AND Apple Working to Solve the Case!" *Perez Hilton* (blog). http://perezhilton.com/2014-09-02-jennifer-lawrence-kirsten-dunst-nude-leak-fbi -investigating-apple-problem.

———. 2014b. "Jennifer Lawrence & Us." *Perez Hilton* (blog). http://perezhilton.com /2014-09-01-jennifer-lawrence-perez-hilton-nude-photos-scandal

———. 2014c. "Jennifer Lawrence Talks Perez in *Vanity Fair*—And Here's His Response!" *Perez Hilton* (blog). http://perezhilton.com/2014-10-20-jennifer -lawrence-talks-perez-in-vanity-fair-and-heres-his-response.

———. 2014d. "MORE Jennifer Lawrence Nude Pics Leak Too! When Will This End?!" *Perez Hilton* (blog). http://perezhilton.com/2014-09-21-jennifer - lawrence-nude-photos-released.

———. 2014e. "Protect Yourself from a Nude Photo Hack! Here's How!" *Perez Hilton* (blog). http://perezhilton.com/2014-09-22-how-to-protect-yourself-from-a-nude -photo-hack-email-hack.

———. 2014f. "Rihanna's Full Frontal & Big Booty Are Spread All over the Internet!" *Perez Hilton* (blog). http://perezhilton.com/2014-09-21-rihanna-nude-photos -leaked-hacked.

————. 2015. "'Fappening' Update: Investigators Believe the Nudes Leak Is Bigger Than Initially Reported & They Know Where the Hack Originated!" *Perez Hilton* (blog). http://perezhilton.com/2015-06-10-nude-leaks-fbi-investigators-fappening-icloud.

Hine, Gabriel Emile, Jeremiah Onaolapo, Emiliano De Cristofaro, Nicolas Kourtellis, Ilias Leontiadis, Riginos Samaras, Gianluca Stringhini, and Jeremy Blackburn. 2017. "Kek, Cucks, and God Emperor Trump: A Measurement Study of 4chan's Politically Incorrect Forum and Its Effects on the Web." In *International Conference on Web and Social Media,* 92–101. https://www.aaai.org/ocs/index.php/ICWSM/ICWSM17/paper/viewFile/15670/14790.

Hobson, Janell. 2017. "Celebrity Feminism: More Than a Gateway." *Signs: Journal of Women in Culture and Society* 42 (4): 999–1007. https://doi.org/10.1086/690922.

Hoby, Hermione. 2014. "Taylor Swift: 'Sexy? Not on My Radar.'" *The Guardian,* August 23. https://www.theguardian.com/music/2014/aug/23/taylor-swift-shake-it-off.

Hocking, Bree. 2015. "It's Not about the Dress?" *US News & World Report,* February 25. //www.usnews.com/opinion/blogs/opinion-blog/2015/02/24/askhermore-misses-the-mark-at-the-academy-awards.

Hodgson, Claire. 2015. "Reese Witherspoon Promotes #AskHerMore on the Oscars Red Carpet." *Cosmopolitan,* February 23. http://www.cosmopolitan.co.uk/entertainment/news/a33679/reese-witherspoon-askhermore-oscars/.

Hogue, Ilyse. 2016. "If u think . . ." Twitter. August 24. https://twitter.com/ilyseh/status/768552911097954305

Holmes, Mary. 2004. "Feeling beyond Rules: Politicizing the Sociology of Emotion and Anger in Feminist Politics." *European Journal of Social Theory* 7 (2): 209–227. https://doi.org/10.1177/1368431004041752.

Honan, Mat. 2015. "It's Just a Matter of Time before Everyone Sees Your Nude Pics." *Slate,* February 18. https://slate.com/technology/2015/02/nudes-online-cloud-software-enables-hackers-to-access-racy-photos.html.

hooks, bell. 2014. *Ain't I a Woman: Black Women and Feminism.* 2nd ed. New York: Routledge.

Hope, Clover. 2015. "The Nightly Show's Panel of Black Women Responds to Patricia Arquette." Jezebel, February 27. https://jezebel.com/the-nightly-shows-panel-of-black-women-responds-to-patr-1688421291.

Horton, Donald, and R. Richard Wohl. 1956. "Mass Communication and Para-social Interaction: Observations on Intimacy at a Distance." *Psychiatry* 19 (3): 215–229.

Hutchby, Ian. 2001. "Technologies, Texts and Affordances." *Sociology* 35 (2): 441–456.

Iqbal, Nosheen. 2015. "Patricia Arquette: 'There's a Lot of Pressure on Actresses to Look Strange and Unrealistic.'" *The Guardian,* February 2. https://www.theguardian.com/film/2015/feb/02/patricia-arquette-boyhood-feminism-ageing.

Jackson, Sarah J., Moya Bailey, Genie Lauren, and Brooke Foucault Welles. 2020. *#HashtagActivism: Networks of Race and Gender Justice.* Cambridge, MA: MIT Press.

Jenkins, Henry. 2008. *Convergence Culture: Where Old and New Media Collide.* Rev. ed. New York: NYU Press.

Jerslev, Anne. 2014. "Talking about Angelina: Celebrity Gossip on the Internet." *Northern Lights: Film & Media Studies Yearbook* 12 (1): 105–122. https://doi.org/info:doi/10.1386/nl.12.1.105_1.

Jones, Leslie. 2016. "If u think . . ." Twitter. July 18. https://twitter.com/lesdoggg/status/755140563184259072.

Jusino, Teresa. 2016. "The Cissexism No One's Talking About in Gloria Steinem's Bill Maher Interview." February 8. https://www.themarysue.com/gloria-steinem-bill -maher-cissexism/.

Juzwiak, Rich. 2014. "You'll Never Get to See Judge Judy's Nudes Since She Destroyed Them." Gawker, September 8. https://www.gawker.com/youll-never-get-to-see -judge-judys-nudes-since-she-dest-1632201320.

Kai, Maiysha. 2016. "More Than Microaggression: The Danger of White Oblivious- ness." The Root, July 21. https://www.theroot.com/more-than-microaggression-the -danger-of-white-obliviou-1790856111.

Kaiser. 2014. "Cele|bitchy | Kim Kardashian's Leaked/Hacked Nude Photos Were Posted on 4chan, Reddit." Celebitchy (blog), September 21. https://www.celebitchy .com/388313/kim_kardashians_leakedhacked_photos_were_posted_on_4chan _reddit_too/.

Kantor, Jodi, Arya Sundaram, Melena Ryzik, and Cara Buckley. 2021. "Turmoil Was Brewing at Time's Up Long before Cuomo." New York Times, August 21. https:// www.nytimes.com/2021/08/21/us/times-up-metoo-sexual-harassment.html.

Kantor, Jodi, and Megan Twohey. 2017. "Harvey Weinstein Paid Off Sexual Harass- ment Accusers for Decades." New York Times, October 5. https://www.nytimes .com/2017/10/05/us/harvey-weinstein-harassment-allegations.html.

Kashner, Sam. 2014. "Cover Exclusive: Jennifer Lawrence Calls Photo Hacking a 'Sex Crime.'" Vanity Fair, October 7. https://www.vanityfair.com/hollywood/2014/10 /jennifer-lawrence-cover.

Keegan, Rebecca. 2021. "Time's Up Healthcare Controversy Sparks Mutiny, Mass Resignations." Hollywood Reporter (blog), March 11. https://www .hollywoodreporter.com/business/business-news/times-up-healthcare-controversy -4147447/.

Keegan, Rebecca, and Tatiana Siegel. 2020. "When Time's Up Didn't Step Up." Hollywood Reporter (blog), June 5. https://www.hollywoodreporter.com/business /business-news/time-s-up-didnt-step-up-1296938/.

Kendall, Mikki. 2020. Hood Feminism: Notes from the Women That a Movement Forgot. New York: Viking.

Kim, Mimi E. 2018. "From Carceral Feminism to Transformative Justice: Women-of- Color Feminism and Alternatives to Incarceration." Journal of Ethnic and Cultural Diversity in Social Work 27 (3): 219–233. https://doi.org/10.1080/15313204.2018.1474827.

———. 2020. "Anti-carceral Feminism: The Contradictions of Progress and the Possibilities of Counter-hegemonic Struggle." Affilia 35 (3): 309–326. https://doi .org/10.1177/0886109919878276.

Knuttila, Lee. 2011. "User Unknown: 4chan, Anonymity and Contingency." First Monday 16 (10). http://firstmonday.org/ojs/index.php/fm/article/viewArticle /3665.

Koerner, Allison. 2016. "22 Celebs Who Stand with Leslie Jones in the Face of That Horrific Twitter Abuse." Bustle, July 19. https://www.bustle.com/articles/173558-22 -celebs-who-stand-with-leslie-jones-in-the-face-of-that-horrific-twitter-abuse.

Kurtzleben, Danielle. 2021. "When Republicans Attack 'Cancel Culture,' What Does It Mean?" NPR, February 10. https://www.npr.org/2021/02/10/965815679/is -cancel-culture-the-future-of-the-gop.

Kwateng-Clark, Danielle. 2016. "Black Men Just Unified to Show Love for Leslie Jones." HelloBeautiful (blog), August 27. https://hellobeautiful.com/2896805/leslie -jones-love/.

Lange, Ariane. 2018. "Activists Who Attended the Golden Globes Say Women in Hollywood 'Are Trying to Learn from Us.'" BuzzFeed News, January 9. https://www.buzzfeednews.com/article/arianelange/activists-golden-globes-times-up.

Lanius, Candice. 2019. "Torment Porn or Feminist Witch Hunt: Apprehensions about the #MeToo Movement on /r/AskReddit." *Journal of Communication Inquiry* 43 (4): 415–436. https://doi.org/10.1177/0196859919865250.

Lapowsky, Issie. 2016. "The Good People of the Internet Love Leslie Jones." *Wired* (blog), August 24. https://www.wired.com/2016/08/good-people-internet-love-leslie-jones/.

Lawson, Caitlin E., and Jimmy Draper. 2021. "Working the Red Carpet: A Framework for Analysing Celebrities' Red Carpet Labour." *Celebrity Studies* 12 (4): 635–648. https://doi.org/10.1080/19392397.2020.1750969.

Lazare, Sarah. 2016. "Dear Madeleine Albright and Gloria Steinem: Feminism Demands We Reject America's Deadly Imperialism." Salon, February 10. https://www.salon.com/2016/02/10/dear_madeline_albright_and_gloria_steinem_feminism_demands_we_reject_americas_deadly_imperialism_partner/.

"Leslie Jones on Her Twitter Trolls." 2016. *Late Night with Seth Meyers*. NBC. https://www.youtube.com/watch?v=5KxhU_yZLG8.

"A Letter on Justice and Open Debate." 2020. *Harper's*, July 7. https://harpers.org/a-letter-on-justice-and-open-debate/.

Levy, Emanuel. 2002. *All about Oscar: The History and Politics of the Academy Awards*. London: Continuum.

Lewis, Dave. 2017. "11 of the Most Political Moments in Oscar History." *Los Angeles Times*, February 24. https://www.latimes.com/entertainment/movies/la-et-mn-controversial-oscar-moments-20170226-story.html.

Lilburn, Sandra, Susan Magarey, and Susan Sheridan. 2000. "Celebrity Feminism as Synthesis: Germaine Greer, *The Female Eunuch* and the Australian Print Media." *Continuum* 14 (3): 335–348. https://doi.org/10.1080/713657725.

Linabary, Jasmine R., Danielle J. Corple, and Cheryl Cooky. 2020. "Feminist Activism in Digital Space: Postfeminist Contradictions in #WhyIStayed." *New Media and Society* 22 (10): 1827–1848. https://doi.org/10.1177/1461444819884635.

Lind, Dara. 2016. "Bernie Bros, Explained." Vox, February 4. https://www.vox.com/2016/2/4/10918710/berniebro-bernie-bro.

Lockett, Dee. 2015. "Patricia Arquette's Badass, Feminist Oscars Speech." Vulture, February 22. https://www.vulture.com/2015/02/patricia-arquette-supporting-actress-oscar-speech.html.

Lorde, Audre. 1997. "The Uses of Anger." *Women's Studies Quarterly* 25 (1/2): 278–285.

Loza, Susana. 2014. "Hashtag Feminism, #SolidarityIsForWhiteWomen, and the Other #FemFuture." *Ada: A Journal of Gender, New Media, and Technology*, no. 5. http://adanewmedia.org/2014/07/issue5-loza/?utm_source=rss&utm_medium=rss&utm_campaign=issue5-loza.

Lutz, Helma, Maria Teresa Herrera Vivar, and Linda Supik. 2011. *Framing Intersectionality: Debates on a Multi-faceted Concept in Gender Studies*. Farnham: Ashgate.

Mack, Ashley Noel, and Bryan J. McCann. 2019. "Recalling Persky: White Rage and Intimate Publicity after Brock Turner." *Journal of Communication Inquiry* 43 (4): 372–393. https://doi.org/10.1177/0196859919867265.

Macmillan, Hayley. 2018. "These Are the Celebrities Who Wore Black at the Golden Globes." *Allure*, January 8. https://www.allure.com/gallery/celebrities-wearing-black-golden-globes-2018-red-carpet.

Maddaus, Gene. 2021. "Time's Up Dissolves Advisory Board That Included Natalie Portman, Jessica Chastain and Reese Witherspoon." *Variety* (blog), September 10. https://variety.com/2021/film/news/times-up-advisory-board-natalie-portman-jessica-chastain-reese-witherspoon-1235060159/.

Malone, Noreen. 2017. "The Woman Targeted by Gamergate on Surviving a World-Altering Trolling Attack." Intelligencer, July 26. https://nymag.com/intelligencer/2017/07/zoe-quinn-surviving-gamergate.html.

Marcotte, Amanda. 2016. "Dowd, Steinem Take the Bait: Sexist 'Catfight' Narrative around the Clinton Campaign Takes Hold in Latest Case of Nasty Gender Politics." Salon, February 9. https://www.salon.com/2016/02/08/dowd_steinem_take_the_bait_sexist_catfight_narrative_around_the_clinton_campaign_takes_hold_in_latest_case_of_nasty_gender_politics/.

Marshall, P. David. 1997. *Celebrity and Power: Fame in Contemporary Culture.* Minneapolis: University of Minnesota Press.

Marwick, Alice E. 2021. "Morally Motivated Networked Harassment as Normative Reinforcement." *Social Media + Society* 7 (2). https://doi.org/10.1177/20563051211021378.

Marwick, Alice E., and Robyn Caplan. 2018. "Drinking Male Tears: Language, the Manosphere, and Networked Harassment." *Feminist Media Studies* 18 (4): 543–559. https://doi.org/10.1080/14680777.2018.1450568.

Marwick, Alice, and danah boyd. 2011. "To See and Be Seen: Celebrity Practice on Twitter." *Convergence* 17 (2): 139–58. https://doi.org/10.1177/1354856510394539.

Maschka, Kristin. 2015. "Gloria Feldt on Women, Pay Equity and Patricia Arquette." HuffPost, March 4. https://www.huffpost.com/entry/gloria-feldt-on-women-pay-equity-and-patricia-arquette_b_6792942.

Mashable. 2015. "@PattyArquette Can Have Another Award for That Speech.Pic .Twitter.Com/BqgJCzKgx6." Tweet. @mashable (blog), February 22. https://twitter.com/mashable/status/569697071621672960.

Massanari, Adrienne. 2017. "#Gamergate and the Fappening: How Reddit's Algorithm, Governance, and Culture Support Toxic Technocultures." *New Media and Society* 19 (3): 329–346. https://doi.org/10.1177/1461444815608807.

Massey, Rebecca. 2016. "The Pressures of Feminism from Heroines Like Gloria Steinem." HuffPost, February 11. https://www.huffpost.com/entry/the-pressures-of-feminism_b_9212200.

Matamoros-Fernandez, Ariadna. 2016. "Platformed Racism: The Mediation and Circulation of an Australian Race-Based Controversy on Twitter, Facebook and YouTube." http://eprints.qut.edu.au/101370/.

McCosker, Anthony. 2015. "Social Media Activism at the Margins: Managing Visibility, Voice and Vitality Affects." *Social Media+ Society* 1 (2): 2056305115605860.

McCosker, Anthony, and Amelia Johns. 2013. "Productive Provocations: Vitriolic Media, Spaces of Protest and Agonistic Outrage in the 2011 England Riots." *Fibreculture Journal*, no. 22 (January): 171–193.

McDonnell, Andrea. 2014. *Reading Celebrity Gossip Magazines.* Malden: Polity.

McDonough, Katie. 2015. "'Fight for Us Now': What Patricia Arquette Got Right (and Wrong) about Equal Pay." Salon, February 23. https://www.salon.com/2015/02/23/fight_for_us_now_what_patricia_arquette_got_right_and_wrong_about_equal_pay/.

McGowan, Rose. 2017. "Ladies of Hollywood . . ." Twitter. October 6. https://twitter.com/rosemcgowan/status/916481735835054081.

McGregor, Jena. 2015. "When Shareholders Want to Talk about Pay Equality, But Companies Don't." *Washington Post*, March 3. https://www.washingtonpost.com /news/on-leadership/wp/2015/03/03/when-shareholders-want-to-talk-about-pay -equality-but-companies-dont/.

McIntosh, Whitney. 2016. "Fans Showered Leslie Jones from 'Ghostbusters' with Love Today." Uproxx, July 18. https://uproxx.com/movies/leslie-jones-love-abuse-twitter -fans/.

McKeown, Janet K. L. 2015. "The Hens Are Clucking: Women Performing Gossip in Their Leisure Lives." *Leisure Sciences* 37 (5): 447–457. https://doi.org/10.1080 /01490400.2015.1037472.

McKinney, Kelsey. 2015. "Why Women like Patricia Arquette Continue to White-wash Feminism." Vox, February 23. https://www.vox.com/2015/2/23/8091449 /oscars-patricia-arquette-feminism.

McNamara, Kim. 2011. "The Paparazzi Industry and New Media: The Evolving Production and Consumption of Celebrity News and Gossip Websites." *International Journal of Cultural Studies* 14 (5): 515–530. https://doi.org/10.1177 /1367877910394567.

McRobbie, Angela. 2009. *The Aftermath of Feminism: Gender, Culture and Social Change*. London: Sage.

Mendes, Kaitlynn. 2011. *Feminism in the News: Representations of the Women's Movement Since the 1960s*. New York: Springer.

Mendes, Kaitlynn, Jessica Ringrose, and Jessalynn Keller. 2018. "#MeToo and the Promise and Pitfalls of Challenging Rape Culture through Digital Feminist Activism." *European Journal of Women's Studies* 25 (2): 236–246. https://doi.org/10 .1177/1350506818765318.

———. 2019. *Digital Feminist Activism: Girls and Women Fight Back against Rape Culture*. Oxford: Oxford University Press.

Merry, Sally. 1984. "Rethinking Gossip and Scandal." In *Toward a General Theory of Social Control*, edited by Donald Black. New York: Academic Press.

Meyer, Robinson. 2015. "Here Comes the Berniebro." *The Atlantic*, October 17. https://www.theatlantic.com/politics/archive/2015/10/here-comes-the-berniebro -bernie-sanders/411070/.

Milano, Alyssa. 2017. "If You've Been Sexually Harassed . . ." Twitter. October 15. https://twitter.com/Alyssa_Milano/status/919659438700670976.

Moore, Booth. 2017. "Golden Globes Fashion Preview: A Run on Black Gowns in Hollywood." *Hollywood Reporter* (blog), December 21. https://www.hollywood reporter.com/news/general-news/golden-globes-fashion-preview-a-run-black -gowns-hollywood-1069848/.

Morath, Eric. 2015. "Behind Arquette's Oscar Speech: Hollywood's Pay Gap Looks a Lot Like Ours." *Wall Street Journal*, February 23. https://www.wsj.com/articles /BL-REB-30926.

Mouffe, Chantal. 2005. *On the Political*. New York: Routledge.

Munro, Ealasaid. 2013. "Feminism: A Fourth Wave?" *Political Insight* 4 (2): 22–25. https://doi.org/10.1111/2041-9066.12021.

Nakamura, Lisa. 2013. *Cybertypes: Race, Ethnicity, and Identity on the Internet*. New York: Routledge.

———. 2015. "The Unwanted Labour of Social Media: Women of Colour Call Out Culture as Venture Community Management." *New Formations* 86 (86): 106–112. https://doi.org/10.3898/NEWF.86.06.2015.

Nakashima Brock, Rita. 2016. "A Place in Hell or Hell on Earth?" HuffPost, February 10. https://www.huffpost.com/entry/a-place-in-hell-or-hell-on_b_9202214.

Nast, Condé. 2017. "Shailene Woodley Is a Feminist Now, but Seems Confused about What That Means." *Allure*, August 22. https://www.allure.com/story/shailene-woodley-confused-feminist.

NBC Newsnight. 2016. "New Hampshire Primary 2016: Election Results—NBC News." https://www.nbcnews.com/politics/2016-election/primaries/NH.

Nguyen, Tina. 2015. "Patricia Arquette Loses Feminist Goodwill with Comments Backstage at Oscars." *Mediaite* (blog), February 23. https://www.mediaite.com/online/patricia-arquette-loses-feminist-goodwill-with-comments-backstage-at-oscars/.

Noble, Safiya Umoja. 2018. *Algorithms of Oppression: How Search Engines Reinforce Racism*. New York: NYU Press.

"No Jokes: Jay Pharoah Defends Leslie Jones against Hackers and Online Harassment." 2016. *Bossip* (blog), August 29. https://bossip.com/1348512/no-jokes-jay-pharoah-defends-leslie-jones-against-hackers-and-online-harassment-43081/.

Ohlheiser, Abby. 2017. "Rose McGowan Blocked from Twitter after Tweeting about Harvey Weinstein and Ben Affleck." *Washington Post*, October 12. https://www.washingtonpost.com/news/the-intersect/wp/2017/10/12/rose-mcgowan-blocked-from-twitter-after-tweeting-about-harvey-weinstein-and-ben-affleck/.

Oluo, Ijeoma. 2016. "Leslie Jones' Twitter Abuse Is a Deliberate Campaign of Hate." *The Guardian*, July 19. https://www.theguardian.com/commentisfree/2016/jul/19/leslie-jones-twitter-abuse-deliberate-campaign-hate.

———. 2018. *So You Want to Talk about Race*. New York: Seal Press.

Oremus, Will. 2014. "How to Not Back Up Your Naked Selfies to the Cloud." *Slate*, September 2. https://slate.com/technology/2014/09/jennifer-lawrence-nude-photos-hack-how-to-turn-off-icloud-backup-for-your-photos.html.

"Oscars 2015: Reese Witherspoon Wants Red Carpet Reporters to #AskHerMore." n.d. *People*. https://people.com/awards/oscars-2015-reese-witherspoon-wants-red-carpet-reporters-to-askhermore/.

Page, Allison, and Jacquelyn Arcy. 2019. "#MeToo and the Politics of Collective Healing: Emotional Connection as Contestation." *Communication, Culture and Critique*, November 18. https://doi.org/10.1093/ccc/tcz032.

Pain, Paromita. 2021. "'It Took Me Quite a Long Time to Develop a Voice': Examining Feminist Digital Activism in the Indian #MeToo Movement." *New Media and Society* 23 (11): 3139–3155. https://doi.org/10.1177/1461444820944846.

Panzar, Javier. 2015. "Patricia Arquette Puts a Spotlight on How California's New Equal-Pay Law Will Affect Hollywood." *Los Angeles Times*, December 30. https://www.latimes.com/politics/la-pol-ca-patricia-arquette-equal-pay-bill-california-20151230-story.html.

Papacharissi, Zizi. 2014. *Affective Publics: Sentiment, Technology, and Politics*. Oxford: Oxford University Press.

Park, Andrea. 2017. "More Than 12M 'Me Too' Facebook Posts, Comments, Reactions in 24 Hours." https://www.cbsnews.com/news/metoo-more-than-12-million-facebook-posts-comments-reactions-24-hours/.

Parker, Kathleen. 2016. "Sorry Gloria, We've Moved On." *Washington Post*, February 10, 23.

Paul, Kari, and Jim Waterson. 2019. "Facebook Bans Alex Jones, Milo Yiannopoulos and Other Far-Right Figures." *The Guardian*, May 2. https://www.theguardian.com/technology/2019/may/02/facebook-ban-alex-jones-milo-yiannopoulos.

People Staff. 2015. "Giuliana Rancic-Zendaya Controversy: Part of Joke Was Edited Out, Source Says." *People*. https://people.com/celebrity/giuliana-rancic-zendaya -controversy-part-of-joke-was-edited-out-source-says/.

Perry, Katy. 2016. "Do not give you . . ." Twitter. August 24. https://twitter.com /katyperry/status/768540189043986432.

Petersen, Anne Helen. 2009. "Smut Goes Corporate: TMZ and the Conglomerate, Convergent Face of Celebrity Gossip." *Television & New Media* 11 (1): 62–81. http://journals.sagepub.com/doi/10.1177/1527476409338196.

———. 2010. "Celebrity Juice, Not from Concentrate: Perez Hilton, Gossip Blogs, and the New Star Production." *Jump Cut*. https://www.semanticscholar.org/paper /Celebrity-juice-%2C-not-from-concentrate-%3A-Perez-%2C-%2C-Petersen/293115 5b485a5219b3e015311c305b94e61dbe30.

———. 2014. "Those Jennifer Lawrence Pictures Aren't Scandalous." BuzzFeed News, September 1. https://www.buzzfeednews.com/article/annehelenpetersen/not-a -scandal.

Petrarca, Emilia. 2018. "Why We Won't Be Ranking Golden Globes Fashion." The Cut, January 3. https://www.thecut.com/2018/01/golden-globes-red-carpet-fashion -ranking.html.

Phillips, Abby. 2018. "At the Golden Globes, Celebrities Wanted to Talk Equal Pay. But Congress Has Been Mostly Silent for More than 50 Years." *Washington Post*, January 8. https://www.washingtonpost.com/news/the-fix/wp/2018/01/08/at-the -golden-globes-celebrities-wanted-to-talk-equal-pay-but-congress-has-been-mostly -silent-for-more-than-50-years/.

Phillips, Kami. 2018. "Girl Power Pieces to Rock in Support of the TIME'S UP Movement." *People*, January 8. https://people.com/style/fashion-that-gives-back-to -feminist-womens-groups/.

Phillips, Whitney. 2015. *This Is Why We Can't Have Nice Things: Mapping the Relationship between Online Trolling and Mainstream Culture*. Cambridge, MA: MIT Press.

———. 2019. "It Wasn't Just the Trolls: Early Internet Culture, 'Fun,' and the Fires of Exclusionary Laughter." *Social Media + Society* 5 (3). https://doi.org/10.1177 /2056305119849493.

Pinson, Laurel. 2018. "Amber Tamblyn, Uzo Aduba, and Tessa Thompson on Wearing Black at the Golden Globes." *Glamour*, January 6. https://www.glamour.com/story /amber-tamblyn-uzo-aduba-and-tessa-thompson-on-times-up-and-why-wearing -black-at-the-golden-globes-matters.

Portlock, Sarah. 2015. "Gender Wage Gap in Eight Charts." *Wall Street Journal*, April 14. https://www.wsj.com/articles/BL-REB-31898.

Puente, Maria. 2015a. "Kaley Cuoco-Sweeting Apologizes for Saying She's Not a Feminist." *USA Today*, January 2. https://www.usatoday.com/story/life/tv/2015/01 /02/kaley-cuoco-sweeting-apologizes-for-feminism-comment/21200379/.

———. 2015b. "Patricia Arquette Chided over Backstage Oscar Remarks." *USA Today*, February 24. https://www.usatoday.com/story/life/movies/2015/02/24/patricia -arquette-chided-on-backstage-oscar-remarks/23937935/.

Questlove. 2016. "these acts against . . ." Twitter. https://twitter.com/questlove/status /768505647457562624.

Rabideau, Camryn. 2018. "Golden Globes 2018: Actresses Bring Activist Guests." *InStyle*, January 7. https://www.instyle.com/news/actresses-bringing-activist -guests-golden-globes.

Rachael the Lord. 2016. "How (White) Feminism Failed Gabby Douglas, Leslie Jones, Normani Kordei & Many Other Black Women." *Medium* (blog), December 29. https://medium.com/@LordRach/how-white-feminism-failed-gabby-douglas -leslie-jones-normani-kordei-many-other-black-women-c2825f07cf3f.

Rancic, Giuliana. 2015. "Dear @Zendaya, I'm Sorry I Offended You and Others. . . ." Tweet. @GiulianaRancic (blog), February 23.

Rappeport, Alan. 2016. "Gloria Steinem and Madeleine Albright Rebuke Young Women Backing Bernie Sanders." *New York Times*, February 7. https://www .nytimes.com/2016/02/08/us/politics/gloria-steinem-madeleine-albright-hillary -clinton-bernie-sanders.html.

Ratajkowski, Emily. 2016. "Here is my entire speech for Bernie Sanders #feelthebern." Facebook video, February 8. https://www.facebook.com/Officialemilyratajkowski /videos/846785232099639/.

The Representation Project. 2014. "#AskHerMore: How the Media Talks to Women on the Red Carpet." https://www.youtube.com/watch?v=0EKc3q2h1Hs.

Rich, Adrienne. 1980. "Compulsory Heterosexuality and Lesbian Existence." *Signs: Journal of Women in Culture and Society* 5 (4): 631–660.

Risam, Roopika. 2015. "Toxic Femininity 4.0." *First Monday, Volume 20, Number 4*, April. https://digitalcommons.salemstate.edu/english_facpub/2.

Robehmed, Natalie. 2018. "With $20 Million Raised, Time's Up Seeks 'Equity and Safety' in the Workplace." *Forbes*, February 6. https://www.forbes.com/sites /natalierobehmed/2018/02/06/with-20-million-raised-times-up-seeks-equity-and -safety-in-the-workplace/.

Romano, Aja. 2016. "The Leslie Jones Hack Is the Flashpoint of the Alt-Right's Escalating Culture War." Vox, August 26. https://www.vox.com/2016/8/26 /12653474/leslie-jones-hack-alt-right-culture-war.

Rose, Gillian. 2007. *Visual Methodologies: An Introduction to the Interpretation of Visual Materials*. Sage.

Rose, Rebecca. 2015. "Patricia Arquette: 'I Blame Myself for Stupid Wording' after Oscar Comments Backlash." *Cosmopolitan*, December 10. https://www.cosmopolitan .com/entertainment/news/a50595/patricia-arquette-clarifies-oscar-speech/.

Rowling, J. K. 2020. "J. K. Rowling Writes about Her Reasons for Speaking Out on Sex and Gender Issues." *J. K. Rowling* (blog), June 10. https://www.jkrowling.com /opinions/j-k-rowling-writes-about-her-for-speaking-out-on-sex-and -gender-issues/.

Ruffo, Jillian. 2018. "Every Red Power Lip at the 2018 Golden Globe Awards." *People*, January 8. https://people.com/style/red-lipstick-at-the-golden-globes-2018/.

Ryan, Patrick. 2015. "#AskHerMore Calls Out Sexist Carpet Q's." *USA Today*, February 22. https://www.usatoday.com/story/life/awardcentral/2015/02/22/celebs -sexist-red-carpet-questions-ask-her-more-campaign/23854953/.

Ryzik, Melena. 2016. "Patricia Arquette Says She Lost Work over Speech at Oscars." *New York Times*, April 20. https://www.nytimes.com/2016/04/21/movies/patricia -arquette-says-she-lost-work-over-speech-at-oscars.html.

Salter, Michael. 2013. "Justice and Revenge in Online Counter-publics: Emerging Responses to Sexual Violence in the Age of Social Media." *Crime, Media, Culture* 9 (3): 225–242. https://doi.org/10.1177/1741659013493918.

Sandler, Monica Roxanne. 2015. "PR and Politics at Hollywood's Biggest Night: The Academy Awards and Unionization (1929–1939)." *Media Industries Journal* 2 (2). https://doi.org/10.3998/mij.15031809.0002.201.

Saturday Night Live. 2016. "Mr. Robot—SNL." https://www.youtube.com/watch?v
=pz-mCjHA6Ak.

Sawaoka, Takuya, and Benoît Monin. 2018. "The Paradox of Viral Outrage." *Psychological Science* 29 (10): 1665–1678. https://doi.org/10.1177/0956797618780658.

Sayers, Janet Grace, and Deborah Jones. 2014. "Fifty Shades of Outrage: Women's
Collective Online Action, Embodiment and Emotions." *Labour and Industry:
A Journal of the Social and Economic Relations of Work* 24 (4): 272–285. https://doi
.org/10.1080/10301763.2014.978969.

Schickel, Richard. 2000. *Intimate Strangers: The Culture of Celebrity.* Chicago:
Ivan R. Dee.

Schulman, Michael. 2015. "Grading the Oscar Speeches: Patricia Arquette Gets an
A+." *New Yorker,* February 23. http://www.newyorker.com/culture/culture-desk
/grading-oscar-speeches-patricia-arquette-gets.

Schwiegershausen, Erica. 2015. "How Much Are Celebrities Paid to Wear Dresses?"
The Cut, June 2. https://www.thecut.com/2015/06/how-much-are-celebrities-paid
-to-wear-dresses.html.

Setoodeh, Ramin. 2015. "Equal Pay Revolution: How Top Actresses Are Finally
Fighting Back." *Variety* (blog), November 10. https://variety.com/2015/film/news
/hollywood-gender-pay-gap-inequality-1201636553/.

Shugerman, Emily. 2021. "Insiders Say #MeToo Powerhouse Time's Up Has Lost Its
Way." *The Daily Beast,* April 9. https://www.thedailybeast.com/insiders-say-metoo
-group-times-up-has-lost-its-way.

Silver, Nate. 2016. "N.H. Democratic Primary Forecasts." FiveThirtyEight, January 12.
http://projects.fivethirtyeight.com/election-2016/primary-forecast/new-hampshire
-democratic/.

Sony Pictures Entertainment. 2016. "GHOSTBUSTERS—Official Trailer (HD)."
https://www.youtube.com/watch?v=w3ugHP-yZXw.

Spacks, Patricia Meyer. 2012. *Gossip.* New York: Knopf Doubleday.

Spangler, Todd. 2014. "Google Threatened with $100 Million Lawsuit over Hacked
Celeb Photos." *Variety* (blog), October 2. https://variety.com/2014/digital/news
/google-threatened-with-100-million-lawsuit-over-hacked-celeb-photos-1201319374/.

———. 2016. "Twitter CEO Jack Dorsey: 'We Need to Do Better' at Curbing
User-Targeted Abuse | Variety." *Variety,* July 26. http://variety.com/2016/digital
/news/twitter-ceo-jack-dorsey-user-abuse-1201823778/.

Squirrell, Tim. 2019. "Platform Dialectics: The Relationships between Volunteer
Moderators and End Users on Reddit." *New Media and Society* 21 (9): 1910–1927.
https://doi.org/10.1177/1461444819834317.

Steiger, Kay. 2015. "Patricia Arquette Calls for Wage Equality during the Oscars."
ThinkProgress (blog), February 23. https://archive.thinkprogress.org/patricia
-arquette-calls-for-wage-equality-during-the-oscars-7db15dd18052/.

Steinem, Gloria. 2016. "In a Case of Talk-Show Interruptus . . ." Facebook, February 7.
https://www.facebook.com/GloriaSteinem/posts/10153237059092854.

Steinmetz, Katy. 2014. "Which Word Should Be Banned in 2015? Vote Now!" *Time.*
November 12. https://time.com/3576870/worst-words-poll-2014/.

Sternheimer, Karen. 2011. *Celebrity Culture and the American Dream: Stardom and
Social Mobility.* New York: Routledge.

Stockman, Farah. 2018. "Women's March Roiled by Accusations of Anti-Semitism."
New York Times, December 23. https://www.nytimes.com/2018/12/23/us/womens
-march-anti-semitism.html.

Stuever, Hank. 2018. "Review | Golden Globes: A Watchable Revolution, with Oprah Leading the Way." *Washington Post*, January 7. https://www.washingtonpost.com /entertainment/tv/golden-globes-a-watchable-revolution-with-oprah-leading-the -way/2018/01/07/3324301a-f3d1-11e7-beb6-c8d48830c54d_story.html.

Tamblyn, Amber. 2018. "Opinion | Amber Tamblyn: Redefining the Red Carpet." *New York Times*, January 7. https://www.nytimes.com/2018/01/07/opinion/sunday /amber-tamblyn-golden-globes-metoo.html.

Taylor, Anthea. 2017. *Celebrity and the Feminist Blockbuster*. New York: Springer.

Tchen, Tina. 2020. "From Pandemic to Possibility: A New World for Women at Work." Annual Report. Time's Up. https://timesupnow.org/times-up-2020-annual-report/.

@TeenVogue. 2018. "Tonight, We're Doing the #GoldenGlobes a Bit Differently . . ." Twitter, January 7. . https://twitter.com/TeenVogue/status/950098713548115968.

Telusma, Blue. 2015. "Dear Patricia Arquette: Blacks and Gays Owe White Women Nothing," TheGrio, February 23. https://thegrio.com/2015/02/23/patricia-arquette -blacks-gays-white-women/.

Thalen, Mikael. 2016. "Wikileaks Goes Head-to-Head with Twitter CEO over Milo Ban." *InfoWars* (blog), July 21. https://www.infowars.com/wikileaks-goes-head-to -head-with-twitter-ceo-over-milo-ban/.

Tobar, Héctor. 2018. "The Time's Up Initiative Built upon the Work Done by These Labor Activists." *Smithsonian Magazine*, December. https://www.smithsonianmag .com/innovation/times-upinitiative-built-upon-work-labor-activists-180970720/.

Today Show. "Gloria Steinem under Fire for Remark about Female Bernie Sanders Supporters." NBC, February 8, 2016.

Today Show. 2018. "America Ferrera Speaks Out about 'Time's Up' Anti-harassment Plan." *Today*, January 4. https://www.today.com/video/america-ferrera-speaks-out -about-time-s-up-anti-harassment-plan-1129134147610.

Traister, Rebecca. 2019. *Good and Mad: The Revolutionary Power of Women's Anger*. Repr. ed. New York: Simon and Schuster.

Turkos, Alison. 2021. "Enough Is Enough: An Open Letter from Survivors to TIME'S UP + National Women's Law Center." *Medium* (blog), September 14. https:// aturkos.medium.com/enough-is-enough-an-open-letter-from-survivors-to-times -up-c1351bcf7673.

Turner, Graeme. 2010. "Approaching Celebrity Studies." *Celebrity Studies* 1 (1): 11–20.

Tuters, Marc, and Sal Hagen. 2020. "(((They))) Rule: Memetic Antagonism and Nebulous Othering on 4chan." *New Media and Society* 22 (12): 2218–2237. https://doi.org/10.1177/1461444819888746.

United Nations. 2014. "Emma Watson at the HeForShe Campaign 2014—Official UN Video." https://www.youtube.com/watch?v=gkjW9PZBRfk.

Valenti, Jessica. 2014. "Beyoncé's 'Flawless' Feminist Act at the VMAs Leads the Way for Other Women." *The Guardian*, August 25. https://www.theguardian.com /commentisfree/2014/aug/25/beyonce-flawless-feminist-vmas.

———. 2016. "Don't Reduce Debate on Hillary Clinton and Female Voters to a Cat-Fight." *The Guardian*, February 10. https://www.theguardian.com/us-news /2016/feb/10/hillary-clinton-women-millennial-voters-argument-inter -generational-fight.

Valenti, Lauren. 2018. "At the 2018 Golden Globes, This Beauty Statement Was a Symbol of Female Empowerment." *Vogue*, January 8. https://www.vogue.com /article/golden-globes-red-lipstick-red-carpet-beauty-times-up-statement-claire-foy -jessica-chastain.

van Dijck, José. 2013. *The Culture of Connectivity: A Critical History of Social Media*. New York: Oxford University Press.

van Dijck, José, Thomas Poell, and Martijn de Waal. 2018. *The Platform Society: Public Values in a Connective World*. New York: Oxford University Press.

Vaynshteyn, Gina. 2015. "#AskHerMore: The Movement That Calls Out Reporters for Asking Female Celebs Sexist Questions." HelloGiggles, January 18. https://hellogiggles.com/lifestyle/askhermore-movement-calls-reporters-asking-female-celebs-wrong-questions/.

Vincent, Isabel, and Paula Froelich. 2020. "Star-Studded Time's Up Charities Spent Big on Salaries, Little on Helping Victims." *New York Post* (blog), November 28. https://nypost.com/2020/11/28/star-studded-times-up-charities-spent-big-on-salaries-not-victims/.

Warren, Rossalyn. 2015. "A Twitter Campaign Is Demanding Reporters Ask Women More Than 'Who Are You Wearing?'" BuzzFeed. https://www.buzzfeed.com/rossalynwarren/do-you-do-that-to-the-guys.

Warzel, Charlie. 2014. "What Kind of Creep Sells a Celebrity's Naked Photos on the Internet?" BuzzFeed News, October 2. https://www.buzzfeednews.com/article/charliewarzel/what-kind-of-creep-sells-a-celebritys-naked-photos-on-the-in.

Washington, Kerry. 2018. "Read this." Twitter. https://twitter.com/kerrywashington/status/950105010146181120.

Weiner, Rachel. 2018. "Former Va. High School Teacher Admits Role in Celebrity Nude Photo Hack." *Washington Post*, October 22. https://www.washingtonpost.com/local/public-safety/former-va-high-school-teacher-admits-role-in-celebrity-nude-photo-hack/2018/10/22/b1c7d4a4-d610-11e8-a10f-b51546b10756_story.html.

Williams, Jessica. 2016. "Breaking Down the Vagina Vote." *The Daily Show with Trevor Noah*, February 9. https://www.cc.com/video/qplr40/the-daily-show-with-trevor-noah-breaking-down-the-vagina-vote.

Wilson, Julie. 2010. "Star Testing: The Emerging Politics of Celebrity Gossip." *The Velvet Light Trap*, March, 25–38. https://doi.org/10.5555/vlt.2010.65.25.

Witherspoon, Reese. 2015. "Reese Witherspoon on Instagram: '♥ This Movement #AskHerMore..Have You Heard of It? It's Meant to Inspire Reporters to Ask Creative Questions on the Red Carpet. I Love the....'" Instagram, Accessed September 22, 2021. https://www.instagram.com/p/zaiCxKihVo/.

Wolff, Josephine. 2015. "Your IP Address or Mine?" *Slate*, June 11. https://slate.com/technology/2015/06/fappening-affidavit-the-celeb-nude-photo-investigation-and-the-problem-with-catching-hackers.html.

Woodruff, Betsy. 2015. "The Gender Wage Gap Is Especially Terrible in Hollywood." Slate, February 23. https://slate.com/human-interest/2015/02/gender-wage-gap-in-hollywood-it-s-very-very-wide.html.

Yahr, Emily. 2017. "Harvey Weinstein's Behaviour Was a Dark Inside Joke on Shows like 'Entourage' and '30 Rock.'" *The Toronto Star*, October 14. https://www.thestar.com/entertainment/television/2017/10/14/harvey-weinsteins-behaviour-was-a-dark-inside-joke-on-shows-like-entourage-and-30-rock.html.

Yang, Guobin. 2016. "Narrative Agency in Hashtag Activism: The Case of #BlackLivesMatter." *Media and Communication* 4 (4): 13–17. https://doi.org/10.17645/mac.v4i4.692.

Yiannopoulos, Milo. 2016. "Teenage Boys with Tits: Here's My Problem with Ghostbusters." Breitbart, July 18. http://www.breitbart.com/tech/2016/07/18/milo-reviews-ghostbusters/.

Yuhas, Alan. 2016. "Hacker Who Stole Nude Photos of Celebrities Gets 18 Months in Prison." *The Guardian*, October 27. https://www.theguardian.com/technology/2016/oct/27/nude-celebrity-photos-hacker-prison-sentence-ryan-collins.

Zacharek, Stephanie, Eliana Dockterman, and Haley Sweetland Edwards. 2017. "TIME Person of the Year 2017: The Silence Breakers." *Time*. https://time.com/time-person-of-the-year-2017-silence-breakers/.

Zakaria, Rafia. 2021. *Against White Feminism: Notes on Disruption*. New York: W. W. Norton.

Zeisler, Andi. 2016. *We Were Feminists Once: From Riot Grrrl to CoverGirl, the Buying and Selling of a Political Movement*. New York: Public Affairs.

Zimmerman, Amy. 2016. "Meryl Streep's Divisive Feminism: How White Feminists Silence People of Color." *The Daily Beast*, February 13. https://www.thedailybeast.com/articles/2016/02/13/meryl-streep-s-divisive-feminism-how-white-feminists-silence-people-of-color.

Zirin, Dave. 2015. "Patricia Arquette's Equal Pay Message Needs a Drastic Rewrite." *The Nation*, February 23. https://www.thenation.com/article/archive/patricia-arquettes-equal-pay-message-needs-drastic-rewrite/.

Index

Note: Page numbers in italics indicate figures in the book.

Academy Awards, 17, 21, 41; capitalistic goals, 68–69; focus on fashion, 47–48; hashtag activism and, 48–57; nomination of Ava Duvernay and, 43–44; objectives of creating, 68; as platform for social agitation and political statements, 46–47; unions and history of, 46, 68; wage disparities and, 44. *See also* #AskHerMore campaign

Academy of Motion Picture Arts and Sciences, 43–44, 46, 48

Access Hollywood, 61, 130, 131

accountability, digital, 4, 96, 111, 113–116, 146. *See also* calling out; "cancel culture"; hashtag activism

accumulation, 6–7, 33, 147, 149

activism and activists: anger and, 152; use of social media, 12; white celebrities/white feminist positions amplified over positions of, 7; Women's March (2017), 117–118. *See also* #AskHerMore campaign; calling out; Golden Globes Blackout (2018); hashtag activism; #MeToo movement; Time's Up

Adams, Amy, 44

Adichie, Chimamanda Ngozi, 16

Aduba, Uzo, 135–136

agonistic pluralism, 74–75

Ahmed, Sara, 98, 112

Ailes, Roger, 1

Albright, Madeleine (comments by), 17, 21, 41; criticisms of hypocrisy by, 90–91; on female solidarity, 88, 89; framing of conflict between young voters and, 76–77; at Hillary Clinton rally, 85–86; identity politics and, 87–88; on symbolic value of a female president, 88, 89; "There's a special place in hell for women who don't help each other" comment by, 73, 85–86

Alex Jones Show, The, 111–112

Alianza Nacional de Campesinas, 123, 124

American Hustle (film), 44

Amit, Reut, 29

amplification, 6, 7, 147–148

anger and angriness, 70–71, 151–154; directed towards Albright, 90; political power of, 74–75; in response to Gloria Steinem's comments, 79, 80; in response to Madeleine Albright's comments, 87; risks and, 74, 75, 76; on social media, 75–76; of young feminists, 78

AnonIB (imageboard), 24, 25, 26; about, 34; landing page, *36, 37;* nude photo hack and, 30–31, 38; terms used to describe, 35–36

anonymity, 12, 24, 26, 34, 35, 40

antiblackness, 18

Argento, Asia, 118

Armani, Giorgio, 47

Arquette, Patricia (on wage equality), 41, 44, 45, 58–67, 68, 110, 125; acceptance speech of, 59–60; acknowledging her lack of intersectionality, 65; backstage comments of, 60; calling out, 58, 61–62; capitalism and, 69; contesting the labor of calling out, 62–65; defenders of, 60–62; as the face of the wage equality debate, 65–67; *The Guardian* interview with, 58; on men and women as equally valuable commodities, 58–59; providing insight into role of calling out, 57–58; reactions to acceptance speech of, 59–60; response to lack of intersectionality by, 60–62; roles of, 58

#AskAWhiteFeminist, 64

#AskHerMore campaign, 42, 44–45, 68–69; capitalist system and, 69; critiques of, 54–57; cross-platform flow and, 49; networked public's affirmative response to, 52–54; Poehler's Smart Girls and, 49, 53; The Representation Project (TRP) and, 48–49; results on the red carpet, 52; Twitter users posting alternative questions for red carpet reporters and, 50–51; Witherspoon's Instagram post and, 49–50, 53–54

Atlantic, The, 72, 135

Aykroyd, Dan, 103–104, 105

backlash to popular feminism, 21

Bailey, Moya, 9, 100, 109

Banet-Weiser, Sarah, 69, 121, 150–151

Bannon, Steve, 98

Barnes, Brooks, 119

Barrow, Jo, 29

#BeenRapedNeverReported, 121

Belgrad, Doug, 44

Benjamin, Ruha, 12, 97

Bernstein, Michael, 34

BET, 105

Beyoncé, 16, 72

Biden, Joe, 140

Bitcoin, 38

Black audiences, media targeted at, 105

Black feminists/feminist thought, 9, 18, 109, 119

#BlackMenSupportLeslie, 104, 105

Black women: Arquette's comments and, 62–64; #AskHerMore and, 57; #MeToo and, 119; misogynoir and, 9, 100; as objects of harassment in digital spaces, 42; Oscar awards (2015) and, 43–44; stories of sexual assault, 120. *See also* celebrities of color; intersectionality; Jones, Leslie (harassment of); women of color

Bland, Bob, 117

Blodgett, Bridget, 112

Boyhood (film), 58

Boylan, Lindsey, 141

Brady, Anita, 14

Brady, William J., 75–76

Braithwaite, Andrea, 19

Brando, Marlon, 47

brands, celebrity, 8

Breitbart, 95, 98, 99, 114

Breitbart, Andrew, 98

Bridesmaids (film), 94

Bridget Jones's Diary, 10

Brown, Jerry, 67

Buckley, Cara, 55–56

Buffy the Vampire, 10

Burgess, Jean, 19

Burke, Tarana, 2, 119, 128–130, 136–138, 143

BuzzFeed, 25, 28, 29, 30, 37, 38, 39, 52

BuzzFeed News, 136

California Fair Pay Act, 66–67

calling out, 4, 13, 21, 43; about, 58; contesting the labor of, 62–65; falling on shoulders of women of color, 64–65; Patricia Arquette, 58, 61–62; Ricky Gervais about nude photo hack tweet, 29; Steinem and Albright, 71; throughout 2018 and 2019, 145

"cancel culture," 13, 22, 29, 97, 111, 145–146

capitalism: Arquette's call for wage equality and, 69; celebrities and, 8, 45; feminist negotiation campaigns and, 45–46; objectives of Academy of Motion Picture Arts and Sciences and, 68–69; popular feminism and, 13–14

carceral feminism, 122

case study approach, 6–7

catfight narrative of feminism, 76–77, 85

Celebitchy, 25, 28, 29, 32, 35

celebrities: as commodities, 8, 58–59; connection between politics and, 115–116; feminism as cool for, 15–16; Golden Globe ceremony (2018), 128–134; as hypermediated, 8; hypervisibility of, 3, 7, 120; as "just like us," 28, 30–31; newsworthiness of, 7, 48, 54, 66, 121, 138, 142, 147, 154; nude photos of, 24; objectification of, 44; sympathy for, in online discourse about nude photo hack, 2626; as victims, 28–33; at Women's March (2017), 117–118. *See also* white celebrities

celebrities of color: Golden Globes Blackout coverage and, 136; speaking out against harassment of Leslie Jones, 104; white celebrities and white feminist positions amplified over, 7

celebrity blogs, 27

celebrity brands, 8

celebrity culture: amplification and, 7; boundary work around feminism and, 6; "canceled," 145–146; intersections with digital platforms and feminism, 2–3; #MeToo movement and, 2; white feminist perspective in, 18. *See also* celebrities; white celebrities

celebrity feminism/feminists, 22, 147; debates about, 14–15; in the digital age, 13–15; expectations of, from #AskHerMore campaign, 51–52; mainifesting structural changes in wage equality, 67; myopia of white privilege of, 3; popularity of, 15–16; praised in commentary about Golden Globe Blackout (2018), 134–139; skepticism and criticism of, 13–14; Time's Up and, 123–125; transforming, 5–7; visibility and, 150–151

celebrity gossip, 20–21, 24, 25–26, 27, 32, 33, 133

Chemaly, Soraya, 49

Chicago Tribune, 55

"choice feminism," 81–85

Choo, Esther, 140, 143

cisgender white women, discourse focused on, 18, 84

Clemente, Rosa, 130, 143

Clinton, Bill, 90–91

Clinton, Hillary (campaign), 17, 21, 41; Albright's endorsement of, 85–86; catfight narrative in the media and, 76–77; controversy surrounding, 71; Donald Trump and, 93; Gloria Steinem and, 72–73; identity politics and, 87; intergenerational conflict and, 92–93; Madeleine Albright and, 73, 85; nonintersectionality and, 84, 90–91; rival of, presidential campaign (2016), 71–72; sexism and, 89; speaking out against Leslie Jones's harassers, 103, 105; Steinem on young women's dislike for, 78; symbolism of a female president and, 88–89; young female voters and, 72

Cobb, Shelley, 66

Cochrane, Kira, 10

Cocks, Heather, 55

Collins, Gail, 89

Collins, Ryan, 157n1

commodities, celebrities as, 58–59

"competitive anti-fandom," 98

Conservative Political Action Conference, 114

content filters, on Twitter, 106

Cooper, Brittney, 63–65, 67

Cosby, Bill, 1

Cosgrave, Bronwyn, 55

counternarratives, 12, 64, 102, 110, 111–112

Crenshaw, Kimberlé, 5, 9

critical discourse analysis, 19, 20

Crocker, Lizzie, 61

Crockett, M. J., 75–76

cross-platform data collection, 25

cross-platform sharing, 49, 50, 52, 102, 148

Cuoco, Kaley, 16, 24

Cuomo, Andrew, 141

Cut, The, 80, 133, 135

Daily Beast, The, 44, 61

Daily Show, The, 87

Dangerous.com, 114

data collection/analysis, 19, 20

Davis, Angela, 117

Davis, Bette, 46

Dawson, Rosario, 136

deplatforming, 108, 113–115

Depression Quest (video game), 23

Dern, Laura, 131

designer dresses, 47, 54–55

de Waal, Martijn, 11, 106

Dietrich, Marlene, 47
digital accountability practices. *See* calling out; hashtag activism
digital activism. *See* activism and activists
digital community formation, 12
digital feminisms, 2, 12–13, 121
digital platforms: celebrity feminism and, 13–15; celebrity gossip and, 27–28; claims to neutrality, 106–107; debates about feminism around celebrity culture, 3–4; definition, 11; disinhibition of, 34; filtration systems on, 6; fourth wave of feminism and, 10; hate and resistance on, 11–13; intersection of celebrity culture and feminism with, 2–3; more voices heard on, 68; programmability and, 11; sociality and, 11–12. *See also* networked publics; online news and commentary; social media; YouTube; *individual names of digital platforms*
Dior, Christian, 47
discourse, definition, 20
disinhibition, on message boards, 34
"dominant conceptions," 6
Dorsey, Jack, 100, 106
"dragging," 13
Drudge Report, 100
Dunham, Lena, 15, 16, 54, 103, 119
DuVernay, Ava, 43–44, 140, 141

E! Entertainment Television, 44, 57
Elle magazine, 53
"Emma Watson? Jennifer Lawrence? These Aren't the Feminists You're Looking For" (Gay), 14
Emmy Awards, 107
empathy, 28, 33
ephemerality, on imageboards, 25, 34, 35
E! Red Carpet & Award Shows, 128
Erevelles, Nirmala, 20
Essence, 105
ET Canada, 103

Facebook, 2, 11, 89, 108; Steinem's apology posted to, 79; Tarana Burke's statement on, 136–138; Yiannopoulos and, 114–115
Fair Pay Act, 67
Fantastic Beasts and Where to Find Them (film), 146

Fappening, The, 24, 35, 40
farmworkers, harassment of, 123
farmworkers, harassment of female, 123–124
far right, the, 10, 21–22, 35; attack on Leslie Jones and, 109–110; condemning Twitter for marginalizing voices of, 97; inversions by, 110; online harassment of Leslie Jones by, 96; victimized mentality of, 110–113
Farrow, Ronan, 1, 118
Fasanella, Kaleigh, 133
fashion, 47–48, 49, 54–57, 133, 135
Feig, Paul, 94–95, 97
female objectification, 21, 29, 43, 44
female solidarity, 92
femininity, female anger and, 75
feminism(s): anger and, 75; Arquette's speech/backstage comments and, 61, 62; boundary work around celebrity culture and, 6; catfight narrative and, 76–77; celebrity culture and, 5–6; first wave of, 8; "fourth wave," 10; intersection with digital platforms and celebrity culture, 2–3; "new visibility" (2010s), 10; postfeminism, 10; role of celebrity feminists in, 79–80; second wave, 8–9, 79–81, 84–85; social media discourse on, 3; third wave, 9–10, 81; *Time's* survey of Words to Ban in 2015 and, 16; transphobic, 146; what to gain in visibility of, 150–151. *See also* celebrity feminism/feminists; popular feminism(s); postfeminism; white feminism/feminists
feminist celebrities. *See* Albright, Madeleine (comments by); Steinem, Gloria
Feminist Mystique, The (Friedan), 9
feminist negotiations. *See* calling out; hashtag activism
feminist politics of choice. *See* politics of choice
Ferrera, America, 117, 123, 125, 127, 129
filtration, 6
Fiorina, Carly, 88
first wave of feminism, 8
Forstater, Maya, 146
Foster, Kimberly, 103
Foucault, Michel, 20
4chan, 23, 25, 26, 30, 34, 35–36

Fox News, 88
framing, 7
"free speech," 13, 106, 108, 111, 112, 145–146
Friedan, Betty, 9
Friedman, Ann, 80
Friedman, Jaclyn, 49

Gamergate, 10, 19, 20, 23–24, 95–96, 98
Garcia, Arturo, 49
Garelick, Rhonda, 133–134
Gawker, 25, 29, 30, 35, 36, 37, 38–39
Gay, Roxane, 13–14, 80
gay community. *See* LGBTQIA
   community
geek masculinity, 39, 95, 112
gender: identity politics and, 88–89;
   victimization and, 29; young women
   voters in presidential campaign (2016)
   and, 72
Gere, Richard, 47
Gervais, Ricky, 28–29
Ghostbusters, 17, 95–100. *See also* Jones,
   Leslie (harassment of)
Gibson, Caitlin, 109
Gillespie, Tarleton, 106
Gill, Rosalind, 10, 52, 54
Girls (television series), 15
Gjoni, Eron, 23
Glamour, 55, 66
Go Fug Yourself (blog), 55
Golden Globes Blackout (2018), 17, 22, 120,
   127, 128–134, 143
Goldie Blox, 53
Goldstein, Jessica, 55
Goodwin, Michael, 88
Google, 11, 19, 132
Google Hangouts, 49
gossip. *See* celebrity gossip
Gray, Jonathan, 98
Grayson, Nathan, 23
Grey, Sarah, 84
Grio, The, 62–63
Guardian, The, 13–14, 15, 58, 59
Guardians of Peace, 44
Gumpert, Andrew, 44
Guthrie, Savannah, 125, 127

Halliday, Nicole, 145
Hamade, Bryan, 38–39, 157n1

Harper's Bazaar, 146
Harper's Magazine, 13
hashtag activism, 4, 12, 21, 43, 48. *See also*
   #AskHerMore campaign; #MeToo
   movement; #OscarsSoWhite campaign
HBO Max, 140, 146
Heat, The (film), 94
#HeForShe movement, 15
HelloBeautiful, 105
Hermes, Joke, 27
Hess, Amanda, 29–30, 30–31
Hilton, Perez, 25, 28, 31, 32–33, 36–37, 40
Hobson, Janell, 14–15
Hocking, Bree, 56
Hogue, Ilyse, 109–110
Hollywood Reporter, 65, 140
Holmes, Mary, 75, 152–153
hooks, bell, 9, 71
Hoover, Kit, 130
Huffington Post, 83–84

iCloud security, 30
identity politics, 86, 87–88, 92
image, Academy Awards focusing on,
   47–48
imageboards. *See* 4chan; AnonIB
   (imageboard)
Imgur, 24
imperatives. *See* intersectional imperative;
   white feminist imperative
individual choice, 87, 92, 150
individuality, 150
InfoWars, 112, 115
innocence, of celebrities in nude photo
   hack, 25, 28, 32, 40
"Inside AnonIB, Where Hacking Is a Sport
   and Women's Bodies Are the Prize"
   (Hess), 31
Instagram, 49–50, 68, 114–115, 136
In Style, 136
intercategorical framework of intersectionality, 20
intergenerational feminist conflicts, 73, 74,
   78–85, 86–89, 91
intersectional imperative, 4; about, 5, 148;
   far right's victimization and, 110, 111;
   feminist politics of choice and, 73–74;
   LGBTQIA, elision of, 18; #Me Too
   movement and, 120; white feminism

intersectional imperative (cont.)
 and, 3–5, 7, 44–46, 91–93; white
 feminist perspective (Academy Awards)
 and, 41, 44, 45; Women's March and
 tensions with white feminist imperative,
 118. *See also* intersectionality
intersectionality, 5; anger over Steinem's
 comments and, 81; Arquette's backstage
 comments and, 60–62, 65; #AskHer-
 More campaign and, 57; definition, 5;
 discourse on, spreading to celebrity
 culture, 109; discourse on Leslie Jones
 issue and, 109, 115; discourse on nude
 photo hack, 41; feminist movement and, 9;
 fourth wave of feminism and, 10; Hillary
 Clinton and, 84, 90–91; "intercategorical
 framework of intersectionality," 20;
 second wave feminism and, 80–81;
 Time's Up and, 123–125, 127, 138, 139,
 142; white feminist perspective and, 5, 7;
 women of color's experience of sexism
 and, 9; young women choosing Sanders
 over Clinton and, 90–91. *See also*
 intersectional imperative
issue publics, 19

Jackson, Hannah-Beth, 66–67
Jenner, Caitlyn, 84
Johansson, Scarlett, 117
Jones, Alex, 110, 111–112, 114, 115
Jones, Leslie (harassment of), 17, 21–22, 42;
 attacks on, motivated by racism and
 sexism, 95–96, 108–109; Black voices
 marginalized in response to, 104–105;
 far right and attack on, 109–110; in
 Ghostbusters, 95, *95;* hacking of personal
 website of, 96, 100; intersectionality and
 discussion of, 109, 115; inversions by the
 far right and, 110–113; on *Late Night
 with Seth Meyers*, 102–103, *103;* messages
 of support for, 100–105; push for
 intervention against online hate and,
 105–108; security patches and, 96–97;
 stand-up comedy, 95; using her platform
 to argue for change to social media
 policy, 107; white celebrities speaking
 out against harassment of, 102–104
Jones, Rashida, 136
Judd, Ashley, 118, 119, 131, 141

Jusino, Teresa, 84
Just Be, 119
Justice, Victoria, 28

Kai, Maiyisha, 107
Kantor, Jodi, 1, 118, 119
Kaplan, Roberta, 141, 143
Kardashian, Kim, 32
"karma," on Reddit, 34–35
Keller, Jessalynn, 102, 121
Kendall, Mikki, 10
Kidman, Nicole, 131
Kosik, Alison, 111
Kotb, Hoda, 125, 127
Kravitz, Zoë, 131

Larry Wilmore Show, The, 62
Larson, Brie, 119, 136
Late Show with Seth Meyers, The, 102–103, *103*
Lawrence, Jennifer, 24, 30, 31, *31,* 33, 39,
 44, 59
Lazare, Sarah, 91
legacy media outlets: amplification and, 7;
 #AskHerMore campaign and, 54–55;
 calling out Arquette's comments, 62;
 data collection, 19, 25; defense of Patricia
 Arquette on, 68; Leslie Jones incident
 and, 102–104
legal defense fund (Time's Up), 22, 123, 125,
 131, 132, 139, 144
"Letter on Justice and Open Debate, A"
 (*Harper's,* July 2020), 13
LGBTQIA community: Arquette's
 anti-intersectional comments and, 60,
 62; celebrity feminism's intersection
 with, 18; second wave feminism and, 9;
 visibility, 18
liberal feminisms, 4
Linklater, Richard, 58
Littlefeather, Sacheen, 47
Longoria, Eva, *134*
Loomer, Laura, 114
Lopez, Jennifer, 60, 130
Lorde, Audre, 9, 75, 81, 91, 122
#LoveForLeslieJ, 105

Mad Max: Fury Road, 94
magazines, 7. *See also individual magazine
 titles*

magazines, data collection and, 19
Maher, Bill (show), 77–79
male celebrities, nude photo hack and, 29
Malory, Tamika, 117
man-hating, new popular reimagining of feminism and, 15–16
"Manosphere," digital, 35, 39
Marcotte, Amanda, 77
"marketplace feminism," 14. *See also* popular feminism(s)
Marlow, Alex, 114
Marwick, Alice, 76
masculinity, 39, 111, 112
Mashable, 61
Massanari, Adrienne, 35, 106
Massey, Rebecca, 83–84
masturbation, 38, 39, 40
Matamoros-Fernández, Ariadna, 19
Mayer, Louis B., 46, 68
McCarthy, Melissa, 95, *95,* 103
McGowan, Rose, 119
McKinney, Kelsey, 63
McKinnon, Kate, *95,* 103
media objects, mapping and analyzing, 19, 20
Medium (television series), 58
Mendes, Kaitlynn, 102, 121
#MeToo movement, 17, 22, 42, 142; "Me too" tweet, 119; shift in popular feminisms and, 120; start of, 119–120; understood as restorative, transformative justice, 121–123
Meyer, Robinson, 72
Meyers, Seth, 102–103, *103,* 107
Milano, Alyssa, 2, 119, 120, 125
Minear, Andrea, 20
misogynoir, 9, 10, 21, 57, 97, 100, 104, 109, 110
misogyny, 10; Gamergate and, 23–24; Leslie Jones harassment and, 100; nude photo hack and, 29–30; rise in, 10, 110–111
Monáe, Janelle, 118
Monroe, Marilyn, 30
Moore, Michael, 47
Morgan, Jessica, 55
Mouffe, Chantal, 74–75, 153
MTV Video Music Awards, 16
multiplatform discourse analysis, 19

multiplatform mapping techniques, 19
Munro, Ealasaid, 10

Nakamura, Lisa, 64
NARAL ProChoice America, 109
Native Americans, 47
negotiations, 148–149
networked misogyny, 2, 20, 23
networked publics, 3, 4, 6; affirmative response to #AskHerMore campaign, 52–54; celebrity blogs and, 27; contesting white feminist perspective, 45; defending Patricia Arquette, 60–62; description of nude photo hackers and, 35–39; feminist negotiations and, 21; feminist politics of choice and, 73; power to destroy individuals for perceived wrongdoing, 13; response to Leslie Jones harassment, 96; Ricky Gervais's tweet on nude photo hack and, 29. *See also* calling out; hashtag activism
#NeverHillary, 93
"New Jim Code," 12
news and commentary: on #AskHerMore, 52–57; catfight narrative of feminist conflict in, 76–77; Golden Globe Blackout (2018), 132–134. *See also* legacy media outlets; networked publics; online news and commentary
Newsom, Jennifer Siebel, 48
newspapers, 7. *See also individual titles*
newspapers, data collection and, 19
newsworthiness, of celebrities, 7, 48, 54, 66, 121, 138, 142, 147, 154
New Yorker, 1, 61, 118
New York Post, 88
New York Times, 1, 55, 76, 89, 118, 119, 123, 135, 143
Noah, Trevor, 87
Noble, Safiya, 12, 97
"normies," 34
#NotHereForBoys, 83
nude photo hack, 20, 24–25, 43; analyzing online discourse about the, 25–26; celebrities as victims and, 28–33; celebrity blogs and, 27; coverage of hackers and sharers, 40; digital communities soliciting and circulating, 34–39; outrage at hackers and, 70

objectification. *See* female objectification
Oluo, Ijeoma, 153
online harassment, 12. *See also* Gamergate;
  Jones, Leslie (harassment of); nude
  photo hack
online news and commentary: about nude
  photo hack, 20, 24, 25–26, 28, 34–39; on
  celebrity victimization, 28–33; data
  collection and, 19; on Leslie Jones
  incident, 101–102, 115. *See also* networked
  publics; news and commentary;
  individual websites and platforms
On the Record (documentary), 140–141, 142
On the Record with Greta Van Susteren, 88
"Open Letter to Gloria Steinem on
  Intersectional Feminism" (Grey), 84
Opinión, La, 123
O'Reilly, Bill, 1
Oscar awards. *See* Academy Awards;
  #AskHerMore campaign
#OscarsSoWhite campaign, 44, 48,
  57, 120
outrage, 70–71, 73, 75–76. *See also* anger
  and angriness

Papacharissi, Zizi, 113
parasocial relationships, 27
Parker, Kathleen, 83
Pascal, Amy, 44
patriarchy, 4, 9, 24, 25, 29, 30, 40, 42, 75,
  124. *See also* white supremacist
  patriarchal authority
People, 53, 133
people of color: Arquette's backstage
  comments and, 60; marginalized voices
  of, in response to Leslie Jones harassment, 104–105; messages of support for
  Leslie Jones, 104. *See also* Black women;
  race and racism; women of color
Perez, Carmen, 117
Perry, Katy, 72, 103, 109, *109*
Petersen, Anne Helen, 27, 29–30
Poehler, Amy, 49, 53
Poell, Thomas, 11, 106
politicized anger, 74–75
politics: Albright on women in, 86;
  connection between celebrity/popular
  culture and, 115–116; at the Oscars,
  46–47; voting for women in, 87–89

politics of choice, 21, 72–74, 92–93, 150
Poo, Ai-Jen, 136
popular feminism(s): #AskHerMore
  campaign and, 45, 50; digital platforms
  and transformation of, 2, 3; LGBTQIA
  rights and, 18; "marketplace feminism," 14;
  #MeToo movement and, 120; popularity
  of, 15–16; postfeminist readings of, 83;
  transforming and negotiating, 147–149;
  white women at center of, 5. *See also*
  celebrity feminism/feminists
"popular misogyny," 121
pornography, 34, 43
Portman, Natalie, 72, 123
Portwood-Stacer, Laura, 69
postfeminism, 2, 10, 14; Arquette's
  acceptance speech and, 60; #AskHer-
  More and, 48; entanglements of feminist
  ideals and ideals of, 48, 52, 150; Golden
  Globes Blackout commentary and,
  132–133; politics of choice and, 74;
  Steinem's comments and, 81, 83, 84
presidential campaign (2016), 21, 71. *See also*
  Clinton, Hillary (campaign)
pressure(s): #AskHerMore and, 51–52;
  calling out and, 58; hashtag activism and,
  48; types of, 70; white feminist
  imperative, 4–5. *See also* intersectional
  imperative; white feminist imperative
privacy: iCloud security, discourse on nude
  photo hack and, 30; Kim Kardashian's
  exposure and, 32; nude photo hack and,
  30, 32, 33; removing a tweet and, 28–29
pseudonymity, 12, 26, 34

Questlove, 109
Quinn, Zoe, 23, 24, 98

Rabideau, Camryn, 136
race and racism, 18; anti-Black, 17, 18;
  #AskHerMore campaign and, 56–57;
  harassment of Leslie Jones and, 103, 104,
  108–109; intersectionality and, 9; labor
  of calling out, 64–65; online harassment
  and, 12; Oscars (2015) and, 43–44;
  #OscarsSoWhite campaign and, 44, 48,
  57, 120; rise in, 10; shaping women's
  experience of sexism and, 9; white
  feminist imperative and, 4; Zendaya,

comments about, 57. *See also* Black women; intersectionality; Jones, Leslie (harassment of); people of color

Rachael the Lord, 103

radicalism and radical feminists, 9, 78, 85, 92

Ramírez, Monica, 123–125, 127, 136

Rancic, Giuliana, 57

Rappeport, Alan, 76–77

Ratajkowski, Emily, 89

Reade, Tara, 140

Real Time with Bill Maher, 77–79

Red Cross, 46

Reddit, 23, 25, 26, 34–36, 98, 108

Reign, April, 120

research design, 19–20, 25

Rhimes, Shonda, 54, 123

Ridley, Daisy, 94

right-wing news, 88, 98. *See also* far right, the

Ringrose, Jessica, 102, 121

Roberts, Robin, 52

Rock, Chris, 95

Rogen, Seth, 119

Romano, Aja, 110

Root, The, 107

Rose, Gillian, 20

Ross, Tracee Ellis, 136–137

Rowling, J. K., 146

Russell, David O., 44

Salon, 64

Salter, Anastasia, 112

Sanders, Bernie (supporters), 71–72, 73, 76, 77, 78, 82–85, 88–93

Sarandon, Susan, 87, 130, 158n4

Sarkeesian, Anita, 23

Sarsour, Linda, 117

Saturday Night Live, 95, 107

Seacrest, Ryan, 128

second wave feminism/feminists, 8–9, 73–74, 79–81, 84–85, 87

security, patches to correct vulnerabilities in, 96–97, 105

Selma (film), 43–44

"serious gossip," 26

sexism: Bernie Sander's supporters and, 72; Clinton campaign and, 89; critiques of Hillary Clinton and, 71; harassment of Leslie Jones and, 108–109; intersectionality and, 9; online harassment and, 12;

women of color's experience of, 9. *See also* intersectionality

sex scandals, celebrity, 32

sexual commodities, women as, 43

sexual harassment: Golden Globes Blackout and, 131, 135, 137; shared on Twitter, 2; Time's Up and, 42, 139, 140–141; Weinstein allegations, 1–2. *See also* nude photo hack

sexuality, nude photo hack and, 39, 40–41

Shriver, Maria, 54

silence, sexual assault and, 120

Simmons, Blake, 104

Simmons, Russel, 140

sisterhood, 150

60 Minutes, 91

Slate, 25, 29–30, 35

Smart Girls, 49, 53

social justice: anger and, 151–154; asking celebrities about their work for, 51. *See also* activism and activists

social media: amplification and, 7; anger and outrage on, 75–76; Bernie Sanders supporters on, 72. *See also* calling out; digital platforms; Facebook; hashtag activism

sociopolitical platform of feminism, 2

solidarity: celebritized media logics of individuality *versus* activist logics of, 142–143; female, 10, 87–88, 89, 91–92, 150; Golden Globes Blackout and, 131; with Leslie Jones, 101–102, 104–105

Sony hack, 21, 44, 58, 66

Sony Pictures, 43, 44

Sorvino, Mira, 118

Spacks, Patricia, 26

spear phishing scam, 24

Spy (film), 94

#StandWithLeslie, 105

Star Wars: The Force Awakens, 94

Steinem, Gloria, 17, 21, 41, 54; anger over comments by, 79; "choice feminism" and, 81–85; Clinton's campaign and, 72–73; comments on Bill Maher show, 73, 77–78; framing of conflict between young voters and, 76–77; as nonintersectional, 84; on radicalism, 92; role as celebrity feminist within feminism, 79–80; at Women's March (2017), 117; on young women/voters, 77–79

stereotypes: of feminists, 9, 15; of geeks and
   tech nerds, 38, 39
Streep, Meryl, 60, 61
Stuever, Hank, 134
subreddits, 34, 35
supportive counterpublics, Leslie Jones
   and, 21–22, 100–105, 110, 113
Swift, Taylor, 15, 16

Tamblyn, Amber, 123, *124*, 135–136
Tchen, Tina, 141, 142
Telegram, 114
television: amplification and, 7; data
   collection and, 19; messages of support
   for Leslie Jones on, 102–104. *See also
   individual television programs*
Telusma, Blue, 62–63
The Representation Project (TRP), 48–49,
   52, 54
Theron, Charlize, 94
ThinkProgress, 61
third wave feminism, 9–10, 81
Thompson, Tessa, 135–136
Time magazine Person of the Year, 2
Time's Up, 17, 42, 120, 121; "Dear Sisters"
   letter, 123, *124;* fall of, 141–142; Golden
   Globes Blackout (2018) and, 127,
   128–134; intersectionality and, 123, 125;
   launching of, 123–127; legal defense
   fund, 22, 131, 132, 139, 144; as organization of wealthy and privileged people,
   142; power struggle between logics of
   celebrity *versus* activism, 142–143; praise
   for celebrity feminists and, 136–139;
   scandals associated with, 139–141, 143;
   statement posted in Twitter, 126; Tamara
   Burke's Facebook post, 136–138; *Today
   Show* interview and, 125, 127
Time's Up Foundation, 139–140
Time's Up Now, 139–140
Today Show, 76, 125, 128
Top Five (film), 95
toxic technocultures, 35, 40
transformation, of popular feminism,
   147–149
transformative justice, understanding
   #MeToo as, 121–123
transmisogyny, Gloria Steinem and, 84
transphobic feminism, 146

trans visibility/activism, 18
trolling, 34, 111
Tropes vs. Women in Video Games
   (YouTube series), 23
True Romance (film), 58
Trump, Donald: anti-trans legislation, 18;
   deplatforming and, 115; Leslie Jones
   harassment and, 96, 109–110; Women's
   March following inauguration of, 117;
   Yiannopoulos, 98
Twitter: anger and, 75; Arquette's
   comments about wage equality on, 65;
   #AskHerMore campaign, 50–51, 53, 54;
   birth of #MeToo on, 2; calling out
   Arquette on, 63–64; data collection and,
   19; Gamergate and, 23; lacking methods
   to combat harassment, 97; of Leslie
   Jones, 96; messages of support for Leslie
   Jones on, 100–101, 104–105; #MeToo
   movement and, 2, 119–120; nude photo
   hack and, 28; Oscar conversations, 44;
   Poehler's Smart Girls on, 49, 53; push for
   intervention against online hate on,
   105–108; racism encoded into, 97;
   removing a tweet on, 28–29; response to
   Steinem's comments on, 79–80, 83, 84;
   rhetoric of neutrality by, 11; security
   patches and, 105; Yiannopoulos and, 100,
   110, 111–112, 114–115
Twohey, Megan, 1, 118, 119

unions, history of the Academy Awards
   and, 46, 68
United Nations women goodwill ambas-
   sador, 15
Upton, Kate, 24, 28, *31*
UpWorthy, 53

Valenti, Jessica, 77
van Dijck, José, 11, 76, 106
Vanity Fair, 33
Variety, 25, 28, 35–36, 66, 104
victimization: the far right and, 100–113;
   nude photo hack and, 28–33, 40, 41
video game industry, 23. *See also*
   Gamergate
"viral outrage," 76
Vogue UK, 66
Vox, 63, 110

vulnerability(ies) (digital), 150; of celebrities, 28; of the far right, 111–112; gendered digital, 24, 31, 41; Leslie Jones and, 105, 113; security patches and, 96–97, 105; Sony hack and, 44; of women of color, 96, 101

wage equality/inequality, 21, 41, 44, 65, 66–67. *See also* Arquette, Patricia (on wage equality)
Warzel, Charlie, 38
Washington, Kerry, 123, 136
Washington Post, 83, 134, 135
Watson, Emma, 15, 16
Watson, Paul Joseph, 88
web series, 12
Weinstein, Harvey, 1, 17, 22, 118–120, 140–141, 142
white celebrities: amplification of positions of, 7, 68; concept of intersectionality and, 5; Golden Globes Blackout (2018) coverage, 136, 142; #Me Too movement and, 120–121; speaking out against Leslie Jones's harassers, 103–104; as victims, 29
white-centric feminism, 41
white feminism/feminists: amplification of positions of, 7, 104, 105; Arquette's anti-intersectional comments and, 60–63; calling out Arquette and, 61–62, 63–65; catfight narrative and, 77; challenges to, 149; definition, 4; intersectional imperative and, 3–5, 7, 44–46, 91–93; Leslie Jones harassment and, 103, 104; response to women of color who criticize, 62; rewarded for statements in mainstream media, 105; Time's Up and, 123–125; women of color and, 10, 18. *See also* celebrity feminism/feminists
white feminist imperative, 4, 42, 148; #AskHerMore campaign and, 44–45; Women's March and tensions with intersectional imperative, 118. *See also* white feminism/feminists
white nationalist movements, 35
white privilege, 3, 105, 124
white supremacist patriarchal authority, 14, 99, 110, 122, 144
white supremacy, 35, 104, 107

white voice, in the media, 105, 109
white women: Arquette's backstage comments and, 60; #AskHerMore campaign and, 44–45; Brittney Cooper calling out Arquette and, 64–65; celebrity feminism focused on, 18; lack of support for Leslie Jones, 103; sexual assault and, 120. *See also* white feminism/feminists
Wiig, Kristen, 95, *95,* 103
Williams, Jessica, 87
Williams, Michelle, 128, 130, 143
Winfrey, Oprah, 72, 140–141
Witherspoon, Reese, 49–50, 52, 53–54, 123, 131, 136, 143
#WOCAffirmation, 120
"woke"/"wokeness," 5, 97, 119, 145
women: Albright's call for solidarity among, 85–87, 91–92; casting in roles previously led by men, 93–94; gossip's function for, 26–27; identity politics and, 88–89; narrative framing of feminist conflict among, 76–77; objectification of, 21, 29, 43, 44; "voting with my vagina" and, 87. *See also* Black women; white women; women of color
#WomenBoycottTwitter, 120
women of color: Arquette correcting comments about wage equality and, 65; Arquette's anti-intersectional comments and, 62–65; Arquette's message and, 62; #AskHerMore campaign and, 57; Clinton's campaign and, 90; digital feminist work of, 12–13; Golden Globes Blackout (2018) coverage on, 136; labor of calling out by, 64–65; response to critique of white feminism by, 62; second wave feminism and, 9; sexual assault and, 120; sexual violence and, 119–120; white celebrities and white feminist positions amplified over feminisms of, 7; white feminist imperative and, 4, 10. *See also* Black women; celebrities of color
Women's March (2017), 117–118
Woodley, Shailene, 16, 131
Wruble, Vanessa, 117
Wu, Brianna, 23

xenophobic politics, 35

Yiannopoulos, Milo, 95–96, 98–100, 108, 110–112, 113–115
young women/voters/feminists: Albright's comments directed toward, 91–92; on a female president, 89; identity politics and, 87–88; on individual choice, 92; on progressive feminism, 92; response to Albright's comments, 85–87; Steinem's comments about, 76–79, 77–79;

Steinem's comments directed toward, 91; Trump presidency and, 93
YouTube: #AskHerMore campaign and, 49; *Ghostbusters* trailer on, 98; multiplatform mapping techniques, 19; Perez Hilton's video apology on, 32; videos supporting Leslie Jones on, 102

Zakaria, Rafia, 4, 10
Zeisler, Andi, 14, 54
Zendaya, *56*, 57, 65

About the Author

CAITLIN E. LAWSON is assistant professor of communication and media at Emmanuel College in Boston. She received her PhD in communication and media from the University of Michigan.